TO EAT OR NOT TO EAT MEAT

HOW VEGETARIAN DIETARY CHOICES INFLUENCE OUR SOCIAL LIVES

༁

Charlotte J. S. De Backer
Maryanne L. Fisher
Julie Dare
Leesa Costello

Published by Rowman & Littlefield
An imprint of The Rowman & Littlefield Publishing Group, Inc.
4501 Forbes Boulevard, Suite 200, Lanham, Maryland 20706
www.rowman.com

6 Tinworth Street, London SE11 5AL, United Kingdom

British Library Cataloguing in Publication Information Available

Library of Congress Cataloging-in-Publication Data Is Available

ISBN 978-1-5381-1496-4 (cloth : alk. paper)
ISBN 978-1-5381-1497-1 (electronic)

∞™ The paper used in this publication meets the minimum requirements
of American National Standard for Information Sciences—Permanence of
Paper for Printed Library Materials, ANSI/NISO Z39.48-1992.

Rowman & Littlefield Studies in Food and Gastronomy

General Editor: Ken Albala, Professor of History, University of the Pacific (kalbala@pacific.edu)

Rowman & Littlefield Executive Editor: Suzanne Staszak-Silva (sstaszak-silva@rowman.com)

Food studies is a vibrant and thriving field encompassing not only cooking and eating habits but also issues such as health, sustainability, food safety, and animal rights. Scholars in disciplines as diverse as history, anthropology, sociology, literature, and the arts focus on food. The mission of **Rowman & Littlefield Studies in Food and Gastronomy** is to publish the best in food scholarship, harnessing the energy, ideas, and creativity of a wide array of food writers today. This broad line of food-related titles will range from food history, interdisciplinary food studies monographs, general interest series, and popular trade titles to textbooks for students and budding chefs, scholarly cookbooks, and reference works.

Appetites and Aspirations in Vietnam: Food and Drink in the Long Nineteenth Century, by Erica J. Peters

Three World Cuisines: Italian, Mexican, Chinese, by Ken Albala

Food and Social Media: You Are What You Tweet, by Signe Rousseau

Food and the Novel in Nineteenth-Century America, by Mark McWilliams

Man Bites Dog: Hot Dog Culture in America, by Bruce Kraig and Patty Carroll

A Year in Food and Beer: Recipes and Beer Pairings for Every Season, by Emily Baime and Darin Michaels

Celebraciones Mexicanas: History, Traditions, and Recipes, by Andrea Lawson Gray and Adriana Almazán Lahl

The Food Section: Newspaper Women and the Culinary Community, by Kimberly Wilmot Voss

Small Batch: Pickles, Cheese, Chocolate, Spirits, and the Return of Artisanal Foods, by Suzanne Cope

Food History Almanac: Over 1,300 Years of World Culinary History, Culture, and Social Influence, by Janet Clarkson

Cooking and Eating in Renaissance Italy: From Kitchen to Table, by Katherine A. McIver

Eating Together: Food, Space, and Identity in Malaysia and Singapore, by Jean Duruz and Gaik Cheng Khoo

Nazi Hunger Politics: A History of Food in the Third Reich, by Gesine Gerhard

The Carrot Purple and Other Curious Stories of the Food We Eat, by Joel S. Denker

Food in the Gilded Age: What Ordinary Americans Ate, by Robert Dirks

Urban Foodways and Communication: Ethnographic Studies in Intangible Cultural Food Heritages Around the World, by Casey Man Kong Lum and Marc de Ferrière le Vayer

Food, Health, and Culture in Latino Los Angeles, by Sarah Portnoy

Food Cults: How Fads, Dogma, and Doctrine Influence Diet, by Kima Cargill

Prison Food in America, by Erika Camplin

K'Oben: 3,000 Years of the Maya Hearth, by Amber M. O'Connor and Eugene N. Anderson

As Long As We Both Shall Eat: A History of Wedding Food and Feasts, by Claire Stewart

American Home Cooking: A Popular History, by Tim Miller

A Taste of Broadway: Food in Musical Theater, by Jennifer Packard

Pigs, Pork, and Heartland Hogs: From Wild Boar to Baconfest, by Cynthia Clampitt

Sauces Reconsidered: Après Escoffier, by Gary Allen

Pot in Pans: A History of Eating Weed, Robyn Griggs Lawrence

Screen Cuisine: Food and Film from Prohibition to James Bond, by Linda Civitello

To Eat or Not to Eat Meat: How Vegetarian Dietary Choices Influence Our Social Lives, edited by Charlotte De Backer; Julie Dare and Leesa Costello

Nomadic Food, by Jean Pierre Williot and Isabelle Bianquis

Dedicated to our families, friends,
and all others with whom we enjoy sharing meals

CONTENTS

FOREWORD

WHY WE COLLECTED STORIES ABOUT VEGETARIANISM

"Who is the vegetarian today?!" A loud and clear voice shouted out these words, directed to the only vegetarian at a summer barbecue. That vegetarian was me, Charlotte De Backer, the lead editor of this volume. It was a relaxed Sunday afternoon in Antwerp, Belgium, and I was attending a barbecue with a crowd of distant friends and acquaintances. I had fairly recently decided to ban all meat from my diet, a decision that was triggered by reading some of the stories for this book. I was in my forties, had never been vegetarian in my entire life and generally had paid little attention to those around me who were vegetarian, including my dear academic friend and co-editor of this book, Maryanne Fisher. And, most of all, I had never experienced how the food choices I made had an impact on my social life. That experience came to an abrupt end at that moment at the barbeque, when everyone stopped talking for a minute to look at the only vegetarian in the crowd. For a minute, I felt like I was spoiling everyone's fun, but the moment ended when they started talking again, directing questions to me. "So why are you vegetarian? How long have you been doing this? Do you miss meat? What do you eat on most days? Isn't it hard to see us all eating meat? Can your child eat meat?" They had numerous questions for me, and I found only a few were easy to answer. "Of course our child can eat meat, and no it is not hard to see others eat meat, nor do I miss meat, and if you allow me some time I can recall what I ate in the past weeks," I readily replied. But some questions made me pause: Why, for instance, was I vegetarian? Am I even a vegetarian? I decided to avoid meat a few weeks prior to the barbecue, but was that long enough to become a vegetarian? I still do eat meat when, for instance, I'm invited to dine with family or friends and they have cooked a meal with meat; I won't make a fuss about it. I don't want to be in the center of attention because of what I do and do not eat, but I soon realized that is no option if you genuinely are vegetarian. At that barbecue, where my husband had told the host I had become vegetarian, I suddenly was the center of some weird, awkward attention and it made me very uncomfortable. For the first time in my life, I felt like many people often do: I felt like those who make a personal choice to not eat meat or other animal products, and who get bombarded with questions and oftentimes face critique.

Increasingly meat eaters experience the same critiques. They, too, get questioned about why they (still) eat meat, why they do not feel guilt about their meat consumption, and whether they plan to take responsibility in behaving ethically toward animals and our planet. Vegetarians have grown in numbers and their voices are getting louder, but some, unfortunately, treat those who eat meat in similar ways as they have been treated as vegetarians: as different, incomprehensible, and oftentimes, despicable. The polarization between those who do and do not eat meat escalates differences between groups of otherwise similar groups. It is understandable that distinction according to diet matters, since what we eat not only shapes us physically, but mentally as well. Food and identity are well connected, and what we eat will very much influence who we are, at least in the eyes of others.[1] Yet, it may be time to turn this polarization around, to increase our understanding of each other's food choices, and how these food choices influence our social relations. While much has been written already about food and identity, and how our social context shapes our food choices, scant attention had so far been paid to how food choices shape our social relations.

This neglect is the topic we wanted to explore with this book; we look at the social consequences of dietary choices and take vegetarians as a case study. Vegetarians in this book include all those who exclude meat and fish, regardless of whether other animal products, such as dairy and/or eggs are also excluded. Whereas some may argue that the term ovolactovegetarian may be better suited to use, we follow others'[2] suggestions to use "vegetarian" as the broad overarching term for the eclectic group of people ranging from the ovolactovegetarians (who still eat dairy and eggs) to the vegans (who ban all animal products from their diet and lifestyle). We acknowledge upfront that differences do exist between different types of vegetarianism, and especially vegans can and should be treated as a separate group at times. At times it is necessary to differentiate vegetarians and vegans in this volume, but if we simply talk about vegetarians, vegans are included in this classification.

We stress that this book is by no means pro-vegetarianism (nor anti-vegetarianism). We do not take any position in ongoing debates about the health implications of diets with or without meat, nor do we take any position in ongoing debates about the impact of (not) eating meat on our ecology. We merely and very briefly discuss these debates in the introductory chapter to provide context for the narratives in the rest of the book. In several stories that are collected in this book, health-, animal-, and ecological concerns may have driven those who were interviewed to become vegetarian, but we distance ourselves from these opinions, which are, and remain personal to every participant who was interviewed. Moreover, the scope of this book is not to focus on these motivations to ban meat, but instead to illustrate how a simple choice to avoid meat can have complex consequences for one's social life. We do not want to convince people to avoid meat, nor do we want to scare people away from that decision. What we do intend with this book is to create more awareness about the social consequences of dictary choices. In a world where food influencers increasingly convince people to ban all sorts of foods from their diet,[3] this could easily have been a book about not eating fat, sugar, gluten, or carbs. However, we opted to create a book about not eating meat, as this dietary decision has a long history, exists all over the globe, and continues to spark debates in today's societies worldwide.

The seeds for this book had been planted when I, Charlotte, was in Perth, Australia, working with Julie Dare and Leesa Costello. Leesa and Julie both followed a plant-based diet and introduced me to their dietary habits. Professionally, we were collaborating in a project about the use of stories (particularly narratives) to endorse all sorts of health behavior, including healthy diet choices. Stories are powerful, as humans are literary beings.[4] Our brains are hardwired to process even the most complex stories with greater ease than, for instance, to memorize digital numbers. Fairytales, fictional stories, everyday gossip, and other facts embedded in stories are much more likely to be remembered and shared than even the shortest, factual accounts of information.[5] That finding I knew well enough from my earlier work on gossip, for which I often did and still do collaborate with Maryanne Fisher, who also joined our editorial team because of her expertise and personal interest. What I did not know was that health interventions increasingly apply storytelling techniques to achieve successful outcomes.[6] Marketers, as well, use storytelling to convince their customers.[7] This book is a further example of the power of stories; we rely on storytelling as the most useful tool to reach out to readers and inform them about a controversial topic. Therefore, we collected stories from vegetarians across the globe in order to explore if, and how, their dietary choices had an impact on their social life. None of these stories are fictional; all are true, realistic accounts from people's personal lives. We hope that when readers know that these stories are realistic, a change of attitudes or values is more likely to occur.[8] Although our goal is not to change people's diets, we do hope that people will understand their social relations better. It is time to change the potentially negative attitudes people develop and hold toward others based on their dietary choices.

This book may first appeal to vegetarians, who may recognize themselves in these stories, but we equally hope to reach out to the die-hard meat eaters as well. In many ways, this book has been especially crafted for meat eaters, as we did not want to write a book filled with facts and information about what it is like to be vegetarian, but rather a collection of stories that may look at this topic through the eyes of others. The stories told in this book could be told by anyone and can apply to meat eaters too when they are in the minority in a group setting, for example. The stories illustrate how not eating the same items as the majority eats sets people apart and may even disrupt their social life in ways they had not anticipated and most certainly would not have wanted. If vegetarians are growing in numbers, meat eaters may increasingly be confronted with similar uncomfortable experiences previously felt by vegetarians. We want to help people avoid these sorts of uncomfortable situations. It is important to remember that meat has a central place in the human diet, which we review in the introduction.

We hope this book can convince readers that we must avoid labeling people by what they do or do not eat, and that it is necessary to think about the ways we can all gather around the same table and enjoy food together. After all, few people like to eat alone, and food is what genuinely connects us to each other. The 1960s civil rights activist Cesar Chavez is attributed to have said, "If you really want to make a friend, go to someone's house and eat with him . . . the people who give you their food give you their heart." This sentiment of how food and social interacting go together is the backbone of this book. We go one step further and use the specific diet of vegetarianism to show how individuals grapple with complex issues within their social worlds. Our research, as presented in this book, clearly indicates that simple food choices can lead to complex social consequences, but that in the end everyone can gather at each other's house to enjoy food together.

Charlotte J. S. De Backer
Associate Professor in Communication Sciences,
University of Antwerp Belgium

With support from her co-editors:
Maryanne L. Fisher, Saint Mary's University, Canada
Julie Dare, Edith Cowan University, Perth Australia
Leesa Costello, Edith Cowan University, Perth Australia

REFERENCES

Byrne, Emer, John Kearney, and Claire MacEvilly. "The Role of Influencer Marketing and Social Influencers in Public Health." *Proceedings of the Nutrition Society* 76, no. OCE3 (2017).

Dagnelie Pieter C. and François Mariotti. "Vegetarian diets: Definitions and pitfalls in interpreting literature on health effects of vegetarianism" in *Vegetarian and Plant-Based Diets in Health and Disease Prevention*, ed. François Mariotti (London: Academic Press, 2017), 3–10.

de Graaf, Anneke, Jose Sanders, and Hans Hoeken, "Characteristics of narrative interventions and health effects: A review of the content, form, and context of narratives in health-related narrative persuasion research." *Review of Communication Research*, 4 (2016): 88–131.

Fischler, Claude. "Commensality, society and culture." *Social Science Information* 50, no. 3–4 (2011): 528–48.

Gottschall, Jonathan and David Sloan Wilson. *The Literary Animal: Evolution and the Nature of Narrative*. Evanston, IL: Northwestern University Press, 2005.

Kim, Hyun Suk, Cabral A. Bigman, Amy E. Leader, Caryn Lerman, and Joseph N. Cappella. "Narrative health communication and behavior change: The influence of exemplars in the news on intention to quit smoking." *Journal of Communication* 62, no. 3 (2012): 473–92.

Mariotti, François. *Vegetarian and Plant-Based Diets in Health and Disease Prevention* (London: Academic Press, 2017), 3–10.

Sperber, Dan. "Anthropology and psychology: Towards an epidemiology of representations," *Man* (1985): 73–89.

Urban, Glen L., Renee Gosline, and Jeff Lee. "The power of consumer stories in digital marketing." *MIT Sloan Management Review* 58, no. 4 (2017).

Notes

1. Claude Fischler, "Commensality, society and culture." *Social Science Information* 50, no. 3–4 (2011): 528.

2. Pieter C. Dagnelie and François Mariotti, "Vegetarian diets: Definitions and pitfalls in interpreting literature on health effects of vegetarianism" in *Vegetarian and Plant-Based Diets in Health and Disease Prevention*, ed. François Mariotti (London: Academic Press, 2017), 3–4.

3. Emer Byrne, John Kearney, and Claire MacEvilly, "The Role of Influencer Marketing and Social Influencers in Public Health." *Proceedings of the Nutrition Society* 76, no. OCE3 (2017).

4. Jonathan Gottschall and David Sloan Wilson, *The Literary Animal: Evolution and the Nature of Narrative*. Evanston, IL: Northwestern University Press, 2005.

5. Dan Sperber, "Anthropology and psychology: Towards an epidemiology of representations," *Man* (1985): 73.

6. For an overview work, see e.g., Anneke de Graaf, Jose Sanders, and Hans Hoeken, "Characteristics of narrative interventions and health effects: A review of the content, form, and context of narratives in health-related narrative persuasion research" (2016): 88.

7. See, e.g., Glen L. Urban, Renee Gosline, and Jeff Lee. "The power of consumer stories in digital marketing." *MIT Sloan Management Review* 58, no. 4 (2017).

8. Hyun Suk Kim et al., "Narrative health communication and behavior change: The influence of exemplars in the news on intention to quit smoking." *Journal of Communication* 62, no. 3 (2012): 473.

INTRODUCTION

CHARLOTTE J. S. DE BACKER
AND MARYANNE L. FISHER

While some report a global rise in plant-based eating,[1] other figures[2] show that meat consumption is also on the rise. This pattern is not only seen in America and Europe, but increasingly also in China, India, and other emerging countries. Even in India, known for its considerable higher percentage of vegetarians, being a so-called non-veg has become a status symbol in India's thriving cities.[3] Nevertheless, India still outscores all other countries with their highest percentage of vegetarians and vegans at 38 percent of the total population. This high percentage is intimately tied to the popularity of religions like Buddhism and Janaism, which both emphasize respect and non-violence to all forms of life.[4] This percentage is staggering in comparison to the numbers of vegetarians and vegans in other countries worldwide, where they are undoubtedly still a minority group. Israel and Taiwan share second place with approximately 13 percent of people excluding meat from their diet. This restriction is again often due to religious prohibitions regarding the consumption of meat, in these cases Judaism (Israel), Hokkien, Hakka, and Buddhism (Taiwan). Next in rank comes Italy (10 percent), which has the highest rates of vegetarianism in Europe, directly followed by Austria and Germany (both 9 percent), and the United Kingdom at about 9 percent. Closing the top ten are Brazil (8 percent), Ireland (6 percent), and Australia (5.5 percent).[5]

Overall, these percentages highlight that vegetarians and vegans are minority groups worldwide, even in countries that are listed to have the highest percentages. In addition, what many of these top ten countries have in common is that religious practices support a vegetarian or vegan diet. Many religions prescribe rules about excluding at least certain forms of meat, but one's motives to be(come) vegetarian and vegan can also be based on philosophical grounds[6] or personal (health-driven) goals, as is discussed later in this chapter.

What is truly fascinating is to realize that the decision of whether to eat or not to eat meat is never an individual process. The decision may be very personal, but the consequences will filter through different layers of social processes. What we eat is inherently connected to our personal identity, as well as our group identities.[7] This sentiment is accurately captured in the well-known "tell me what you eat and I'll tell you who you are" quote of eighteenth-century French gastronome Brillat-Savarin.[8] Food is sociality says Claude Fischler,[9] and he adds an important comment[10] to Brillat-Savarin's quote: If it is really the case that you are what you eat, then what happens when you and I eat the same foods or different foods? Do we then share identities when eating the same foods, and do we feel like different people when the foods we eat are different? These are questions addressed in this book. We investigate the social consequences of individual decisions to not eat meat. We explore if, and how, decisions to ban meat from one's diet can influence who they are and how they interact with others, and we always frame these perceptions using a cultural context.

Food is not just fuel to the body, but also a system of communication.[11] Some even claim that the foods we do or do not eat are the driving forces behind a "transition between nature and culture."[12] Humans are omnivores[13] that need a variety of foods to survive, yet at the same time, not everything in our environment is edible, and some plants or animals can even kill us when we eat them.[14] Knowing what items to eat and what items to avoid is a process of social learning. On top of this layer of learning, social norms about what to eat have become group markers as well, not only dictating what one can or cannot eat to survive, but also what one can or cannot eat to be part of a cultural group. In this light, culture is at the very heart of perceptions about what food is right, or wrong, to eat in specific circumstances. It is key to situate our understanding of vegetarian and veganism within a cultural context. Consequently, the core of this book is the series of personal narratives from countries across the globe that offer insights in how becoming vegetarian is more than just a dietary and/or ethical decision. In all of the narratives, people describe the intricate and enmeshed manner in which food choices are tied to their social worlds.

In this introductory chapter we begin by briefly situating meat in the human diet: When did humans start to eat meat, why did they do so, and with what consequences? This review is necessary in order to understand the historical significance of humans deciding to ban meat from their diet. We will then look at the different motives for vegetarian diet choices in modern age societies. At the end of this introduction, we reach the cornerstone of this book's scope by providing an overview of the theories and scientific findings that help to explain why dietary choices automatically imply consequences for our identity and social interactions.

TO EAT MEAT: A HISTORY OF MEAT IN THE HUMAN DIET

Humans descended from a plant-eating ancestor. However, the pattern of gut anatomy and digestive kinetics typical for ancestral hominoids imposed certain constraints, and meat eating was a solution to bypass these constraints.[15] By starting to routinely include animal proteins in their diet, our human ancestors freed space in their gut, which at that time was still adapted for digesting plant-based foods only. The introduction of meat in the human diet enabled an increase in body size, without the associated costs of developing a bigger gut and consequently losing mobility. Second, the entrance of meat in the human diet can also be linked to the expansion of the human brain and increased sociality.[16] Thus, unlike our relatives the orangutans and gorillas who remained frulivores and developed bigger guts, thereby becoming more passive and less sociable,[17] meat eating enabled our ancestors to become more mobile and social. This change had incredible advantages in terms of our evolutionary trajectory.

The introduction of meat into the human diet has been connected to unique traits that set humans apart from other primates and mammals, such as our long lifespan, an extended period of juvenile dependence, and extreme intelligence.[18] Interestingly, meat eating not only changed our ancestors' physiology (e.g., smaller guts, bigger brains), but also the acquisition and distribution of meat in human groups has played important roles in shaping our psychology and behavior.[19] To support this conjecture, consider the following difference between animals and plants. Plants typically remain in one spot for their existence, and in order to eat them, one simply needs to recall their location, have some knowledge of when they are ready for collection, as well as some idea about how to prepare them if needed. Animals, in comparison, are far more challenging to rely on as a food source, as one must locate the target, possess sufficient skills to successfully hunt, and then process the meat for immediate consumption before it spoils. In ancestral times, high levels of knowledge, skills, strength, and coordination were required to get access to meat, as animals were not domesticated. There was a long learning phase for our young human ancestors to acquire these skills, which at least partly explains the long juvenile period that typifies us as human beings.[20] Killing a large animal also required cooperation with others, which would not be necessary when gathering vegetative matter.

Unlike other meat-eating animals, human hunters used a wealth of information to make context-specific decisions which were dependent on the coordination of the overall group of hunters.[21] This level of decision-making and social cooperation is a key part of the evolution of our species' intelligence. Moreover, there is the important issue of food sharing. Successfully hunting large animals also resulted in large packages of energy-dense food, often more than hunters and their close family could immediately consume. In the absence of modern technologies to store food, it would be difficult to preserve large amounts of meat for long periods of time. This situation leads to an interesting place: hunters of large animals would have a surplus of meat that would spoil rather quickly, yet the meat itself was a valuable commodity due to the skill it took to acquire it. The result was to share food, but to do so in strategic ways. Throughout major parts of human evolutionary history, meat consumption, more than any other food type, was characterized by sharing with related family members and with non-kin group members.[22] Food sharing automatically implies that one must make decisions about how to share, what amount to share, and with whom to share meat. Do we share first with, and give the most to family members (kinship-based food sharing)? Do we share with anyone in the community but rely on rules of reciprocity (I'll share with you if you share with me)? Or can the sharing of large amounts of food, and meat in particular, be best explained by so-called tolerated scrounging; sharing food with others to avoid conflicts or threats (I'll share because I am afraid you may hurt or threaten me)? Researchers who have examined the literature on the prevalence of these different food-sharing strategies in both human foragers and non-human primates conclude that most food sharing is based on rules of reciprocity[23]: I'll share with you if you share with me. Often these transactions did not happen at the same time but were characterized by a delay in time.[24] That is, while today I may have successfully hunted a large animal, or collected a large amount of edible plants, next week I may be less fortunate. If I, however, share my foods with others, they may be likely to share food with me at times when I am less fortunate.

This perspective shows that group living could, and still can, offer food security to its individual members. Of course, this system requires trusting others will return a favor, and fair behavior in that they will return the favor. If a group member refuses to cooperate and share foods with others, or fails to cooperate to acquire food, the best strategy is for the group to impose serious threats such as isolating them from the group or refusing to share with them in the future. Group living was key for our ancestors' survival, and due to the needs to sustain the benefits of group living, a morality system emerged. The (delayed) transactions of food, and meat in particular, shaped our evolved psychology to control collective group actions and to punish cheaters abusing the cooperative system, along with felt emotions of anger (by those *taken* advantage of by a member) and guilt (by those *taking* advantage of others). Large-game meat in particular served as the basis for potential conflicts about fairness and cheating behavior, and by introducing meat into the human diet, a regulating system of morality evolved to ensure group members would contribute to the acquisition of meat, and the fair sharing of meat among the different group members.[25] Or, "If the hypothesis is correct, we can say that, in a sense, *meat made us moral.*"[26]

The introduction of meat into the human diet enabled us to think about treating others fairly, which becomes rather paradoxical if one shifts their view such that the "others" become animals. Ethical reasons to not harm animals are, in fact, the core motive that sets vegans and vegetarians apart from those who do eat meat, including those who reduce their meat intake (flexitarians),[27] as we discuss in more detail further in this chapter. Yet, if it is true that the introduction of meat in the human diet has shaped our morality (i.e., our sense to treat others fairly), then it was the introduction of meat into the human diet that enabled vegetarians and vegans today to consider it unethical to eat animals.

The consumption of meat in today's societies is paradoxical in other ways too. The so-called meat paradox is that most people like animals, even so fondly that they want to keep them as pets, but many include animals in their diet.[28] For vegetarians and vegans having pets can lead to further dilemmas; do they then feed the pets meat or not?[29] These are all cases that can lead to emotional discomfort, or cognitive dissonance.[30] Attitudes like "loving animals" and "harming an animal is bad" conflict with the attitude to "love meat" and the actual behavior of eating meat. Meat eaters often experience unease when being confronted with the fact that animals had to suffer and be killed to become meat.[31,32] The unpleasant experience of unease motivates people to use dissonance, or to find strategies to ease their discomfort.[33] These strategies include seeking (extra) justifications to eat meat,[34] making clear distinctions between animals and meat, for instance by naming them differently (e.g., cow versus beef and pig versus pork),[35] drawing strict(er) lines between humans and animals,[36,37] denial of animal pain and the likelihood of them having a mind,[38,39] and other coping strategies such as eating organic meat, less meat or eventually no meat.[40]

TO NOT EAT MEAT: DRIVERS OF VEGETARIAN DIET CHOICES

Vegetarianism is not new or modern. Even after the introduction of meat into the human diet, plant-based foods remained important resources.[41] Moreover, there have been humans who consciously decided to not eat meat at many moments in humans' ancient history. Buddha and Pythagoras were strong adepts of the ethical principle "to not kill for food" in India and Greece in 500 BC.[42] Whereas many consider vegetarianism to be a fairly modern concept, its roots go back to as early as 600–700 BC in Ancient Greece.[43]

In today's society, ethical grounds to "not kill for food" and other more personal motives, like health concerns, drive people to become vegetarian or vegan. However, there is a plentiful and diverse range of other motives, which are best separated into intrinsic personal motives, intrinsic moral motives (with a clear concern for the well-being of others), and extrinsic social/cultural motives. We start with the intrinsic motives that arise from within the individual and that can be oriented toward personal goals or benefits or toward benefitting others. The first, and most often mentioned intrinsic personal motive to ban meat (and other animal products) from one's diet are health concerns.[44] Like vegetarians or vegans, flexitarians, who consciously reduce their intake of meat, health concerns are important motives to support their diet choice.[45] Some stop eating meat because they believe this will lead to a better health. It should be noted that this link is not entirely scientifically supported, as there is discussion about whether vegetarian or vegan diets are healthier than diets with moderate amounts of meat.[46] Indeed, there is more consensus among researchers that in our modern societies, *reducing* the intake of meat and animal products reduces the risks of cardiovascular issues and a range of chronic diseases.[47]

A second intrinsic personal motive to ban meat (and other animal products) is to lose weight. Low-fat vegan diets can be very effective to lose weight, or at least more effective than low-fat diets that include meat.[48]

Especially among young girls/women veganism or vegetarianism can become a mask to cover up their restrained eating.[49] Third and last, taste preferences also count as important intrinsic personal reasons to both eat or not eat meat. Taste is the most important criterion for sincere meat lovers in supporting their diet.[50] Taste is undeniably important; once people have switched from an omnivore to a vegetarian diet, "missing the taste of meat" is an often mentioned reason to "sin" by eating meat, or even switch back to a diet including meat.[51] Yet, taste, or at least discovering new tastes, is also an important motive to consider a vegetarian diet.[52] This may seem contradictory at first, because omnivores are by definition people that eat everything, exposing themselves to a wider range of tastes, as compared to people who restrict their dietary choices, like vegetarians. The reason why taste is a driver behind (especially die-hard) meat eater's decision to try vegetarian meals is that they are often not acquainted with the foods that one may eat to replace meat. Many meat eaters subsist on meals consisting of meat, starches (potatoes, pasta, rice) and some vegetables on the side, but are not familiar with alternative sources of protein like tofu, seitan, tempeh, nor do they know about many legumes, which are typically central to vegetarian diets.

Intrinsic motives can also be aimed at benefitting others, promoting animal welfare, or include ethical concerns, which are the most commonly mentioned moral motives to be(come) vegetarian.[53] Avoiding meat because of animal concerns is what sets vegetarians and vegans apart from people who consciously reduce their meat intake (flexitarians), which can also be driven by all other personal motives.[54] Having pets during childhood predicts the likelihood that people are/become vegetarian as an adult, and this relationship is mediated by ethical concerns toward animal use.[55] If one is concerned about the well-being of other animals, then meat cannot be part of their diet, at least as long as we have to kill animals to obtain meat. In vitro meat production may change, or at least challenge, this necessity. If meat can be cultivated in a laboratory, without having to kill animals, there are no ethical concerns about animal welfare. In line with this, it has been found that vegetarians and vegans find in vitro meat more appealing than farmed meat. They remain, however, less willing to consume in vitro meat than those who do include animals in their diet.[56] Overall, attitudes toward in vitro meat are mixed and not yet very positive, but it seems likely that consumer acceptance of this novel type of food will change in the coming years, when in vitro meat would become affordable and more available.[57] If, at some point in the future, all meat consumed by humans would be produced in vitro, then arguments to not eat meat because of ethical concerns no longer hold. In other words, vegetarian or vegans who are refusing meat solely due to their concern for animal welfare would have no reason to continue their restricted diet.

In vitro meat production also reduces ecological concerns, which are another intrinsic and moral motivation, as it is an effective way to resolve many ethical and environmental concerns.[58] Those with environmental concerns[59] know that vegetal protein food sources have a lower carbon footprint as compared to animal protein sources,[60] but some argue that meat-based diets can be environmentally sustainable, depending on how meat is being produced.[61] Similar to concerns about animal welfare, ecological motives to not eat meat are being questioned by some, due to the possibilities of in vitro meat production, or the potential of ecological sustainability of eating a small amount of meat. Likewise, there is no clear link between a total absence of meat in one's diet and health advantages. Considering that these three motives are the most important drivers of meatless diets,[62] it is not surprising that those who consciously choose to avoid meat will not be free of critique, and may feel the need to defend their dietary behavior. Vegetarians and vegans often feel silenced by conflict and stereotypes, and frequently engage in several defensive or "face-saving" strategies to avoid confrontations.[63]

Not all vegetarians and vegans are personally, or intrinsically motivated to avoid consuming meat. Some will not eat meat, or at least certain types of meat, because of external forces such as group norms. There are numerous religious reasons to not eat (certain) meat(s).[64] Religions that originated in ancient India, such as Hinduism and Buddhism, are most known for their vegetarian dietary guidelines. As mentioned at the start of this chapter, these religious practices explain the relatively high prevalence of vegetarians and vegans in India today. Yet also other, smaller religious groups, such as the Seventh-day Adventists, adhere to a strict vegetarian diet.[65] In such cases of extrinsic religious or other social motives, an individual's choice to avoid meat fits with the group norms that apply to other members of their community. In these cases, not eating meat is part of their group identity and who they are as a member of that group. In other words, the fact that they restrict their diet is the rule, not the exception, and they have full acceptance of their dietary choices by others in their group. In stark contrast, vegetarians and vegans who have intrinsic motives that drive their diet choices, their decision to avoid meat may set them apart from the actions of others in their social groups. It can be expected that in these latter cases the impact of a simple choice like not eating meat may have a bigger impact on the social lives of these individuals.

YOU ARE (NOT) WHAT YOU EAT: HOW FOOD CHOICES DEFINE OUR IDENTITY AND SOCIAL BEHAVIOR

"Tell me what you eat and I'll tell you who you are,"[66] but while what you *do eat* may reveal part of your identity, what you *do not eat* may do this even better. Food and identity have complex relationships on different levels, ranging from individual to social (group identity) processes.[67,68] On an individual level, some believe that what you do or do not eat influences who you are, or who you will become. This belief is based on the principle that what you incorporate into your body becomes one of your properties, a core part of who you are as an individual.[69] Several cultures strongly believe in this principle. It pops up in indigenous cultures; among the Tairora of Papua New Guinea, for instance, mother's milk is seen as an important route for a mother to pass on her properties to her children. Or, among the Hua in Papua, New Guinea, people believe that you grow fast if you eat "fast-growing food." Not just habitants of indigenous cultures believe in these principles, Westerners also make similar associations. Americans were asked to rate the personality of people from different, fictive, cultures based on short descriptions including information about their dietary habits. In the first experiment, participants were asked to rate people from a culture that ate sea turtles *or* wild boars, while all other descriptive information, such as the name of the clan and their daily activities remained similar. Participants in this study rated the sea turtle eaters as more generous, good natured, phlegmatic, long-lived, restrained, slow-moving, lazy, good swimmers, with no facial hair and green eyes, while the wild boar eaters were perceived as ungenerous, irritable, excitable, short-lived, uncontrolled, fast-moving, industrious, good runners, with beards and brown eyes. In a second follow-up study, the authors contrasted vegetarians versus elephant eaters. In that study hardly any differences in perceptions were noticed, except for the fact that elephant eaters were thought of as having a bigger build as compared to the vegetarian group.[70] This notion of "you are what you (do not) eat" due to the consumption of the properties of the foods consumed is also central to many religious rules about food. Among, for example, modern-day Jews, only foods that are considered *kosher* or "proper" can be eaten, because for Jews, the food they eat becomes part of their soul. If they eat proper food, their soul will be proper, but if they eat non-proper foods, their soul also becomes contaminated.[71] Pork, for example, is not considered kosher food and should be avoided at all times. Muslims too abstain from pork, which according to their cultural norms is not *halal*. For Muslims, halal foods are those Allah has not forbidden in the Quran. Thus, for Muslims, it is not the fear that what they eat will become part of their soul, but rather the prescriptions of Allah that drives eating habits. Most cultures share in this pattern; if religious rules do not dictate what foods can and cannot be eaten, cultural norms do so.

Across centuries and cultures, groups create their identity, in part, by what they eat. After all, food is a system of communication,[72] and the culinary world can be seen as the "transition between nature and culture."[73] To fully understand this link, we need to start from the fact that humans are omnivores.[74] We can eat a huge variety of unique foods, which allows us to easily adapt to new environments with different food systems. We are not restricted by our diet, unlike some animals, however, "this liberty also implies dependence and a constraint—that of variety."[75] We need high levels of variety in our diet to attain all the nutrients we require, but we also must take care while selecting what to eat. Not everything nature offers is edible; some plants (and animal products) can kill us. This dichotomy translates into our paradoxical quest and interest in exploring new tastes and foods (neophilia), yet at the same time being wary about unfamiliar foods we have not seen before (neophobia). Culture, in terms of having the opportunity to observe what others do and hear other's experiences offers solutions to the omnivore's paradox.[76] Cultural norms limit the foods we accept and make us less tolerant toward newer foods. In Western cultures, for example, insects are not food, whereas in Asian cultures they often are.[77] In the past decades this particular example, of eating insects, has become an interesting case in many Western countries, where some have tried to actively endorse insect consumption because of its nutritious properties and environmental benefits. Despite the clear benefits, Westerners remain hesitant to eat insects, in part due to their cultural habits.[78] In this way, cultural norms about what to eat and what not to eat mark the boundaries of a group. During our extensive evolutionary history, food may have operated as this type of cultural marker. Today, this marker carries over, such that eating similar or different foods acts as a signal of trust during interactions even among strangers. That is, when complete strangers meet and eat similar foods, they appear to trust each other more as compared to when strangers meet and eat different foods.[79]

The importance of food cannot be overestimated: what we do and do not eat signals who we are, which group(s) we belong to, and in the end, it greatly influences our social behavior. When you do not eat the foods of the cultural group you belong to, you are not part of that group. This link between eating and group memberships is nicely illustrated by case studies of diaspora when moving to a different culture. Geeta Kothari, for example, describes her personal journey of growing up as a member of an Indian family in the United States.[80] At home, the Kothari's ate Indian food, as part of a long-standing cultural tradition. Indian food marked their group identity, their cultural heritage. Yet at school Geeta Kothari felt different from her classmates who ate American or Mexican food. Even at a young age, she experienced how it felt to be "different" from other children merely based on the fact that what she ate was different from what other children were eating. Food, and especially the consumption of different foods, created a divide between her (and also her family) and American people who ate different foods. She felt Americans expected her and her family to adapt to the American food culture, by eating what Americans eat. When she is sent to school in London, years later, she experiences this set of feelings all over again. Her story clearly signals how food is an important cultural marker. Many Indian Americans,[81] Asian-Americans[82,83] and diaspora worldwide have experienced "feeling different" or "feeling excluded" from the dominant group, merely based on what they ate. Immigrants worldwide understand and play with their multiple identities through culinary habits and so do people worldwide who avoid eating animals.

Identity is far from a simple construct to fully discuss, but when mixed with food, it quickly becomes even more complex. Zooming in on how food and (social) identities are interrelated for vegetarians and vegans, the Unified Model of Vegetarian Identity[84] proposes at least ten dimensions to capture the many identity-related aspects of a vegetarian diet. These dimensions can be grouped into contextual, internalized, and externalized levels. Contextual dimensions, which include the historical embeddedness, timing, and duration, situate vegetarian diet choices into the broader historical, sociocultural, and lifespan contexts. Being vegetarian and also being vegan, for example, is different today as compared to a few decades ago, because veganism has enjoyed increasing popularity.[85] Or, being vegetarian in India, where avowing meat is more common, is different as compared to being vegetarian in Brazil, where meat consumption is much higher and still on the rise. Yet, regardless of when and where one is or becomes vegetarian, lifespan contexts are also crucial. Food preferences and dietary choices evolve over the lifespan,[86] and this finding is especially true for vegetarian dietary processes. Few vegetarians are born and raised as vegetarians; most make a conscious decision later in life to abandon meat.[87] Furthermore, while dietary changes can last a lifetime for some, they may not for others. Especially in the West, vegetarianism is seldom practiced for one's full lifetime, but more often it is the choice of a "convert" who has "subjected more traditional foodways to critical scrutiny and has subsequently made a deliberate decision to change their eating habits."[88] By doing so, they also take on a different identity, both at an individual and a group level. Using the Unified Model of Vegetarian Identity, this shift shows the context factors that underlie the internalizations and externalizations of vegetarian identities.[89] The internalized level dimensions of this model cover, on the one hand, the motives to (be)come vegetarian, but also focus on how people reflect on their personal vegetarian identity and their overall sense of self. Externalized dimensions focus on the behavior of vegetarians; their behavior toward foods (what they do and do not eat at certain occasions, and how strictly they follow their diets), as well as their behavior toward other people, including the ways vegetarians express their identity. It may also be that they do *not* express their vegetarian identity, or their true self; several studies indicate vegetarians sometimes do not (wish to) express their dietary preferences because they are afraid to be, or are fed up with being judged and stereotyped by omnivores.[90] Researchers have documented how people are perceived based on their choice to eat or not eat animals, contrasting vegetarian and vegan diets to general omnivorous diets. They conclude that vegetarians, and especially vegans are perceived differently, and specifically to be less masculine.[91] In part, this stereotype is due to the fact that people who eat meat, red meat in particular, are seen as strong because of the blood they consume.[92] For vegetarians, this gender stigma appears to have declined in the past years,[93] but for vegans the perception to be less masculine still stands strongly, and it is especially the *choice* to be(come) vegan that leads to these biased perceptions.[94] This perception of decreased masculinity may represent a special challenge for men to opt for a vegan (or even a vegetarian) diet. Some argue that any promotion for a meatless, or even a meat-reduced diet focusing on animal, health, or ecological issues will not convince a large population of men who feel a sense of "maleness" because of their meat consumption.[95] For some men, meat is an essential part of their identity. Other men, however, do consciously decide to be(come) vegan, and they challenge our traditional way of thinking about gender norms, the stereotypes revolving around identity and masculinity and femininity; with their diet choice they alter the definition of being "a man."[96]

Whereas stereotyping may affect men who are vegetarians more so than women who are vegetarians, both sexes report cases of being attacked by omnivores. Herein lies another paradox. Die-hard meat eaters do not like to be confronted by vegetarians, possibly because it is perceived as criticism about their own meat-eating diet choices. When meat eaters interact with vegetarians the former engage in cognitive dissonance; knowing there are profound reasons to not eat meat, yet simultaneously feeling a strong love or craving for meat. Meat eaters must seek out ways to overcome cognitive dissonance. For example, they may find reasons to justify their diet, or they may opt to avoid interactions with vegetarians.[97] Yet, what would happen if an omnivore and vegetarian are family members, friends, or lovers? Avoiding interaction then becomes more difficult and painful, but it does happen. In a study where forty vegans were interviewed in the UK, thirty-three reported to receive negative reactions from friends and family.[98] Becoming vegan, especially in a family of meat eaters can be very challenging, leading to serious conflicts and even family disruptions.[99] Consider, for example this quote from a vegetarian who married an omnivore: "If I really want to make myself sick, I worry that my husband will one day leave me for a meat-eater, for someone familiar who doesn't sniff him suspiciously for signs of alimentary infidelity."[100] The divide is created from both sides; some meat eaters may (or do) avoid vegetarians, but also some vegetarians explicitly avoid contact with omnivores. Taken to an extreme, some vegans refuse to be intimately involved with meat eaters; this so-called vegansexuality has sparked considerable debate from both sides,[101] and further fuels the divide between those who do and do not consume animals.

Not surprisingly, those who become vegetarian often almost entirely abandon their omnivorous social group membership and become a member of a new social group: the meat-avoiders.[102] Many vegans actively seek out new friendships with like-minded people[103] and even join online forums for this purpose.[104] This new membership may, however, come with a more complex identity structure. There are many distinct motives that can and do sustain meatless diets, but, in addition, among those who "avoid meat," very different patterns in what they do and do not eat also occur. Pesco-vegetarians abandon meat, but still eat fish; lacto-ovo-vegetarians exclude meat and fish but still eat eggs and dairy; lacto-vegetarians exclude meat, fish, and eggs but not dairy; ovo-vegetarians exclude meat, fish, dairy but not eggs; and vegans exclude all foods from animal origin, and often call themselves "strict vegetarians." Even this latter group can be further divided into those who only apply the "no animal product" (e.g., gelatin) to their diet (which the French call being "vegetalienne"), and those who apply this rule to their overall lifestyle by not wearing leather, wool, or other materials from animal origins (which in French are the true "vegans"). This brief overview shows how eclectic the group of meat-avoiders is, and how many different terms exist to label, and hence potentially divide, their core group. In terms of identity, being a meat-avoider comes at a higher price as compared to being an omnivore. What one does and does not eat places individuals into a subgroup of a minority group, but also the motives behind the dietary choices will become more crucial than ever in defining social identity and others' perceptions. The distinction between personal and moral motives for not eating meat can create frictions among members of this eclectic meat-avoiding group. Even those who follow an identical diet, let's say a vegan diet, may clash if one person is driven by personal health concerns and other vegans are driven by moral animal and ecological concerns. Morally-driven vegans in particular appear to eschew health-driven vegans, whom they view as unauthentic.[105] This nicely illustrates the complexity of vegetarian diets that the Unified Model of Vegetarian Identity[106] aimed to capture; it is not just about what you eat, but why you make your dietary choices, and what others think of your decisions. There is little doubt, as revealed in the stories contained in the chapters of this volume, that becoming and being vegetarian is challenging on many levels. It is critical to note, though, that while such complexity exists, the eclectic community of meat-avoiders can also form a strong community, embracing its diversity by clearly marking itself differently from those who do eat meat. Vegetarians, for example, typically feel closer to vegans as compared to omnivores who do eat meat.[107] It is the people we eat with, as well as the groups we (want to) belong to, that influence *what* we eat, and how we use these food choices to manage and express current, future, and aspired identities.[108] Yet we cannot and should not create a world where omnivores and vegetarians live separately; there must be ways in which we can all join in, and above all, share the dinner table for a communal meal.

YOU ARE THE SAME AS THOSE YOU EAT WITH (OR NOT): WHY COMMENSALITY AND THE SHARING OF FOOD MATTERS MORE THAN WE THINK

Conviviality, or commensality, defined as the act of eating together, is good for us, both in terms of physical as well as mental well-being. Conviviality is central to the Mediterranean Diet model and considered a crucial cultural component that sustains a healthy dietary pattern.[109] It is well acknowledged that commensality, and especially commensal family meals lead to several nutritional benefits for both younger and older individuals.[110,111] Preschoolers, whose parents often worry that they eat too much meat and too few fruits and vegetables, are more likely to consume fruits, and especially vegetables when eating in the company of an adult, which can either be a parent[112,113] or another child-care provider, such as a teacher at daycare or school.[114] Although eating together has not always been found to be a sufficient predictor of an increased vegetable consumption at this very young age,[115] the association between commensal meals and healthy dietary patterns is more evident in older children and adolescents.[116] Adolescents especially benefit from commensal family meals, as they protect against the risk of obesity,[117] and guarantee healthier dietary patterns in (young) adulthood.[118] During adulthood, commensality seems to matter less in terms of dietary outcomes,[119] but the benefits reappear later in life when not obesity, but undernourishment becomes a burden. For elderly people, commensality leads to a higher consumption of more varied foods.[120,121,122] Moreover, for elderly who suffer from dementia, family-style meals can also result in modest increases of well-being and even communication.[123] Based on all the evidence that commensality leads to nutritional benefits throughout the lifespan, some[124] have urged the general public to invest more in family meals and support families that experience barriers, often related to time pressures. Not just families must make an effort, however, as commensality can take many forms; friends can also dine together, colleagues can share lunches, and communal gatherings revolving around food are equally important in this context. Those who study the Mediterranean Diet Model, including the conviviality aspects of it, have already suggested to start using the pleasure of sharing meals as a strategy to endorse healthier diets in this broader range of different settings.[125] They believe that the focus on joining in and eating in a social way will be more successful than a focus on diet and health, because few people like to be told what to eat, whereas most of us do enjoy eating in a social way. After all, let's not forget, "conviviality" refers to the "pleasure of eating together."

In the end, few people like to eat alone. When people do eat alone, they seek out distraction: in front of a window, or a device that lends them social companionship, such as a book or a (TV) screen. Technologists are well aware of this tendency and build tools to enable those who are forced to eat alone, for whatever reason, to be in contact with their loved ones.[126] Eating alone is not part of our human nature, nor is it part of our history. In indigenous societies "food is almost always shared; people eat together; mealtimes are events when the whole family or settlement or village comes together. Food is an occasion for sharing . . . for the expression of altruism."[127] Many anthropologists actually use commensality, food sharing, or joint cooking processes as proxies to indicate the closeness of connections between individuals or groups (families). To define a family unit or household not with respect to "living together under the same roof," but rather "using the same cooking facilities" appears to be the best predictor of closeness.[128] Several families or households may live under the same roof, yet have separate cooking facilities, or if they share the kitchen, they will use it at different times. Sharing a cooking pot and actually eating together are central behaviors to the definition of "household units" used by several anthropologists studying (still active) indigenous societies in Africa,[129] Asia,[130,131] North America,[132] Europe,[133] Oceania,[134] and Russia.[135] Some anthropologists[136] have even suggested to no longer talk about "households" or families, but use more culturally appropriate terms such as "*bokyea*" which among the Ghanaian Akan refers to "cooking-hearth" or "eating-group." Also, archeologists studying ancient cultures in Greece[137] or Mexico[138] use commensality, via traces of shared cooking or eating facilities, to map out spatial organization. These researchers have further emphasized that both eating and cooking together was not restricted to families or other close-knit groups but occurred at the level of the larger community. At larger, celebratory occasions, meat was often involved; Jones[139] describes the importance of meat in his book *Feast*, where he reviews our long history of commensality. On special occasions meat is eaten, because the slaughtering of an animal is part of religious practices,[140] or because meat serves as a status symbol and makes the meal more wealthy or special.[141] In many countries around the world meat is central to special occasions; think of the American Thanksgiving turkey, the Christmas turkey or goose in most of the Western world, or the sheep for the Muslim Feast of Sacrifice. Meat on the table makes a meal more festive, which can be explained by the fact that throughout human history, meat has been a scarce commodity which required cooperation to obtain and resulted in celebration during its consumption.[142] Not just meat was served on these occasions, also plant-based foods were offered and shared, and eating was about the joys of celebrating the successful realization of a variety of foods to share and eat.[143]

In today's societies, this enjoyment of commensality is still omnipresent and can take many forms, as we alluded to earlier in this section. It may range from family dinners, going out to eat with friends, to bigger and more formal banquets with colleagues, and even very big festivities like communal gatherings where food is served.[144] Yet today, more than ever, many people, and especially elderly people, also eat alone.[145] This trend is disheartening when we consider the evidence that for elderly people, commensality relates to a better psychological well-being[146] and can buffer against a depressive mood.[147] In general, across demographics, eating in the company of others leads to an improved psychological well-being.[148] For example, in a large Thai cohort study, it was found that having a meal in the company of other people is a vital part of daily social interactions and contributes to increased happiness.[149] Thai culture, and Asian cultures more broadly, are known for (food) sharing practices and the importance of collective action.[150] Yet, even in a highly individualistic culture, such as the American culture which is often blamed for neglecting commensality,[151] sharing meals is also key in bonding with others and defining friendships.[152] Food also connects at a romantic level. When singles move in with each other, eating together becomes a crucial expression of showing love and affection toward each other.[153,154] Food offering is a means to increase positive affect,[155] an expression of love used, for instance, within couples or by mothers feeding their family.[156] Women in particular often select to cook their partner's or children's favorite foods and even set aside their own food preferences to express their fondness.[157] For children, the benefits of commensality are not only about getting favorite meals and feeling loved, but also about everyday dinner routines. Practical assignments like helping to dress the table and emotional rituals embedded in mealtime conversations (e.g., reminiscing about the day) contribute to children's well-being and support their feelings of belonging to their family.[158,159] When children share a meal with their parents, family, or even at school, they feel connected and they get a more developed sense of their identity. Food relates to identity not only because of "we are *what* we eat," but also because of "we are *with whom* we eat."[160]

Parents will understand, however, that in reality, family meals are most often not about cooking together, dressing a nice table, and sharing a meal everyone loves while reminiscing about everyone's day. Instead, reality is often discord between parents and children, who may yell and scream in clear disagreement over food, especially if it involves a disliked food item. As much as commensality can connect us, it also creates significant tensions.[161] Sharing food often results in negotiations or contests.[162] From a very young age onward, mealtimes are an arena to negotiate power.[163] Young children may resist eating certain food and try to negotiate with their parents. Such occasions are often more about a power struggle than about the food itself, as refusing food is one of the first and strongest power signals young children possess.[164] For families with young children, meal times can therefore become a real burden, and as children grow older, pickiness over food, and also conflicts about meal planning, food preparations, time spent at the table, and shared cleaning up may emerge.[165] Yet, despite these food conflicts most parents do consider family meals to be crucial, in part because they can be used as good teaching moments,[166] which in itself is critical in developing a healthy relation between food and sociality. For children and adolescents, meal-times are an important arena of socialization, and we should treat "mealtimes as cultural sites for the socialization of persons into competent and appropriate members of a society."[167] Both the spoken and unspoken elements of meal-times matter in this socialization process. Dinner conversations contribute to language socialization, while a range of other, mostly unspoken, rituals teach children about the cultural norms that govern a society. Children need to learn, for instance, about the order in which food is being served. Depending on cultures and occasions some foods will be served first, second, and so on, while others will be last. In most cultures it is also inappropriate to take the foods of others, and greediness in general is not appreciated. "Embedded in the socialization of commensality are messages regarding the morality of food distribution and consumption and the rights of adults and children to determine how, when, and how much family members will eat."[168] All of this communication of norms not only applies to children, but to adults as well, and novices (e.g., new members of a cultural group) in particular. When adults meet over food, negotiations and conflicts are also likely.[169] For adults too, commensal meals are ideal occasions to remind each other to treat others fairly, to not be greedy, to wait until others are served, and to be thankful to those who prepared the meal. These actions can be very subtle, at an unspoken, minimal level, while the consequences can be much bigger than anticipated. It has been shown, for instance, that the more young adults have been exposed to food sharing during their childhood, the more often they tend to act pro-socially as an adult, by offering help to family, friends, acquaintances, and even complete strangers.[170] Importantly, however, not all occasions of commensality matter equally. There is a difference between "eating together," where everyone at the table has their own plate/meal, and "sharing food," where everyone around the table is eating from the same pots/foods. Eating together is common when we dine out, but increasingly also happens at home, during family meals. In an attempt to avoid conflict, some families will serve different meals that cater to every individual preference. In contrast, sharing food is about everyone having the same food, served from shared plates and pots. Only in these occasions does moral socialization happen; the sharing of food and not the mere act of eating together deals with the unspoken rules of who is to be served first, and who gets which portion of each dish.[171] Those who are fond of meatballs, and children in particular, will count how many balls are in the pot, how many end up on their plate, and the number on the plates of others. Any unequal distribution will generate conflict and a request to get a fair(er) share. For similar reasons, children's birthday parties fare much better in leading to moral socialization when there is one big cake rather than several individual cupcakes. Cupcakes are comfortable, because all children receive a cake of approximately the same size and can all take their individual cake at the same time, by which families avoid conflict. Conflict, instead, may emerge if one large celebration cake is served, as the last child needs to wait a long time to receive perhaps the last tiny piece of cake. However, this conflict may potentially remind several children about treating each other nicely; that it is considerate to give a bigger piece first to the birthday boy, and that it is painful if not everyone gets an equal share of the cake. Disliked foods will generate the same process; as much as children may monitor how meatballs are being distributed, they will also monitor how, for example, brussels sprouts are served. Do they get more than other family members? Is this fair? Meals where foods are shared have the power to socialize individuals into becoming prosocial persons, whereas merely eating together cannot achieve this outcome to the same extent. In the study with the young adults, it was the frequencies of childhood food-sharing occasions that predicted their adult prosocial behavior, not the frequencies of how often they ate in the company of others.[172] For adults too, food sharing appears to matter, perhaps much more than we realize. When adults eat the same food, they trust each other more as compared to when they eat different foods.[173] When adults share plates, or feed each other (sharing utensils), they are perceived as very close, intimately involved.[174] Eating from the same pot, sharing utensils, sharing plates, and so on are all occasions where those who eat together may contaminate each other. For such occasions, trust is a necessity; people need to trust the chef who prepared the meal, as much as they need to trust everyone at the table with whom they share food. Every occasion of sharing food is, in the end, an occasion where people can poison each other, and exactly this threat makes the sharing of food such a strong signal of trust and unity.[175]

TO EAT OR NOT EAT MEAT: HOW (VEGETARIAN) DIETARY CHOICES INFLUENCE OUR SOCIAL LIFE

"To be or not to be?" asked Shakespeare's Prince Hamlet bemoaning the pain and unfairness of life, yet at the same time realizing that the alternative may even be worse. "To (eat) meat or not to (eat) meat?" is a similar question we raise here. For some, eating meat is painful and unfair to other animals, but the consequences of not eating meat may become painful and unfair to themselves. If it is true that what really connects us is the food we share, Claude Fischler's remark that "if you and I eat similar foods we are the same, whereas if you and I eat different foods we are different"[176] boils down to much more than the relation between food and identity. Food is part of our identity, and sharing food is necessary in building and maintaining close relationships. Our goal with the current volume was to explore what happens when people exclude foods from their diet, and in particular when these are foods most other people do eat, such as meat and other animal products. In the 1990s, an anthropologist[177] studied this topic in India, known for its relatively large community of vegetarians. The choice to eat or not eat meat in India is also related to their caste system, and sex differences, with especially women and higher caste Brahmins opting for a vegetarian diet, and relatively more men and lower caste non-Brahmins eating meat. This case study showed how vegetarian Brahmins struggled with everyday interactions because of their vegetarian food choice. When they left their house, and especially when they traveled to other countries, Brahmins experienced difficulties with sticking to their diet, resulting in some individuals even skipping meals for days in a row. They also found occasions where people of different communities met, including those with the vegetarian/non-vegetarian divide, to be challenging. Such events required careful planning, and hosts had to decide whether to opt to offer a pure all-vegetarian menu, or two categories of food (meat and vegetarian) that were kept separate and pure at all times. At weddings, where different caste backgrounds meet, most often vegetarian Brahmin food is served, even if the caste of the host is non-vegetarian. Or when, especially women, meet at clubs, awkwardness may also occur when vegetarian and non-vegetarian members eat together. In this study, Indian women who ate out and joined clubs were often more liberal in their ideas and dietary practices and were keen on mutual respect. They valued commensality very highly and treated it as a form of sociality and civility. Joining and eating in a social way was used to overcome caste differences, as well as religious differences between Hindus, Christians, and Muslims.[178] Food, and the sharing of food, was seen as a crucial element of living together in harmony. The price they may have paid for this harmony was that they had to be personally liberal and tolerant toward their own dietary choices as well, allowing themselves to deviate from some of the restricting rules.

Since the 1990s vegetarianism has grown in many other countries across the globe, and in the next chapters we explore if and how vegetarians in countries other than India experience changes in their identity and social life when they decide to ban meat from their diet. We have contributions from fifteen countries: Australia, Austria, Belgium, Brazil, Canada, Finland, Germany, Ireland, Israel, Italy, the Netherlands, South Africa, Turkey, the United Kingdom, and the United States. In all of these randomly sampled countries we contacted scholars with a simple request to interview one or more vegetarian individuals about their experiences with being vegetarian. Some included personal experiences, others captured the experience of different vegetarian profiles. Each chapter starts with a brief contextual introduction about the prevalence of vegetarianism in that specific country, followed by some background information about the motives to ban meat from the diet of those interviewed. Each chapter then reflects on how these dietary choices, along with their motives, may have influenced identities and social interactions. The chapters are offered in the alphabetical order of the covered countries but should not necessarily be read in that order. Each chapter stands on its own, and while overlap may occur, each chapter tells a unique story. At the end of this book, a short conclusion summarizes some key observations, highlighting the similarities and differences in what was collected from the fifteen participating countries. The conclusion offers opportunities for future research on this topic, along with practical tips and tricks to ease any ongoing disputes between those who do and do not eat meat. In the end, we believe that the only one who should answer the question "to eat or not eat meat?" should be the person asking this question of their own behavior. Food choices are individual choices, with a wide array of interesting, and until now, previously undocumented social consequences.

Suggested Readings

Alley, Thomas R., Lauren W. Brubaker, and Olivia M. Fox. "Courtship feeding in humans?," *Human Nature* 24, no. 4 (2013): 430–43.

Altus, Deborah E., and R. Mark Mathews. "Using family-style meals to increase participation and communication in persons with dementia." *Journal of Gerontological Nursing* 28, no. 9 (2002): 47–53.

Barr, Susan I., and Gwen E. Chapman. "Perceptions and practices of self-defined current vegetarian, former vegetarian, and nonvegetarian women." *Journal of the American Dietetic Association* 102, no. 3 (2002): 354–60.

Barthes, Roland. "Towards a Psychosociology of Contemporary Food Consumption." *Food and Culture: A Reader*. Ed. Carole Counihan and Penny Van Esterik. New York: Routledge (1997): 20–27.

Beardsworth, Alan, and Teresa Keil. "The vegetarian option: Varieties, conversions, motives and careers." *The Sociological Review* 40, no. 2 (1992): 253–93.

Berge, Jerica M., Melanie Wall, Tsun-Fang Hsueh, Jayne A. Fulkerson, Nicole Larson, and Dianne Neumark-Sztainer. "The protective role of family meals for youth obesity: 10-year longitudinal associations." *The Journal of Pediatrics* 166, no. 2 (2015): 296–301.

Bisogni, Carole A., Margaret Connors, Carol M. Devine, and Jeffery Sobal. "Who we are and how we eat: A qualitative study of identities in food choice." *Journal of Nutrition Education and Behavior* 34, no. 3 (2002): 128–39.

Bloch, Maurice. "Commensality and poisoning." *Social Research* (1999): 133–49.

Brillat-Savarin, Jean Anthelme. *The Physiology of Taste: Or Meditations on Transcendental Gastronomy*. New York: Knopf Doubleday Publishing, 2009.

Bryant, Christopher, and Julie Barnett. "Consumer acceptance of cultured meat: A systematic review." *Meat Science* 143 (2018): 8–17.

Caplan, Pat. "Crossing the veg/non-veg divide: Commensality and sociality among the middle classes in Madras/Chennai." *South Asia: Journal of South Asian Studies* 31, no. 1 (2008): 118–42.

Carsten, Janet. "The substance of kinship and the heat of the hearth: Feeding, personhood, and relatedness among Malays in Pulau Langkawi." *American Ethnologist* 22, no. 2 (1995): 223–41.

Charles, Nickie, and Marion Kerr. *Women, food, and families*. Manchester: Manchester University Press, 1988.

Chemnitz, Christine, and Stanka Becheva. "The meat atlas." Accessed September 4, 2018, https://www.boell.de/sites/default/files/meat_atlas2014_kommentierbar.pdf.

Christopher, Allison, John Bartkowski, and Timothy Haverda. "Portraits of veganism: A comparative discourse analysis of a second-order subculture." *Societies* 8, no. 3 (2018): 55.

Chuter, Robyn. "Finding companionship on the road less travelled: A netnography of the Whole Food Plant-Based Aussies Facebook group" (2018), Accessed October 23, 2018, http://ro.ecu.edu.au/theses_hons/1517.

Cooke, L. J., J. Wardle, E. L. Gibson, M. Sapochnik, A. Sheiham, and M. Lawson. "Demographic, familial and trait predictors of fruit and vegetable consumption by pre-school children." *Public Health Nutrition* 7, no. 2 (2004): 295–302.

De Backer, Charlotte J. S., Maryanne L. Fisher, Karolien Poels, and Koen Ponnet. "'Our' food versus 'my' food. Investigating the relation between childhood shared food practices and adult prosocial behavior in Belgium." *Appetite* 84 (2015): 54–60.

De Backer, Charlotte J. S. and Liselot Hudders. "From meatless Mondays to meatless Sundays: Motivations for meat reduction among vegetarians and semi-vegetarians who mildly or significantly reduce their meat intake." *Ecology of Food and Nutrition* 53, no. 6 (2014): 639–57.

De Backer, Charlotte J. S. and Liselot Hudders. "Meat morals: Relationship between meat consumption consumer attitudes towards human and animal welfare and moral behavior." *Meat Science* 99 (2015): 68–74.

DeVault, Marjorie L. *Feeding the Family: The Social Organization of Caring as Gendered Work*. Chicago: University of Chicago Press, 1994.

Dikkanen, Siri Lavik. 1965. "Sirma: Residence and work organization in a Lappish-speaking community." *Samiske Samlinger*. Oslo, Norway: Norsk Folkemuseum, http://ehrafworldcultures.yale.edu/document?id=ep04-015.

Dinu, Monica, Rosanna Abbate, Gian Franco Gensini, Alessandro Casini, and Francesco Sofi. "Vegetarian, vegan diets and multiple health outcomes: A systematic review with meta-analysis of observational studies." *Critical Reviews in Food Science and Nutrition* 57, no. 17 (2017): 3640–49.

Dong, Lan. "Eating Different, Looking Different: Food in Asian American Childhood." *Critical Approaches to Food in Children's Literature*. Ed. Kara K. Keeling and Scott T. Pollard. New York: Routledge (2008): 137–47.

Dwyer, Laura, April Oh, Heather Patrick, and Erin Hennessy. "Promoting family meals: A review of existing interventions and opportunities for future research." *Adolescent Health, Medicine and Therapeutics* 6 (2015): 115.

Eisenberg, Marla E., Rachel E. Olson, Dianne Neumark-Sztainer, Mary Story, and Linda H. Bearinger. "Correlations between family meals and psychosocial well-being among adolescents." *Archives of Pediatrics & Adolescent Medicine* 158, no. 8 (2004): 792–96.

Fenton, Tanis, and Chelsia Gillis. "Plant-based diets do not prevent most chronic diseases." *Critical Reviews in Food Science and Nutrition* (2018): 1–2.

Festinger, Leon. *A Theory of Cognitive Dissonance*. Vol. 2. Stanford: Stanford University Press, 1962.

Fiese, Barbara H., Kimberly P. Foley, and Mary Spagnola. "Routine and ritual elements in family mealtimes: Contexts for child well-being and family identity." *New Directions for Child and Adolescent Development*, 2006, no. 111 (2006): 67–89.

Fischler, Claude. "Food, self and identity." Information (International Social Science Council) 27, no. 2 (1988): 275–92.

Fischler, Claude. "Commensality, society and culture." *Social Science Information* 50, no. 3–4 (2011): 528–48.

Fischler, Claude. "Gastro-nomy, Gastro-anomy, Gastro-autonomy and the Invention of choice." *Plenary Lecture at IEHCA 2017 the Third International Conference on Food History and Food Studies.* Tours: University Francois-Rabelais, 2017, June 1.

Fox, Robin. "Food and eating: An anthropological perspective." *Social Issues Research Centre.* Ed. SIRC. SIRC, n.d. Web. 1 Oct. 2014, http://www.sirc.org/publik/foxfood.pdf.

Fulkerson, Jayne A., Mary Story, Dianne Neumark-Sztainer, and Sarah Rydell. "Family meals: Perceptions of benefits and challenges among parents of 8- to 10-year-old children." *Journal of the American Dietetic Association* 108, no. 4 (2008): 706–709.

Fulkerson, Jayne A., Nicole Larson, Melissa Horning, and Dianne Neumark-Sztainer. "A review of associations between family or shared meal frequency and dietary and weight status outcomes across the lifespan." *Journal of Nutrition Education and Behavior* 46, no. 1 (2014): 2–19.

Giacoman, Claudia. "The dimensions and role of commensality: A theoretical model drawn from the significance of communal eating among adults in Santiago, Chile." *Appetite* 107 (2016): 460–70.

Gilbody, Simon M., Sara FL Kirk, and Andrew J. Hill. "Vegetarianism in young women: Another means of weight control?" *International Journal of Eating Disorders* 26, no. 1 (1999): 87–90.

Graça, João, Maria Manuela Calheiros, and Abílio Oliveira. "Situating moral disengagement: Motivated reasoning in meat consumption and substitution." *Personality and Individual Differences* 90 (2016): 353–64.

Greenebaum, Jessica. "Veganism, identity and the quest for authenticity." *Food, Culture & Society* 15, no. 1 (2012): 129–44.

Greenebaum, Jessica. "Managing impressions: 'Face-saving' strategies of vegetarians and vegans." *Humanity & society* 36, no. 4 (2012): 309–25.

Greenebaum, Jessica, and Brandon Dexter. "Vegan men and hybrid masculinity." *Journal of Gender Studies* 27, no. 6 (2018): 637–48.

Grevet, Catherine, Anthony Tang, and Elizabeth Mynatt. "Eating alone, together: New forms of commensality." In *Proceedings of the 17th ACM international conference on Supporting group work*, pp. 103–106. ACM, 2012.

Hamburg, Myrte Esther, Catrin Finkenauer, and Carlo Schuengel. "Food for love: The role of food offering in empathic emotion regulation." *Frontiers in Psychology* 5 (2014): 32.

Hanson, Kobena T. "Rethinking the Akan household: Acknowledging the importance of culturally and linguistically meaningful images." *Africa Today* (2004): 27–45.

Heiss, Sydney, and Julia M. Hormes. "Ethical concerns regarding animal use mediate the relationship between variety of pets owned in childhood and vegetarianism in adulthood." *Appetite* 123 (2018): 43–48.

Hirschler, Christopher A. "'What pushed me over the edge was a deer hunter': Being vegan in North America." *Society & Animals* 19, no. 2 (2011): 156–74.

Hu, Frank B. "Plant-based foods and prevention of cardiovascular disease: An overview." *The American journal of clinical nutrition* 78, no. 3 (2003): 544S–551S.

Hye-Cheon Kim, Karen, Wm Alex Mcintosh, Karen S. Kubena, and Jeffery Sobal. "Religion, social support, food-related social support, diet, nutrition, and anthropometrics in older adults." *Ecology of Food and Nutrition* 47, no. 3 (2008): 205–28.

Ishikawa, Midori, et al. "'Eating together' is associated with food behaviors and demographic factors of older Japanese people who live alone." *The Journal of Nutrition, Health & Aging* 21, no. 6 (2017): 662–72.

Jaeggi, Adrian V., and Michael Gurven. "Reciprocity explains food sharing in humans and other primates independent of kin selection and tolerated scrounging: A phylogenetic meta-analysis." *Proceedings of the Royal Society of London B: Biological Sciences* 280, no. 1768 (2013): 20131615.

Jones, Martin. *Feast: Why Humans Share Food* (2007). Oxford: Oxford University Press.

Julier, Alice P. *Eating Together: Food, Friendship and Inequality*. Champaign: University of Illinois Press, 2013.

Kaplan, Hillard, Kim Hill, Jane Lancaster, and A. Magdalena Hurtado. "A theory of human life history evolution: Diet, intelligence, and longevity." *Evolutionary Anthropology: Issues, News, and Reviews* 9, no. 4 (2000): 156–85.

Kimura, Yumi, T. et al. "Eating alone among community-dwelling Japanese elderly: Association with depression and food diversity." *The Journal of Nutrition, Health & Aging* 16, no. 8 (2012): 728–31.

King, Stacie M. "4 Remembering one and all: Early postclassic residential burial in coastal Oaxaca, Mexico." *Archeological Papers of the American Anthropological Association* 20, no. 1 (2010): 44–58.

Kothari, Geeta. "If you are what you eat, then what am I?" *Kenyon Review* (1999): 6–14.

Kremmer, Debbie, Annie S. Anderson, and David W. Marshall. "Living together and eating together: Changes in food choice and eating habits during the transition from single to married/cohabiting." *The Sociological Review* 46, no. 1 (1998): 48–72.

Kunst, Jonas R., and Sigrid M. Hohle. "Meat eaters by dissociation: How we present, prepare and talk about meat increases willingness to eat meat by reducing empathy and disgust." *Appetite* 105 (2016): 758–74.

Lamphere, Louise. 1977. "To Run After Them: Cultural and Social Bases f Cooperation in a Navajo Community." Tucson: University of Arizona Press, http://ehrafworld-cultures.yale.edu/document?id=nt13-193.

Larson, Nicole, Jayne Fulkerson, Mary Story, and Dianne Neumark-Sztainer. "Shared meals among young adults are associated with better diet quality and predicted by family meal patterns during adolescence." *Public Health Nutrition* 16, no. 5 (2013b): 883–93.

Lévi-Strauss, Claude. *The Raw and the Cooked*. London: Jonathan Cape, 1970.

Li, Tania Murray. "Working separately but eating together: Personhood, property, and power in conjugal relations." *American Ethnologist* 25, no. 4 (1998): 675–94.

Lokuruka, Michael NI. "Meat is the meal and status is by meat: Recognition of rank, wealth, and respect through meat in Turkana culture." *Food & Foodways* 14, no. 3–4 (2006): 201–29.

Loughnan, Steve, Nick Haslam, and Brock Bastian. "The role of meat consumption in the denial of moral status and mind to meat animals." *Appetite* 55, no. 1 (2010): 156–59.

Loughnan, Steve, Brock Bastian, and Nick Haslam. "The psychology of eating animals." *Current Directions in Psychological Science* 23, no. 2 (2014): 104–8.

Lymperaki, Marianna, Dushka Urem-Kotsou, Stavros Kotsos, and Kostas Kotsakis. "Household scales: What cooking pots can tell us about households in the Late Neolithic Stavroupoli (Northern Greece)." *Open Archaeology* 2, no. 1 (2016).

Mameli, Matteo. "Meat made us moral: A hypothesis on the nature and evolution of moral judgment." *Biology & Philosophy* 28, no. 6 (2013): 903–31.

Mannur, Anita. "Culinary fictions: Immigrant foodways and race in Indian American literature." *Asian American Studies after Critical Mass*. Ed. By Kent. A. Ono, Malden, MA: Blackwell Publishing (2008): 56–70.

Marshall, David W. and Annie S. Anderson. "Proper meals in transition: Young married couples on the nature of eating together." *Appetite* 39, no. 3 (2002): 193–206.

Meiselman, Herbert. L., ed. *Dimensions of the meal: The science, culture, business and art of eating*. Aspen: Gaithersburg, 2000.

Milton, Katharine. "A hypothesis to explain the role of meat-eating in human evolution." *Evolutionary Anthropology Issues News and Reviews* 8, no. 1 (1999): 11–21.

Mishori, Daniel. "Environmental vegetarianism: Conflicting principles, constructive virtues." *The Law & Ethics of Human Rights* 11, no. 2 (2017): 253.

Motta, Roberto Mauro Cortez. "Meat and feast: The Xango religion of Recife, Brazil." (1990): 0722-0722.

Mullee, Amy et al., "Vegetarianism and meat consumption: A comparison of attitudes and beliefs between vegetarian, semi-vegetarian, and omnivorous subjects in Belgium." *Appetite* 114 (2017): 299–305.

Nemeroff, Carol, and Paul Rozin. "'You are what you eat.' Applying the demand-free 'impressions' technique to an unacknowledged belief." *Ethos* 17, no. 1 (1989): 50–69.

Nestle, Marion. "Animal v. plant foods in human diets and health: Is the historical record unequivocal?," *Proceedings of the Nutrition Society* 58, no. 2 (1999): 211–18.

Newton, Janice. 1985. "Orokaiva Production and Change." *Pacific Research Monograph.* Canberra: Development Studies Centre, Australian National University, http://ehrafworldcultures.yale.edu/document?id=oj23-029.

Nicklas, Theresa A., Tom Baranowski, Janice C. Baranowski, Karen Cullen, LaTroy Rittenberry, and Norma Olvera. "Family and child-care provider influences on preschool children's fruit, juice, and vegetable consumption." *Nutrition Reviews* 59, no. 7 (2001): 224–35.

Nijdam, Durk, Trudy Rood, and Henk Westhoek. "The price of protein: Review of land use and carbon footprints from life cycle assessments of animal food products and their substitutes." *Food Policy* 37, no. 6 (2012): 760–70.

Nijs, Kristel, Cees De Graaf, Els Siebelink, Ybel H. Blauw, Vincent Vanneste, Frans J. Kok, and Wija A. Van Staveren. "Effect of family-style meals on energy intake and risk of malnutrition in Dutch nursing home residents: A randomized controlled trial." *The Journals of Gerontology Series A: Biological Sciences and Medical Sciences* 61, no. 9 (2006): 935–42.

Oberst, Lindsay. "Vegan Statistics: Why the Global Rise in Plant-Based Eating Isn't a Fad." Accessed September 4, 2018, https://foodrevolution.org/blog/vegan-statistics-global/.

Ochs, Elinor, and Merav Shohet. "The cultural structuring of mealtime socialization." *New Directions for Child and Adolescent Development* 2006, no. 111 (2006): 35–49.

Onwezen, Marleen C., and Cor N. van der Weele. "When indifference is ambivalence: Strategic ignorance about meat consumption." *Food Quality and Preference* 52 (2016): 96–105.

Patrick, Heather, and Theresa A. Nicklas. "A review of family and social determinants of children's eating patterns and diet quality." *Journal of the American College of Nutrition* 24, no. 2 (2005): 83–92.

Phull, Surinder, Wendy Wills, and Angela Dickinson "Is it a pleasure to eat together? Theoretical reflections on conviviality and the Mediterranean diet." *Sociology Compass,* 9(11) (2015a): 977–86.

Phull, Surinder, Wendy Wills, and Angela Dickinson. "The Mediterranean diet: Socio-cultural relevance for contemporary health promotion." *The Open Public Health Journal* 8 (2015b): 35–40.

Potts, Annie, and Jovian Parry. "Vegan sexuality: Challenging heteronormative masculinity through meat-free sex." *Feminism & Psychology* 20, no. 1 (2010): 53–72.

Pulleyn, Simon. "Why vegetarianism wasn't on the menu in early Greece." *Ethical Vegetarianism and Veganism,* Ed. Andrew Linzey and Clair Linzey (2018): 72–81.

Quick, Brian L., Barbara H. Fiese, Barbara Anderson, Brenda D. Koester, and Diane W. Marlin. "A formative evaluation of shared family mealtime for parents of toddlers and young children." *Health Communication* 26, no. 7 (2011): 656–66.

Rao, Nirmala, and Sunita Mahtani Stewart. "Cultural influences on sharer and recipient behavior: Sharing in Chinese and Indian preschool children." *Journal of Cross-Cultural Psychology* 30, no. 2 (1999): 219–41.

Reicks, Marla, Jinan Banna, Mary Cluskey, Carolyn Gunther, Nobuko Hongu, Rickelle Richards, Glade Topham, and Siew Sun Wong. "Influence of parenting practices on eating behaviors of early adolescents during independent eating occasions: implications for obesity prevention." *Nutrients* 7, no. 10 (2015): 8783–8801.

Rosenfeld, Daniel L., and Anthony L. Burrow. "The unified model of vegetarian identity: A conceptual framework for understanding plant-based food choices." *Appetite* 112 (2017): 78–95.

Rosenfeld, Daniel L. "The psychology of vegetarianism: Recent advances and future directions." *Appetite* 131 (2018): 125–38.

Rouse, Ian L., Bruce K. Armstrong, and Lawrence J. Beilin. "Vegetarian diet, lifestyle and blood pressure in two religious populations." *Clinical and Experimental Pharmacology and Physiology* 9, no. 3 (1982): 327–30.

Rothgerber, Hank. "A meaty matter. Pet diet and the vegetarian's dilemma." *Appetite* 68 (2013): 76–82.

Rothgerber, Hank. "Efforts to overcome vegetarian-induced dissonance among meat eaters." *Appetite* 79 (2014): 32–41.

Rothgerber, Hank. "Real men don't eat (vegetable) quiche: Masculinity and the justification of meat consumption." *Psychology of Men & Masculinity* 14 (2013): 363–75.

Rozin, Paul. "The meaning of food in our lives: A cross-cultural perspective on eating and well-being." *Journal of Nutrition Education and Behavior* 37 (2005): S107–S112.

Rozin, Paul, Maureen Markwith, and Caryn Stoess. "Moralization and becoming a vegetarian: The transformation of preferences into values and the recruitment of disgust." *Psychological Science* 8, no. 2 (1997): 67–73.

Ruby, Matthew B., and Steven J. Heine. "Too close to home. Factors predicting meat avoidance." *Appetite* 59, no. 1 (2012): 47–52.

Sawe, Benjamin Elisha. "Countries with the highest rates of vegetarianism. Worldatlas." Accessed February 9, 2018, https://www.worldatlas.com/articles/countries-with-the-highest-rates-of-vegetarianism.html (May 1, 2017).

Scholliers, Peter. *Food, Drink and Identity: Cooking, Eating and Drinking in Europe since the Middle Ages.* Oxford: Berg, 2001.

Spencer, Colin. *Vegetarianism: A History.* London: Grub Street, 2000.

Stanford, Craig B., and Henry T. Bunn, eds. *Meat-eating and Human Evolution.* Oxford: Oxford University Press, 2001.

Stevens, Jeffrey R., and Ian C. Gilby. "A conceptual framework for nonkin food sharing: Timing and currency of benefits." *Animal Behaviour* 67, no. 4 (2004): 603–14.

Sweetman, Claire, Laura McGowan, Helen Croker, and Lucy Cooke. "Characteristics of family mealtimes affecting children's vegetable consumption and liking." *Journal of the American Dietetic Association* 111, no. 2 (2011): 269–73.

Tan, Hui Shan Grace, Arnout RH Fischer, Patcharaporn Tinchan, Markus Stieger, L. P. A. Steenbekkers, and Hans CM van Trijp. "Insects as food: Exploring cultural exposure and individual experience as determinants of acceptance." *Food Quality and Preference* 42 (2015): 78–89.

Thomas, Margaret A. "Are vegans the same as vegetarians? The effect of diet on perceptions of masculinity." *Appetite* 97 (2016): 79–86.

Torreiro Pazo, Paula. *Diasporic Tastescapes. Intersections of Food and Identity in Asian American Literature* (2016). Vienna: Lit Verslag GmbH & Co.

Turner-McGrievy, Gabrielle M., Neal D. Barnard, and Anthony R. Scialli. "A two-year randomized weight loss trial comparing a vegan diet to a more moderate low-fat diet." *Obesity* 15, no. 9 (2007): 2276–81.

Twine, Richard. "Vegan killjoys at the table—Contesting happiness and negotiating relationships with food practices." *Societies* 4, no. 4 (2014): 623–39.

Valentine, Gill. "Eating in: Home, consumption and identity." *The Sociological Review* 47, no. 3 (1999): 491–524.

Verbeke, Wim, and Isabelle Vackier. "Profile and effects of consumer involvement in fresh meat." *Meat science* 67, no. 1 (2004): 159–68.

Wilks, Matti, and Clive J. C. Phillips. "Attitudes to in vitro meat: A survey of potential consumers in the United States." *PloS one* 12, no. 2 (2017): e0171904.

Woolley, Kaitlin, and Ayelet Fishbach. "A recipe for friendship: Similar food consumption promotes trust and cooperation." *Journal of Consumer Psychology* 27, no. 1 (2017): 1–10.

Wright, N., L. Wilson, M. Smith, B. Duncan, and P. McHugh. "The BROAD study: A randomised controlled trial using a whole food plant-based diet in the community for obesity, ischaemic heart disease or diabetes." *Nutrition & Diabetes* 7, no. 3 (2017): 256.

Wright, Lucy, M. Hickson, and G. Frost. "Eating together is important: Using a dining room in an acute elderly medical ward increases energy intake." *Journal of Human Nutrition and Dietetics* 19, no. 1 (2006): 23–26.

Wyse, Rebecca, Elizabeth Campbell, Nicole Nathan, and Luke Wolfenden. "Associations between characteristics of the home food environment and fruit and vegetable intake in preschool children: A cross-sectional study." *BMC Public Health* 11, no. 1 (2011): 938.

Yeh, Hsin-Yi. "Voice with every bite: Dietary identity and vegetarians 'the-second-best' boundary work." *Food, Culture & Society* 17, no. 4 (2014): 591–613.

Yiengprugsawan, Vasoontara, Cathy Banwell, Wakako Takeda, Jane Dixon, Sam-ang Seubsman, and Adrian C. Sleigh. "Health, happiness and eating together: what can a large Thai cohort study tell us?" *Global Journal of Health Science* 7, no. 4 (2015): 270.

Ziker, John, and Michael Schnegg. "Food sharing at meals." *Human Nature* 16, no. 2 (2005): 178–210.

Notes

1. Lindsay Oberst, "Vegan Statistics: Why the Global Rise in Plant-Based Eating Isn't a Fad," accessed September 4, 2018, https://foodrevolution.org/blog/vegan-statistics-global/.
2. Christine Chemnitz, and Stanka Becheva, "The meat atlas." Accessed September 4, 2018, https://www.boell.de/sites/default/files/meat_atlas2014_kommentierbar.pdf, 8.
3. Chemnitz, and Becheva, "The meat atlas," 48–49.

4. Elisha Sawe, "Countries with the highest rates of vegetarianism," https://www.worldatlas.com/articles/countries-with-the-highest-rates-of-vegetarianism.html (May 1, 2017). Accessed February 9, 2018.

5. Sawe, "Countries with the highest rates of vegetarianism."

6. Chemnitz, and Becheva, "The meat atlas," 9.

7. Peter Scholliers. *Food, Drink and Identity* (Oxford: Berg, 2001).

8. Jean Anthelme Brillat-Savarin. *The Physiology of Taste* (New York: Knopf Doubleday Publishing, 2009), 15.

9. Claude Fischler. "Commensality, society and culture," *Social Science Information* 50, no. 3–4 (2011): 528–48.

10. Claude Fischler, "Gastro-nomy, gastro-anomy, gastro-autonomy and the invention of choice," *Plenary Lecture at IEHCA 2017,* Tours: Universite Francois-Rabelais, June 1, 2017.

11. Roland Barthes, "Towards a psychosociology of contemporary food consumption," *Food and Culture: A Reader.* Ed. Carole Counihan and Penny Van Esterik. New York: Routledge (1997): 20–27.

12. Claude Lévi-Strauss, *The Raw and the Cooked* (London: Jonathan Cape, 1970), 164.

13. Claude Fischler, "Food, self and identity," 277–79

14. Claude Fischler, "Food, self and identity," 278

15. Katharine Milton, "A hypothesis to explain the role of meat-eating in human evolution," *Evolutionary Anthropology Issues News and Reviews* 8, no. 1 (1999): 11.

16. Milton, "A hypothesis to explain the role of meat-eating in human evolution," 11.

17. Milton, "A hypothesis to explain the role of meat-eating in human evolution," 11.

18. Hillard Kaplan et al., "A theory of human life history evolution: diet, intelligence, and longevity." *Evolutionary Anthropology: Issues, News, and Reviews* 9, no. 4 (2000): 156.

19. Craig Stanford, and Henry Bunn, *Meat-eating and Human Evolution* (Oxford: Oxford University Press, 2001).

20. Kaplan, et al., "A theory of human life history evolution: Diet, intelligence, and longevity," 156.

21. Kaplan, et al., "A theory of human life history evolution: Diet, intelligence, and longevity," 170–71.

22. Kaplan, et al., "A theory of human life history evolution: Diet, intelligence, and longevity," 175.

23. Adrian Jaeggi, and Michael Gurven, "Reciprocity explains food sharing in humans and other primates independent of kin selection and tolerated scrounging: A phylogenetic meta-analysis," *Proceedings of the Royal Society of London B: Biological Sciences* 280, no. 1768 (2013): 1.

24. Jeffrey Stevens, and Ian Gilby, "A conceptual framework for nonkin food sharing: Timing and currency of benefits." *Animal Behaviour* 67, no. 4 (2004): 603..

25. Matteo Mameli, "Meat made us moral: A hypothesis on the nature and evolution of moral judgment," *Biology & Philosophy* 28, no. 6 (2013): 927–28.

26. Mameli, "Meat made us moral: A hypothesis on the nature and evolution of moral judgment," 903.

27. Charlotte De Backer, and Liselot Hudders, "From meatless Mondays to meatless Sundays: Motivations for meat reduction among vegetarians and semi-vegetarians who mildly or significantly reduce their meat intake," *Ecology of Food and Nutrition* 53, no. 6 (2014): 639.

28. Steve Loughnan, et al., "The psychology of eating animals," *Current Directions in Psychological Science* 23, no. 2 (2014): 104.

29. Hank Rothgerber, "A meaty matter. Pet diet and the vegetarian's dilemma," *Appetite* 68 (2013): 76.

30. Leon Festinger, *A Theory of Cognitive Dissonance*. Vol. 2 (Stanford: Stanford University Press, 1962).

31. Marleen Onwezen, and Cor van der Weele, "When indifference is ambivalence: Strategic ignorance about meat consumption," *Food Quality and Preference* 52 (2016): 96.

32. Matthew Ruby, and Steven Heine, "Too close to home. Factors predicting meat avoidance," *Appetite* 59, no. 1 (2012): 47.

33. Festinger, *A Theory of Cognitive Dissonance*, Vol. 2.

34. Hank Rothgerber, "Efforts to overcome vegetarian-induced dissonance among meat eaters," *Appetite* 79 (2014): 34

35. Jonas Kunst, and Sigrid Hohle, "Meat eaters by dissociation: How we present, prepare and talk about meat increases willingness to eat meat by reducing empathy and disgust," *Appetite* 105 (2016): 758.

36. João Graça, et al., "Situating moral disengagement: Motivated reasoning in meat consumption and substitution," *Personality and Individual Differences* 90 (2016): 353.

37. Charlotte De Backer, and Liselot Hudders, "Meat morals: Relationship between meat consumption consumer attitudes towards human and animal welfare and moral behavior," *Meat Science* 99 (2015): 68.

38. Rothgerber, "Efforts to overcome vegetarian-induced dissonance among meat eaters," 33–34.

39. Steve Loughnan, et al., "The role of meat consumption in the denial of moral status and mind to meat animals," *Appetite* 55, no. 1 (2010): 156.

40. Onwezen, and van der Weele, "When indifference is ambivalence: Strategic ignorance about meat consumption," 103.

41. Marion Nestle, "Animal v. plant foods in human diets and health: Is the historical record unequivocal?," *Proceedings of the Nutrition Society* 58, no. 2 (1999): 211.

42. Colin Spencer, *Vegetarianism: A History* (London: Grub Street, 2000).

43. Simon Pulleyn, "Why vegetarianism wasn't on the menu in early Greece," *Ethical Vegetarianism and Veganism* (2018): 72–73.

44. See for instance: Paul Rozin, Maureen Markwith, and Caryn Stoess, "Moralization and becoming a vegetarian: The transformation of preferences into values and the recruitment of disgust," *Psychological Science* 8, no. 2 (1997): 67.

45. De Backer, and Hudders. "From meatless Mondays to meatless Sundays," 639.

46. See, for example, a review paper that demonstrates health benefits of vegetarian and vegan diets: Monica Dinu, et al., "Vegetarian, vegan diets and multiple health outcomes: a systematic review with meta-analysis of observational

studies," *Critical Reviews in Food Science and Nutrition* 57, no. 17 (2017): 3640. Versus other studies that argue against such health claims, like Tanis Fenton and Chelsia Gillis, "Plant-based diets do not prevent most chronic diseases," *Critical Reviews in Food Science and Nutrition* (2018): 1.

47. See a recent longitudinal study by Wright, et al., "The BROAD study: A randomised controlled trial using a whole food plant-based diet in the community for obesity, ischaemic heart disease or diabetes," *Nutrition & Diabetes* 7, no. 3 (2017): e256. Or, for a review, see Frank Hu, "Plant-based foods and prevention of cardiovascular disease: an overview," *The American Journal of Clinical Nutrition* 78, no. 3 (2003): 544S–551S.

48. Gabrielle Turner-McGrievy, et al., "A two-year randomized weight loss trial comparing a vegan diet to a more moderate low-fat diet," *Obesity* 15, no. 9 (2007): 2276.

49. Simon Gilbody, Sara Kirk, and Andrew Hill, "Vegetarianism in young women: Another means of weight control?," *International Journal of Eating Disorders* 26, no. 1 (1999): 87.

50. Wim Verbeke, and Isabelle Vackier, "Profile and effects of consumer involvement in fresh meat," *Meat Science* 67, no. 1 (2004): 159.

51. Susan Barr, and Gwen Chapman, "Perceptions and practices of self-defined current vegetarian, former vegetarian, and nonvegetarian women," *Journal of the American Dietetic Association* 102, no. 3 (2002): 354.

52. Amy Mullee, et al., "Vegetarianism and meat consumption: A comparison of attitudes and beliefs between vegetarian, semi-vegetarian, and omnivorous subjects in Belgium," *Appetite* 114 (2017): 299.

53. Rozin, et al., "Moralization and becoming a vegetarian: The transformation of preferences into values and the recruitment of disgust," 67.

54. De Backer, and Hudders, "From meatless Mondays to meatless Sundays: Motivations for meat reduction among vegetarians and semi-vegetarians who mildly or significantly reduce their meat intake," 639.

55. Sydney Heiss, and Julia Hormes, "Ethical concerns regarding animal use mediate the relationship between variety of pets owned in childhood and vegetarianism in adulthood," *Appetite* 123 (2018): 43.

56. Matti Wilks, and Clive Phillips, "Attitudes to in vitro meat: A survey of potential consumers in the United States," *PloS one* 12, no. 2 (2017): e0171904.

57. Christopher Bryant, and Julie Barnett, "Consumer acceptance of cultured meat: A systematic review," *Meat Science* 143 (2018): 8.

58. Bryant, and Barnett, "Consumer acceptance of cultured meat: A systematic review," 8.

59. De Backer, and Hudders, "From meatless Mondays to meatless Sundays," 639.

60. Durk Nijdam, Trudy Rood, and Henk Westhoek, "The price of protein: Review of land use and carbon footprints from life cycle assessments of animal food products and their substitutes," *Food policy* 37, no. 6 (2012): 760.

61. Daniel Mishori, "Environmental Vegetarianism: Conflicting principles, constructive virtues," *The Law & Ethics of Human Rights* 11, no. 2 (2017): 253.

62. De Backer, and Hudders, "From meatless Mondays to meatless Sundays," 639.

63. Jessica Greenebaum, "Managing impressions: 'Face-saving' strategies of vegetarians and vegans," *Humanity & Society* 36, no. 4 (2012): 309.

64. Kim Hye-Cheon, et al., "Religion, social support, food-related social support, diet, nutrition, and anthropometrics in older adults," *Ecology of Food and Nutrition* 47, no. 3 (2008): 205.

65. Ian Rouse, Bruce Armstrong, and Lawrence Beilin, "Vegetarian diet, lifestyle and blood pressure in two religious populations," *Clinical and Experimental Pharmacology and Physiology* 9, no. 3 (1982): 327.

66. Brillat-Savarin, *The Physiology of Taste* (New York: Knopf Doubleday Publishing, 2009), 15.

67. Claude Fischler, "Food, self and identity," *Information* 27, no. 2 (1988): 277–79.

68. Daniel Rosenfeld, and Anthony L. Burrow, "The unified model of vegetarian identity: A conceptual framework for understanding plant-based food choices," *Appetite* 112 (2017): 78.

69. Claude Fischler, "Food, self and identity," 279.

70. Carol Nemeroff, and Paul Rozin, "'You are what you eat': Applying the demand-free 'impressions' technique to an unacknowledged belief," 59–63.

71. Carol Nemeroff, and Paul Rozin, "'You are what you eat': Applying the demand-free 'impressions' technique to an unacknowledged belief," *Ethos* 17, no. 1 (1989): 50–51.

72. Roland Barthes, "Towards a psychosociology of contemporary food consumption," *Food and Culture: A Reader*. Ed. Carole Counihan and Penny Van Esterik. New York: Routledge (1997): 20–27.

73. Claude Lévi-Strauss, *The Raw and the Cooked* (London: Jonathan Cape, 1970), 164.

74. Claude Fischler, "Food, self and identity," 277–79.

75. Claude Fischler, "Food, self and identity," 278.

76. Claude Fischler, "Food, self and identity," 278–79.

77. Claude Fischler, "Food, self and identity," 285.

78. Hui Shan Grace Tan, et al., "Insects as food: Exploring cultural exposure and individual experience as determinants of acceptance," *Food Quality and Preference* 42 (2015): 78.

79. Kaitlin Woolley, and Ayelet Fishbach, "A recipe for friendship: Similar food consumption promotes trust and cooperation," *Journal of Consumer Psychology* 27, no. 1 (2017): 1–10.

80. Geeta Kothari, "If you are what you eat, then what am I?" *Kenyon Review* (1999): 6–14.

81. Anita Mannur, "Culinary fictions: Immigrant foodways and race in Indian American literature," *Asian American Studies after Critical Mass*. Ed. By Kent. A. Ono, Malden MA: Blackwell Publishing (2008): 56–70.

82. Lan Dong, "Eating Different, Looking Different: Food in Asian American Childhood," *Critical Approaches to Food in Children's Literature*. Ed. Kara K. Keeling and Scott T. Pollard. New York: Routledge (2008): 137–47.

83. Paula Torreiro Pazo, *Diasporic Tastescapes. Intersections of Food and Identity in Asian American Literature* (2016). Vienna: Lit Verslag GmbH & Co.

84. Daniel Rosenfeld, and Anthony L. Burrow, "The unified model of vegetarian identity: A conceptual framework for understanding plant-based food choices," 78.

85. Allison Christopher, John Bartkowski, and Timothy Haverda, "Portraits of Veganism: A Comparative Discourse Analysis of a Second-Order Subculture," *Societies* 8, no. 3 (2018): 55.

86. Carole Bisogni, Margaret Connors, Carol Devine, and Jeffery Sobal, "Who we are and how we eat: a qualitative study of identities in food choice," *Journal of Nutrition Education and Behavior* 34, no. 3 (2002): 136.

87. Daniel Rosenfeld, and Anthony L. Burrow, "The unified model of vegetarian identity: A conceptual framework for understanding plant-based food choices," 91–92.

88. Alan Beardsworth, and Teresa Keil, "The vegetarian option: Varieties, conversions, motives and careers." *The Sociological Review* 40, no. 2 (1992): 253.

89. Daniel Rosenfeld, and Anthony L. Burrow, "The unified model of vegetarian identity: A conceptual framework for understanding plant-based food choices," 78.

90. See Daniel Rosenfeld, "The psychology of vegetarianism: Recent advances and future directions," *Appetite* 131 (2018): 129–30 for a good overview of these works.

91. Margaret Thomas, "Are vegans the same as vegetarians? The effect of diet on perceptions of masculinity," *Appetite* 97 (2016): 79–86.

92. Claude Fischler, "Food, self and identity," 279–80.

93. Margaret Thomas, "Are vegans the same as vegetarians? The effect of diet on perceptions of masculinity," 85.

94. Margaret Thomas, "Are vegans the same as vegetarians? The effect of diet on perceptions of masculinity," 85.

95. Hank Rothgerber, "Real men don't eat (vegetable) quiche: Masculinity and the justification of meat consumption," *Psychology of Men & Masculinity* 14(4) (2013): 363.

96. Jessica Greenebaum, and Brandon Dexter, "Vegan men and hybrid masculinity," *Journal of Gender Studies* 27, no. 6 (2018): 637–48.

97. Hank Rothgerber, "Efforts to overcome vegetarian-induced dissonance among meat eaters," *Appetite* 79 (2014): 32.

98. Richard Twine, "Vegan killjoys at the table—Contesting happiness and negotiating relationships with food practices," *Societies* 4, no. 4 (2014): 629.

99. Christopher Hirschler, "'What pushed me over the edge was a deer hunter': Being vegan in North America," *Society & Animals* 19, no. 2 (2011): 162.

100. Geeta Kothari, "If you are what you eat, then what am I?" *Kenyon Review* (1999): 12.

101. Annie Potts, and Jovian Parry, "Vegan sexuality: Challenging heteronormative masculinity through meat-free sex," *Feminism & Psychology* 20, no. 1 (2010): 53.

102. Daniel Rosenfeld, "The psychology of vegetarianism: Recent advances and future directions," *Appetite* 131 (2018): 125.

103. Richard Twine, "Vegan killjoys at the table—Contesting happiness and negotiating relationships with food practices," 635.

104. Robyn Chuter, "Finding companionship on the road less travelled: A netnography of the Whole Food Plant-Based Aussies Facebook group" (2018), retrieved from http://ro.ecu.edu.au/theses_hons/1517.

105. Jessica Greenebaum, "Veganism, identity and the quest for authenticity," *Food, Culture & Society* 15, no. 1 (2012): 129.

106. Daniel Rosenfeld, and Anthony L. Burrow, "The unified model of vegetarian identity: A conceptual framework for understanding plant-based food choices," 78.

107. Hsin-Yi Yeh, "Voice with every bite: Dietary identity and vegetarians 'the-second-best' boundary work," *Food, Culture & Society* 17, no. 4 (2014): 591.

108. Carole Bisogni, et al., "Who we are and how we eat: A qualitative study of identities in food choice," *Journal of Nutrition Education and Behavior* 34, no. 3 (2002): 128.

109. Surinder Phull, Wendy Wills, and Angela Dickinson, "The Mediterranean diet: Socio-cultural relevance for contemporary health promotion," *The Open Public Health Journal* 8 (2015b): 35.

110. Jayne Fulkerson, Nicole Larson, Melissa Horning, and Dianne Neumark-Sztainer, "A review of associations between family or shared meal frequency and dietary and weight status outcomes across the lifespan," *Journal of Nutrition Education and Behavior* 46, no. 1 (2014): 2.

111. Marla Reicks, et al., "Influence of parenting practices on eating behaviors of early adolescents during independent eating occasions: Implications for obesity prevention," *Nutrients* 7, no. 10 (2015): 8783.

112. Cooke, et al., "Demographic, familial and trait predictors of fruit and vegetable consumption by pre-school children," *Public Health Nutrition* 7, no. 2 (2004): 295.

113. Rebecca Wyse, Elizabeth Campbell, Nicole Nathan, and Luke Wolfenden, "Associations between characteristics of the home food environment and fruit and vegetable intake in preschool children: A cross-sectional study," *BMC Public Health* 11, no. 1 (2011): 938.

114. Theresa Nicklas, et al., "Family and child-care provider influences on preschool children's fruit, juice, and vegetable consumption," *Nutrition Reviews* 59, no. 7 (2001): 224.

115. Claire Sweetman, Laura McGowan, Helen Croker, and Lucy Cooke, "Characteristics of family mealtimes affecting children's vegetable consumption and liking," *Journal of the American Dietetic Association* 111, no. 2 (2011): 269.

116. See Heather Patrick, and Theresa Nicklas, "A review of family and social determinants of children's eating patterns and diet quality," *Journal of the American College of Nutrition* 24, no. 2 (2005) for a thorough overview.

117. See, e.g., Jerica Berge, et al., "The protective role of family meals for youth obesity: 10-year longitudinal associations," *The Journal of Pediatrics* 166, no. 2 (2015): 296.

118. Nicole Larson, Jayne Fulkerson, Mary Story, and Dianne Neumark-Sztainer, "Shared meals among young adults are associated with better diet quality and predicted by family meal patterns during adolescence," *Public Health Nutrition* 16, no. 5 (2013b): 883.

119. Jayne Fulkerson, Nicole Larson, Melissa Horning, and Dianne Neumark-Sztainer, "A review of associations between family or shared meal frequency and dietary and weight status outcomes across the lifespan," 2.

120. Midori Ishikawa, et al., "'Eating together' is associated with food behaviors and demographic factors of older Japanese people who live alone," *The Journal of Nutrition, Health & Aging* 21, no. 6 (2017): 662.

121. Kristel Nijs, et al., "Effect of family-style meals on energy intake and risk of malnutrition in Dutch nursing home residents: A randomized controlled trial," *The Journals of Gerontology Series A: Biological Sciences and Medical Sciences* 61, no. 9 (2006): 935.

122. Lucy Wright, M. Hickson, and G. Frost, "Eating together is important: Using a dining room in an acute elderly medical ward increases energy intake," *Journal of Human Nutrition and Dietetics* 19, no. 1 (2006): 23.

123. Deborah Altus, and Mark Mathews, "Using family-style meals to increase participation and communication in persons with dementia," *Journal of Gerontological Nursing* 28, no. 9 (2002): 47.

124. Laura Dwyer, April Oh, Heather Patrick, and Erin Hennessy, "Promoting family meals: A review of existing interventions and opportunities for future research," *Adolescent Health, Medicine and Therapeutics,* 6 (2015): 115.

125. Surinder Phull, Wendy Wills, and Angela Dickinson, "The Mediterranean diet: Socio-cultural relevance for contemporary health promotion," 35.

126. Catherine Grevet, Anthony Tang, and Elizabeth Mynatt, "Eating alone, together: new forms of commensality," *Proceedings of the 17th ACM International Conference on Supporting Group Work,* pp. 103–6. ACM, 2012.

127. Robin Fox, "Food and Eating: An Anthropological Perspective," *Social Issues Research Centre.* Ed. SIRC. SIRC, n.d. Web. October 1, 2014, http://www.sirc.org/publik/foxfood.pdf.

128. Fox, "Food and eating: An anthropological perspective."

129. Kobena Hanson, "Rethinking the Akan household: Acknowledging the importance of culturally and linguistically meaningful images," *Africa Today* (2004): 27.

130. Janet Carsten, "The substance of kinship and the heat of the hearth: Feeding, personhood, and relatedness among Malays in Pulau Langkawi," *American Ethnologist* 22, no. 2 (1995): 223.

131. Tania Li, "Working separately but eating together: Personhood, property, and power in conjugal relations," *American Ethnologist* 25, no. 4 (1998): 675.

132. Louise Lamphere, 1977. "To run after them: Cultural and social bases of cooperation in a Navajo community." Tucson: University of Arizona Press, http://ehrafworldcultures.yale.edu/document?id=nt13-193.

133. Siri Lavik Dikkanen, 1965. "Sirma: Residence and work organization in a Lappish-speaking community," *Samiske Samlinger.* Oslo, Norway: Norsk Folkemuseum, http://ehrafworldcultures.yale.edu/document?id=ep04-015.

134. Janice Newton, 1985. "Orokaiva production and change." *Pacific Research Monograph.* Canberra: Development Studies Centre, Australian National University http://ehrafworldcultures.yale.edu/document?id=oj23-029.

135. John Ziker, and Michael Schnegg, "Food sharing at meals," *Human Nature* 16, no. 2 (2005): 178.

136. Hanson, "Rethinking the Akan household: Acknowledging the importance of culturally and linguistically meaningful images," 27.

137. Marianna Lymperaki, Dushka Urem-Kotsou, Stavros Kotsos, and Kostas Kotsakis, "Household scales: What cooking pots can tell us about households in the Late Neolithic Stavroupoli (Northern Greece)," *Open Archaeology* 2, no. 1 (2016).

138. Stacie King, "Remembering one and all: Early postclassic residential burial in coastal Oaxaca, Mexico," *Archeological Papers of the American Anthropological Association* 20, no. 1 (2010): 44.

139. Martin Jones, "Feast: why humans share food," Oxford: Oxford University Press, 2007.

140. See, for example, Roberto Motta and Mauro Cortez, "Meat and feast: The Xango religion of Recife, Brazil" (1990): 722.

141. See, for example, Michael Lokuruka, "Meat is the meal and status is by meat: Recognition of rank, wealth, and respect through meat in Turkana culture," *Food & Foodways* 14, no. 3–4 (2006): 201–29.

142. Jones, "Feast: Why humans share food."

143. Jones, "Feast: Why humans share food."

144. Surinder Phull, Wendy Wills, and Angela Dickinson, "Is it a pleasure to eat together? Theoretical reflections on conviviality and the Mediterranean diet," *Sociology Compass*, 9 (11) (2015a): 977.

145. Yumi Kimura, et al., "Eating alone among community-dwelling Japanese elderly: Association with depression and food diversity," *The Journal of Nutrition, Health & Aging* 16, no. 8 (2012): 728.

146. Ishikawa et al., "'Eating together' is associated with food behaviors and demographic factors of older Japanese people who live alone," 662.

147. Kimura, et al., "Eating alone among community-dwelling Japanese elderly: Association with depression and food diversity," 728.

148. Marla Eisenberg, et al., "Correlations between family meals and psychosocial well-being among adolescents," *Archives of Pediatrics & Adolescent Medicine* 158, no. 8 (2004): 792.

149. Vasoontara Yiengprugsawan, et al., "Health, happiness and eating together: What can a large Thai cohort study tell us?" *Global Journal of Health Science* 7, no. 4 (2015): 270.

150. Nirmala Rao, and Sunita Mahtani Stewart, "Cultural influences on sharer and recipient behavior: Sharing in Chinese and Indian preschool children," *Journal of Cross-Cultural Psychology* 30, no. 2 (1999): 219.

151. Paul Rozin, "The meaning of food in our lives: a cross-cultural perspective on eating and well-being," *Journal of Nutrition Education and Behavior* 37 (2005): 107.

152. Alice Julier, "*Eating Together: Food, Friendship and Inequality*" (Champaign: University of Illinois Press, 2013.

153. Debbie Kremmer, Annie S. Anderson, and David W. Marshall. "Living together and eating together: Changes in food choice and eating habits during the transition from single to married/cohabiting," *The Sociological Review* 46, no. 1 (1998): 48.

154. David Marshall and Annie S. Anderson, "Proper meals in transition: Young married couples on the nature of eating together," *Appetite* 39, no. 3 (2002): 193.

155. Myrte Esther Hamburg, Catrin Finkenauer, and Carlo Schuengel, "Food for love: The role of food offering in empathic emotion regulation," *Frontiers in Psychology* 5 (2014): 32.

156. Marjorie DeVault, F*eeding the Family: The Social Organization of Caring as Gendered Work*, Chicago: University of Chicago Press, 1994.

157. DeVault, *Feeding the Family: The Social Organization of Caring as Gendered Work*.

158. Barbara Fiese, Kimberly Foley, and Mary Spagnola, "Routine and ritual elements in family mealtimes: Contexts for child well-being and family identity," *New Directions for Child and Adolescent Development* 2006, no. 111 (2006): 67.

159. Nickie Charles, and Marion Kerr, *Women, Food, and Families*, Manchester: Manchester University Press, 1988: 17.

160. Jeffery Sobal, "Sociability and meals: Facilitation, commensality, and interaction," in *Dimensions of the Meal: The Science, Culture, Business and Art of Eating*, ed. Herbert.L. Meiselman (Aspen: Gaithersburg, 2000), 119.

161. Claudia Giacoman, "The dimensions and role of commensality: A theoretical model drawn from the significance of communal eating among adults in Santiago, Chile," *Appetite* 107 (2016): 460.

162. Gill Valentine, "Eating in: home, consumption and identity," *The Sociological Review* 47, no. 3 (1999): 491.

163. Elinor Ochs, and Merav Shohet, "The cultural structuring of mealtime socialization," *New Directions for Child and Adolescent Development* 2006, no. 111 (2006): 35.

164. Ochs, and Shohet, "The cultural structuring of mealtime socialization," 40–42.

165. Jayne A. Fulkerson, et al., "Family meals: Perceptions of benefits and challenges among parents of 8- to 10-year-old children," *Journal of the American Dietetic Association* 108, no. 4 (2008): 706.

166. Brian L Quick, et al., "A formative evaluation of shared family mealtime for parents of toddlers and young children," *Health Communication* 26, no. 7 (2011): 656.

167. Ochs, and Shohet, "The cultural structuring of mealtime socialization," 35.

168. Ochs, and Shohet, "The cultural structuring of mealtime socialization," 39.

169. Valentine, "Eating in: home, consumption and identity," 520–22.

170. Charlotte De Backer, et al., "'Our' food versus 'my' food. Investigating the relation between childhood shared food practices and adult prosocial behavior in Belgium," *Appetite* 84 (2015): 54.

171. De Backer, et al., "'Our' food versus 'my' food. Investigating the relation between childhood shared food practices and adult prosocial behavior in Belgium," 54–55.

172. De Backer et al., "'Our' food versus 'my' food. Investigating the relation between childhood shared food practices and adult prosocial behavior in Belgium," 54.

173. Woolley, and Fishbach. "A recipe for friendship: similar food consumption promotes trust and cooperation," 1.

174. Thomas R. Alley, Lauren W. Brubaker, and Olivia M. Fox. "Courtship feeding in humans?," *Human Nature* 24, no. 4 (2013): 430.

175. Maurice Bloch, "Commensality and poisoning," *Social Research* (1999): 133.

176. Fischler, "Gastro-nomy, gastro-anomy, gastro-autonomy and the invention of choice."

177. Pat Caplan, "Crossing the veg/non-veg divide: commensality and sociality among the middle classes in Madras/Chennai," *South Asia: Journal of South Asian Studies* 31, no. 1 (2008): 118.

178. Caplan, "Crossing the veg/non-veg divide: Commensality and sociality among the middle classes in Madras/Chennai," 140.

CHAPTER 1

AUSTRALIA

VEGANS, VEGETARIANS, AND AUSTRALIA

LELIA GREEN

A 2016 Roy Morgan poll identified the number of Australian vegetarians as having "risen from 1.7 million people (or 9.7% of the population) [in 2012] to almost 2.1 million (11.2%)."[1] Vegans are a necessary subset of lacto-ovo-vegetarians, in that in qualifying as a vegan, someone also fulfills all the requirements of being a vegetarian. Vegans in Australia are increasingly recognized as a viable "market segment," with Cormack writing in 2016 that Australia is the third fastest growing vegan market after the United Arab Emirates and China. Further, recent predictions indicate that "Australia's packaged vegan food market is currently worth almost $136 million, set to reach $215 million by 2020."[2] Even given Australia's comparatively small population size (24 million in 2016), and the fact that most vegan foods aren't packaged goods that are labelled as "vegan" but vegetable, fruits, nuts, and legumes etc., the $136 million figure makes Australia the world's fourth largest vegan packaged-goods market after the United States ($1.75 billion; 323 million population), Germany ($614 million; 83 million), and the UK ($507 million; 66 million).[3] I'm an Australian vegan, and I am one of the group of people buying those packaged goods.

ME AND MY DIETARY CHOICES

I identify as a 62-year-old female, vegan Australian who was raised in Britain. I became vegan in February 2007, when it was much less common than today, but nobody at that time would have thought I would still be vegan eleven years later. My many dietary weaknesses pre-veganism included comfort food such as bread and (thickly spread) butter, cheese on toast, bacon, roast meats, and ice cream. Further, my personal dietary and health history was a checkerboard record of attempts to address my decades' long issues with being overweight, which was triggered in early adolescence by a traumatic year in boarding school. None of the previous dietary interventions had lasted longer than a year, and each fad and enthusiasm was swiftly replaced by another which also promised to revolutionize my health and my weight. Early social reactions to a newly-minted vegan or vegetarian would often reflect the new convert's previous eating history. In my case, becoming vegan was met with a reaction of resignation mixed with a touch of disbelief.

Over the years, I have become aware that being vegan is tantamount to offering one's self up for moral judgment. Although I identify as a vegan, there are "purer" vegans than me, and others will sometimes point this out. For example, I make an exception for honey: in my vegan diet, honey is permissible. My husband recently began keeping bees in our backyard and even close proximity to these fascinating creatures has not changed my views that honey eating is permissible. I do appreciate that honey harvesting practices involve the destruction of "spare" queens and some loss of worker bees when the honey is extracted from the combs in a process that purer vegans have told me is "the rape of the hive."

It's not only other vegans that judge me as not-vegan-enough, however. A small selection of non-vegans and ex-vegans construct a mostly-vegan lifestyle as a moral statement that invites external judgment. They possibly respond to what they seem to see as an implied criticism of the standard diet (or purer veganism) with attack. For these vegans, I fly too much (certainly more than they do) and create far more global warming than their meat eating would ever do. Wearing clothes which involve wool (or, worse, leather) can sometimes elicit a list of shops that sell synthetic equivalents, along with a tone of voice that implies hurt disappointment: as if they had expected better.

In part, I am guilty as charged in keeping lax vegan standards. I eat too many salted nuts, tortillas, and plain or salt-and-vinegar crisps. I eat hot chips quite often, even if I do combine them with salad. I snack outside meal times. I eat peanut butter sandwiches when the going gets tough. I very much like adulterated processed vegan foods such as Linda McCartney sausages, pies, ice creams, cakes—even traditional Oreos are vegan: Who knew? So, being vegan doesn't stop me from making poor food choices and I wear those choices in my everyday life. I think this also colors how people see my veganism; I think they see me as vegan-light, anti-eating-animals, but not necessarily pro-eating for an optimal me. I sometimes get lectures about plant-based wholefoods and how those are the real keys to health: not just avoiding animal products.

I know that most wine is refined using milk, or egg shells, or (can you believe this!?) fish bladders, but I'm a white wine drinker and so long as the wine is clear, I don't ask too many questions. When I drink wine without looking at the label, however, it's sometimes as though my wider judgmental audience has been trusted with one of my guilty secrets and is willing to keep this lapse quiet. While I don't eat something if I know for certain that it contains milk, or eggs, or animal products, if it's feasible the food might be "uncontaminated" by non-vegan ingredients, then I don't always press the point. Nor do I ask if my vegan food is cooked in the same oil, or on the same griddle, as meat and dairy products.

I justify my accommodation with the everyday in two ways. Firstly, I'm a vegan because I know that it's good for me, and because I believe that it's good for the planet.[4] I want other people to think about becoming vegan. My aim is to project a happy, productive, healthy lifestyle that offers attractive possibilities to non-vegans. In the words of Singer and Mason, I try not to worry about:

> trivial infractions of the ethical guidelines [...] eating ethically doesn't have to be like keeping kosher. [...] Personal purity isn't really the issue. Not supporting animal abuse—and persuading others not to support it—is. Giving people the impression that it is virtually impossible to be vegan doesn't help animals at all.[5]

Secondly, as a vegan who is motivated by health concerns, I accept the findings of, for example, researchers Campbell and Campbell, who do not argue that "the optimum percentage of animal-based products is zero." Their view is that "the lower the percentage of animal-based foods that are consumed the greater the health benefits [but] most of the health benefits are realised at very low, but non-zero levels of animal-based foods."[6] This isn't an excuse to eat animal products at will, but an injunction to concentrate on the big picture, not the minutiae: "The ability to relax about very minor quantities of animal-based foods makes applying this diet much easier—especially when eating out or buying already-prepared foods."[7] Sometimes, those issues can be hard enough without adopting the critical stance that some non-vegans and purer vegans might wish upon me.

MY MOTIVATIONS

My key motivator for becoming vegan was other people's responses to their own encounters with veganism. They were my inspirations, and I hope I have similarly inspired others to explore the dietary change. (If that is the case, I don't know about it: I am more influenced than influencing.) My parents were each raised in a family of four children. Of these eight close relatives in that generation of my family, parents, aunts, and uncles, three survive. Six of these live with or died from cancer: breast, prostate, pancreatic, brain, and lung; a seventh had a fatal health crisis which overtook her national health system's capacity to provide a diagnosis, but it was triggered by white blood cells multiplying to 100 times the normal amount (eosinophilia). The eighth has been vegan since 2004, on the basis of his understanding of the health benefits. In his seventies, my uncle holds down a three-day-a-week responsible professional role while continuing to scuba dive, body surf, sea kayak, and swim with whale sharks. He's a long-distance walker, a novice yoga practitioner and has only recently relinquished white water rafting. He's clearly a role model, but his example alone was not sufficient to persuade me to give veganism a go.

My current practice of veganism is a personal response to the influence of two PhD students, three books, and an eight-week course. Dr. Leesa Costello was my key influence (as well as being an editor of this volume), in cahoots even then with Dr. Julie Dare (also an editor). They were both working with me at the time, as doctoral students and, in Leesa's case, as a researcher in a project that created an online community for people impacted by heart disease. Talking to the participants and reading around the subject, Leesa came across *The China Study*,[8] and recommended that I read it. I later discovered it had also influenced my uncle's decision to become vegan. The older of the father-and-son Campbells, Professor Colin Campbell, had previously been a highly-regarded laboratory researcher and had discovered in experiments with injecting cancer-causing substances into rodent cells and rodents, that: "*nutrition [was] far more important in controlling cancer promotion than the dose of the initiating carcinogen*" and that "*nutrients from animal-based foods increased tumor development while nutrients from plant-based foods decreased tumor development*"[9] (italics in original). That caught my attention.

It was these kinds of under-acknowledged findings that prompted another of my key authors, Professor Jane Plant, who had been given a terminal diagnosis in 1993 after her fifth recurrence of breast cancer, to write in 2007 that she was astonished "to learn precisely how much has been discovered already [about cancer but . . .] not filtered through to the public."[10] My third book-based influencer was a physician, Dr Caldwell Esselstyn. Esselstyn's book, *Prevent and Reverse Heart Disease,*[11] was published during my first year as a vegan and tells the stories of a group of heart patients who had been given up for dead by the medical profession but who went on to lead happy, healthy lives on a strict plant-based whole food diet. One of these patients was brought to Perth as part of publicity for an eight-week course promoted as the Coronary Health Improvement Plan (CHIP), now rebadged and available as a 30-day online course at http://chiphealth.org.au/. Although I wasn't personally concerned about coronary health, I believed that the same diet that works to improve coronary health also reduces cancer risk, so a friend and I signed up to CHIP and committed to two evenings of lectures and cookery classes per week, for an eight-week period. For me, the rest is history; for my friend the diet was eventually unsustainable because of family and other incompatibilities. This latter instance indicates the crucial role played by domestic companions in becoming and staying vegan.

I was lucky on my personal journey to veganism. I was single at the time, sharing my home with two adult children who were bemused and teasing, but mainly supportive. They became keen on cooking meat, eggs, dairy, etc. for themselves; stepping in to prevent their diet from becoming the same as mine, but happy to share a vegan dish or two to provide "the vegetables." In 2011 I began dating again after fifteen years of being single and got the odd negative comment about including "vegan" in my social network profile. I occasionally felt a little like the "Fruitarian" might have done in the movie *Notting Hill* when introduced to Hugh Grant's character. One potential partner even shared his opinion that being vegan must mean that I didn't especially care about food. We agreed to respect our differences and focus on what we had in common, starting a relationship anyway. Some months later he gave veganism a try, experienced a range of health benefits for himself and has been vegan ever since. (We married three years later.)

Like gorillas, horses, elephants, and brontosaurus, I am a large-ish animal that eats plants but still feels strong and capable. I look to my wider family for the results of the traditional Western diet and draw a range of conclusions. I have close relatives who were younger than me, and much lighter than me, when they needed their first hip replacement, then knee replacements. The family member who was keenest on dairy was tragically also the person most troubled by osteoporosis and falls. I didn't need the Campbells to tell me that "Those countries that use the most cow's milk and its products also have the highest fracture rates and the worst bone health";[12] I could see that for myself. Long before we began talking about the risks of low-fat foods I had come to realize that if fat constitutes almost 60 percent of the brain,[13] then maybe we needed to treat fat as a friend, rather than an enemy, provided it was sourced from plants. I speculate that maybe more fat in our diet would be one way to delay cognitive decline in aging.

As I ate less meat for health reasons, I also began to think more about animals for ethical reasons. Like so many other people, I have had companion animals. I know that animals can be happy, sad, scared, angry, hurt, and frightened: I've seen it for myself. I have no doubt that cows, sheep, pigs, chickens, etc., have social repertoires and ways of relating to each other when they are able to enjoy their natural habitats. Once I stopped buying animal products and began to wake up to how they landed at my local supermarket, or on my table,[14] I was horrified. The most positive thing I did in response, apart from being vegan, was to join Animals Australia. Their activities make a positive difference, and I am proud to be a member. Having said that, I still wear and use animal products in my daily life and have developed an awareness of plastics and synthetics that make me concerned about the environmental cost of substituting artificial man-made materials for "natural" products.

The Practicalities of a Vegan Diet

I have many long-suffering friends. My 40-year tussle with being overweight meant that people had become used to me occasionally bringing my own food to social gatherings, including events like Christmas parties and weddings. I started to do that again, but as hummus and other vegan options became more mainstream, people began to provide that for starters, plus cook me extra vegetables with beans or nuts for mains, and offer vegan crumbles or soy ice cream for dessert. This dynamic was partly supported by me inviting my friends to come over for vegan meals at my place, plus meat dish options for mains (sourced from local Indian, Vietnamese, or Italian take-aways). I rationalized that if I hoped that my friends might accommodate my vegan choices eventually, it was only fair that I should consider their carnivorous preferences. When I entertain I try to provide vegan versions of the kinds of food that I think they like: soups, casseroles, etc., demonstrating that vegan food is consistent with people's current dietary preferences.

Eating out in Australia used to be a challenge for vegans, but I soon got into the habit of calling the restaurant a day or two prior to the booking to see if there were vegan choices and got permission to bring my own food if not. I choose not to accommodate the "well you can just pick the cheese out" or "why don't you leave the meat on the side of the plate?" kind of comment. If someone wants to make food that I want to eat, they don't include obvious animal products. When I am at large social functions such as a book launch or hospitality after a public lecture and there's nothing that's labeled vegan, I just do without.

These days it's much easier to be vegan and eat out than it was in 2007, and many restaurants accommodate vegans and vegetarians. Even so, about half of them seem to confuse gluten free with vegan, telling me that I can eat the flourless orange-almond cake even though it is clearly packed with eggs. I generally look puzzled and ask for the ingredients, before politely explaining why the recipe is not a vegan one. People working in food and hospitality should know these differences, but they can be antagonistic to my explanations. Only recently a baker in a bread shop said something to me about veganism being "this month's fad."

Generally, I feel supported in my veganism by family and friends and incredibly supported by my now-vegan partner. I'm not aware of anyone whose friendship I have lost as a result of being vegan. I think I may be judged somewhat by strangers, but that's okay, I probably judge them too.

Our environment is under huge threat and I am personally convinced that much of the danger is related to human activity, especially in the industrialized world. But there is very little awareness about the impact of livestock farming practices upon that calamity, even though the definitive United Nations non-vegan-friendly report was published in the mid-noughties.[15] As well as being responsible for more global warming potential greenhouse gases than the world's transport systems, "livestock production accounts for 70 percent of all agricultural land and 30 percent of the land surface of the planet."[16] Like the data cited earlier about animal protein and tumor growth, there's no general awareness of these uncomfortable truths. There are too many vested interests that stand to lose out if we begin to factor these issues into our consumption choices. We need to inform ourselves and make our choices accordingly—and sometimes that's at the expense of what other people think of us.

Suggested Readings

Campbell, T. Colin and Thomas Campbell. *The China Study: Startling Implications for Diet, Weight Loss and Long-Term Health.* Dallas: Benbella Books, 2004.

Chang, Chia-Yu, Der-Shin Ke, and Jen-Yin Chen. "Essential fatty acids and human brain," *Acta Neurol Taiwan* 18, no. 4 (2009): 231–41.

Cormack, Lucy. "Australia is the third-fastest growing vegan market in the world," *Sydney Morning Herald*, June 4, 2016, https://www.smh.com.au/business/consumer-affairs/australia-is-the-thirdfastest-growing-vegan-market-in-the-world-20160601-gp972u.html.

Esselstyn, Caldwell. *Prevent and Reverse Heart Disease: The Revolutionary, Scientifically Proven Nutrition-Based Cure.* New York: Avery, 2007.

Green, Lelia, Julie Dare, and Leesa Costello. "Veganism, health expectancy, and the communication of sustainability." *Australian Journal of Communication* 37, no. 3 (2010): 87–102.

Morgan, Roy. "The slow but steady rise of vegetarianism in Australia." Roy Morgan: Press Release, August 15, 2016, http://www.roymorgan.com/findings/vegetarianisms-slow-but-steady-rise-in-australia-201608151105.

Plant, Jane. *Your Life in Your Hands: Understand, Prevent and Overcome Breast Cancer and Ovarian Cancer,* 4th Ed. London: Virgin Books, 2007.

Singer, Peter and Jim Mason. *The Ethics of What We Eat: Why Our Food Choices Matter.* Melbourne: Rodale Books, 2007.

Steinfeld, Henning, Pierre Gerber, T. D. Wassenaar, Vincent Castel, Mauricio Rosales, Mauricio Rosales, and Cees de Haan. *Livestock's Long Shadow: Environmental Issues and Options.* Rome: Food & Agriculture Org., 2006.

Notes

1. Roy Morgan, "The slow but steady rise of vegetarianism in Australia," Roy Morgan: Press Release, 15 August 2016, http://www.roymorgan.com/findings/vegetarianisms-slow-but-steady-rise-in-australia-201608151105.

2. Lucy Cormack, "Australia is the third-fastest growing vegan market in the world," *Sydney Morning Herald,* June 4, 2016, https://www.smh.com.au/business/consumer-affairs/australia-is-the-thirdfastest-growing-vegan-market-in-the-world-20160601-gp972u.html.

3. Lucy Cormack, "Vegan market."

4. Lelia Green, Julie Dare, and Leesa Costello. "Veganism, health expectancy, and the communication of sustainability," *Australian Journal of Communication* 37, no. 3 (2010): 87–102.

5. Peter Singer and Jim Mason. *The Ethics of What We Eat: Why Our Food Choices Matter* (Melbourne: Rodale Books, 2007), 258–59.

6. T. Colin Campbell and Thomas Campbell, *The China Study: Startling Implications for Diet, Weight Loss and Long-Term Health* (Dallas: Benbella Books, 2004), 242.

7. Campbell and Campbell, *The China Study,* 244.

8. Campbell and Campbell, *The China Study*.

9. Campbell and Campbell, *The China Study*, 66.

10. Jane Plant, *Your Life in Your Hands: Understand, Prevent and Overcome Breast Cancer and Ovarian Cancer,* 4th Ed. (London: Virgin Books, 2007), 18.

11. Caldwell Esselstyn, *Prevent and Reverse Heart Disease: The Revolutionary, Scientifically Proven Nutrition-based Cure* (New York: Avery, 2007).

12. Campbell and Campbell, *The China Study*, 205.

13. Chia-Yu Chang, Der-Shin Ke, and Jen-Yin Chen. "Essential fatty acids and human brain," *Acta Neurol Taiwan* 18, no. 4 (2009).

14. Singer and Mason, *The Ethics of What We Eat*.

15. Henning Steinfeld, Pierre Gerber, T. D. Wassenaar, Vincent Castel, Mauricio Rosales, Mauricio Rosales, and Cees de Haan. *Livestock's Long Shadow: Environmental Issues and Options* (Rome: Food & Agriculture Org., 2006).

16. Steinfeld, Gerber, Wassenaar, Castel, Rosales, Rosales, and de Haan, *Livestock's Long Shadow*, xxi.

CHAPTER 2

AUSTRALIA

EXPERIENCES OF A VEGAN IN THE AUSTRALIAN JEWISH COMMUNITY

TALIA RAPHAELY AND ASHER MYERSON

This chapter explores the experiences of, and community attitudes toward, a young Jewish, values-driven vegan community leader living in Perth's Jewish community. Research in late 2017 and early 2018 focused on the respondent's dietary choices and the impact of these choices on his social interactions. Jewish ethical meat avoidance is increasingly mainstream, particularly among young adults choosing to participate in a Jewish-values driven vegan vanguard embodying a more holistic, integrated spirituality and ethical Jewish dietary choice.

THE SETTING

Perth, the capital of Western Australia, is the country's fourth most populous city with a population of almost 2 million. Despite being one of the most isolated major cities in the world (surpassed only by Honolulu) it has a cosmopolitan, culturally diverse population with more than half of its residents born overseas.[1] Comprising about 90,000 people (less than 0.4 percent of Australia's total population) and less than 1 percent of the total global Jewish population, Australia has the world's 9th largest Jewish community but Australia's smallest religious group. Home to 7,000 Jews representing the smallest religious group in this city (less than 0.3 percent), Perth has the highest proportion of Jews born overseas—just two out of five people (41 percent) are Australia-born with a very large proportion (28 percent) being South Africa-born.[2] Despite its size, Jewish life in Perth is extensive, inclusive, and embracing. Six different religious congregations cater to its Jewish diversity, a top-rated Jewish day school offers secular and religious education from Kindergarten to year 12 and a Jewish Center which hosts the two largest youth movements among other organizations and forms a focal point of the community.

No specific statistics are available for Jewish vegetarians in Perth, but between 2012 and 2016, the number of Australian adults following a "meat minimal" diet rose from 1.7 million people to almost 2.1 million (9.7 percent to 11.2 percent of the population). In Western Australia, 10.9 percent of adults adopt a meat-free or meat-minimal diet up from 8.7 percent in 2012.[3] Vegetarianism or veganism overall are familiar dietary choices, with most Perth restaurants including vegan offerings on their menu.

THE CONTEXT

Classical Jewish law neither explicitly requires nor prohibits meat consumption. This has stimulated centuries of in-depth religious and philosophical debate regarding consumption of animal flesh and, if so, under what circumstances. These authoritative deliberations contained inter alia in various historic and current books of Jewish law including the Tanach, Jewish literature, writings, and commentaries are complex and beyond this chapter's scope but a simplified summary is offered below to contextualize this ethnography.

Jews almost unanimously believe G-d originally intended humankind to be vegetarian as evidenced by the following biblical description: "And G-d said: Behold, I have given you every herb yielding seed which is upon the face of all the earth, and every tree that has seed-yielding fruit—to you it shall be for food."[4] Adam and Eve were indisputably vegan—G-d did not permit Adam and his wife to kill a creature and to eat its flesh. "Only every green herb shall they eat together."[5] Thirteenth century sage Maimonides reasoned these initial dietary laws recognized animals have a soul and their fear of pain and death makes them similar to humans.[6] Fifteenth century philosopher Rabbi Albo,[7] describes how "killing of animals requires cruelty, rage, and the accustoming of oneself to the bad habit of shedding innocent blood. . . ." However, adherence to philosophical ideals can be difficult and "by Noah's time, humanity was eating limbs torn from living animals"[8] and cannibalism prevailed: "And G-d saw the earth, and behold it was corrupt; for all flesh had corrupted their way upon the earth"[9] and brought the great flood. Upon surviving the inundation, Noah was told, "every moving thing that lives shall be yours to eat; like the green vegetation, I have given you everything."[10] Yet this permission for Jews to eat meat is considered a temporary concession to humanity's weak nature,[11] a transient period until a "brighter era" is reached and people returned to a vegetarian diet.[12]

The very precise laws of kashrut (keeping kosher) remind Jews of the magnitude of the task of killing a living being,[13] discourage the consumption of meat, teach us compassion and "lead us gently to vegetarianism."[14] Multiple Jewish rabbis and sages past and present[15,16] support this opinion and throughout Jewish texts flesh foods are mentioned with distaste, associated with lust, materialism, and lack of control over one's appetite for meat. Numerous biblical and philosophical references describe the moral return to vegetarianism as a virtue of such great value that it cannot be lost forever.[17] There is a midrash (a Jewish lesson, based on Jewish values and tradition, that defines Jewish norms and mores) that "in the future ideal state, just as at the initial period, people and animals will not eat flesh."[18] Rabbi Kook and Joseph Albo, two great Jewish sages and mystics, describe how in the forthcoming enlightened era no one shall hurt nor destroy another living creature and people's lives will not be supported at the expense of the lives of animals.[19] "In the messianic age, the biblical ideal to which all humankind should strive to return, no meat shall be eaten— neither by not by people or other animals."[20] Likewise, "none shall hurt nor destroy in all of God's holy mountain."[21]

Despite these biblical visions and directions toward a better, kinder world most Jews today eat meat. However, although no rabbinic call has formally prohibited meat consumption, there is growing global rabbinical support for veganism, which is particularly apparent among rabbis in Israel.[22] These calls are echoed by numerous health, community, religious, environmental, and animal welfare groups both within and beyond Israel's borders, promoting Jewish values-driven plant-based eating. In 2016, Israel was described as "the most vegan country on earth" with more vegans per capita than any other country in the world.[23] Over 5 percent of Israelis eschew all animal products, a proportion that has doubled since 2010, when

2.6 percent of Israelis were either vegan or vegetarians.[24] Vegan activism is very prominent in Israel, with the largest animal rights protest globally occurring in Tel Aviv in September 2017, with 30,000 protestors carrying placards stating "compassion, justice, veganism."[25] Concerns about animal welfare are driving an exponentially growing conversion to veganism because of concerns regarding animal welfare. In May 2018, following an exposé of conditions on live export vessels from Australia, sixty leading Israeli rabbis signed a ruling that anyone consuming meat from animals shipped from overseas to Israel for slaughter is "partner to an evil crime."[26] Clearly plant-based eating, supported since the time of Adam and Eve, has sustained through the ages as an ethical dietary choice, and although many Jews today consume animal meat and products, there is a fast and powerful, growing movement back toward a veganism driven by traditional Jewish values, including human, environmental, and animal well-being.

A VEGAN JEW IN PERTH: OUR CASE STUDY

This ethnography is based on six months of personal interviews and discussions with "Ben"—a young man, twenty-two years of age, who has strongly identified as vegan since 2015 and is a lifelong committed, proud, and practicing Jew. Melbourne-born, Ben moved to Perth when he was nine and presently leads the local branch of Habonim Dror, an international Jewish Zionist youth movement. Our interviews with Ben, who plays an influential and prominent role as a Jewish vegan youth leader in the Perth Jewish community, gave us a unique window into this community's responses and attitudes to veganism. Research was supplemented with ongoing participant observation and informal interviews. Consistent with an ethic of ethnographic transparency, it is noteworthy that both authors are long-time practicing vegans and Jews living permanently in and as part of the community studied.

This is Ben's story—told largely in his own words: "*I clearly remember as a child being disturbed that meat came from animals but was told by all influences that it was natural and necessary. Whilst attending Carmel, Perth's local Jewish school I became involved in Habonim Dror, my Jewish Youth Movement which I have attended since I was 16. It is a vegetarian movement that further exposed me to the great animal cruelty that exists within the animal industry. My passion for animal rights is what led me to being vegetarian. After school I went to Poland as a part of my Gap Year Program with my youth movement. This experience in Poland affected me greatly. A Jew amongst his Jewish friends returning to the place where Jews had been persecuted, murdered and systematically massacred. I realised from my Poland that you must choose to be a moral person despite living in an immoral world. For me I had always known that my values directly aligned with a vegan diet and on return from Poland I immediately changed from a vegetarian to a vegan diet. I have never looked back."* The history of the Jewish people has had significant initial and ongoing impact on Ben's understanding of himself as both a Jew and a vegan, prefacing his realization that *"There is never a perfect time to do something brave. The time is now."* The horrors of the Holocaust and brave Jewish resistance continued to influence Ben after he finished high school and through continuing involvement in Habonim Dror, supported by other like-minded fellow Jewish vegetarians, his exposure to modern Jewish history increasingly empowered and propelled him toward veganism. The fact that Habonim Dror was heavily involved in resistance during the Holocaust and particularly in the Warsaw ghetto uprising further reinforced Ben's determination to "actualise" his values without further delay.

The more Ben studied Judaism the more convinced he became that there is no such thing as kosher meat. Meat in all its forms, is in direct contradiction of Jewish values concerning human, animal, and planetary welfare and well-being. In Ben's view, there are three core Jewish values or mandates that alone and in combination make it clear to him that a Jewish diet should be a vegan diet. The first core Jewish value he lists is responsibility over the environment: *"In Genesis humankind are declared custodians over the environment. There are also many Jewish values and laws that require Jews to protect the environment. An example of these is Bal Tashchit—the prohibition to waste or destroy resources. A meat-eater destroys 4700 litres of water, 20kg of grain, 3 square metres of forested land and generates 9 kg of Carbon Dioxide a day more than a vegan. This is unnecessarily wasteful thus it is clear that reducing meat consumption is a necessity to live in accordance with the mandate of Bal Tashchit. Another example is Tikkun Olam— the Jewish value of healing and fixing the world which is another example of how meat eating contravenes values integral to Judaism. Climate change is one of the greatest threats to humankind and the planet. The animal industry is the greatest contributor to climate change. To be a Jew therefore requires one to reduce or eliminate meat consumption to behave in accordance with this critical consideration of Tikkun Olam."* The second core Jewish value, he continues *"is Tzaar Baalei Chayim, the prohibition of animal cruelty. The modern animal production industry is in direct violation of this,"* and the third and last Jewish value *"is Pikuach Nefech (preserving one's life). Research confirms current levels of meat consumption are causing wide-ranging diseases and lowering life expectancy."*

Despite these core Jewish values that, in Ben's opinion, lead to a vegetarian or vegan diet, *"the majority of Perth Jews cannot understand why I am vegan. They are ignorant of the Jewish values which have led me and others to this diet or they choose not to see the connections."* Ben's beliefs are not yet a widely held belief among Perth's Jewry where one of the local rabbis is a kosher slaughterer, supplying "kosher" meat for religious members of the community. Ben seems to have mixed feelings about this: *"Jews who are not entirely vegan do not bother me although I struggle a bit with the disconnect they seem to live with which is similar to the disconnect in the broader Perth community. How can people know about environmental destruction, cruelty to sentient beings and damage to personal and community health yet still participate in its cause? I feel that Jews, more than any other race or nationality, should adopt veganism in order to truly align entirely with Jewish values and intentions of causing no harm to people, the planet or animals. Having said which, I am encouraged to know there is a growing number of Jews like me, who have become vegan, vegetarian or flexitarian. What does bother me significantly is when Jews eat meat several times a day, because this is a blatant and clear violation of our Jewish values and law. More Rabbis and other Jewish leaders need to lead the way and encourage Jews to shift their diets in accordance with Jewish values. They feel very comfortable encouraging people to eat food that is 'kosher.' But there is no such thing as kosher meat . . . I find it difficult that Jewish organisations even cater meat. If that the event is the only time they are eating meat for the entire week, so be it. It could be improved, but it is satisfactory. If they are eating meat once or twice a day, it is highly problematic for me and I struggle with this on a regular basis because for me to be completely Jewish—in all intents and purposes—intrinsically requires one to be vegan!"*

When asked if his dietary choices have influenced his identity, Ben explains that it is rather his Jewish identity that influences his dietary choices: *"As I've said my veganism and Judaism are so interrelated. My veganism is rooted in my Judaism. From my perspective my diet is inherently Jewish. If I was not Jewish, which is an incredibly difficult hypothetical to comprehend, I think I would eat meat."* Yet he does add to this that *"Being vegan has also become important to my identity. My values bind me to not eat any animal products. In Judaism there is such a great emphasis on responsibility over the environment, the prohibition of animal cruelty and preservation of one's life, that a diet rich in meat is a contradiction of Jewish law, tradition and culture."*

In understanding veganism as a Jewish necessity contemporizing biblical teachings including compassion, Jewish responsibility over the environment, and personal health and wellbeing, Ben exemplifies Jewish ethical dietary decision-making. Consistent with research in this area, what we eat influences those with whom we eat.[27] Through his dietary-decisions and in his role as a youth leader, Ben is clearly influencing others. Through his leadership role Ben is filling the role of an innovator or early adopter— leading the way toward a more vegan Judaism. Although the idea of veganism is by no means new in Judaism—having its roots in the biblical story of creation—it is still not widespread in the Jewish community in Perth. Rather however than feeling alienated or marginalized in any way, Ben feels socially empowered by his choices and feels a responsibility to similarly empower others: *"I don't feel isolated or strange. I feel part of something so critical and integral to the future of the planet. I strive to be the change I wish to see in the world, to make this a better place for all and I seek for more Jews in the community to recognise this and join me in this Jewish diet. The best I can do is lead by example. In 2015, when I was living in a commune in Israel with 20 people, after I went vegan two of my friends followed me and then 4/20 of us were vegan. We always used to make sure there were vegan options for every meal we made and eventually all 20 of us stopped eating meat totally. Today I find most of my friends and family are very supportive. My parents have started cooking and eating less meat. In fact my mother went vegan a month ago, which is amazing."*

In this journey, Ben has mostly felt supported: *"I have always had my family's support for me acting upon my values, but some family members have worried that I am not prioritising my health, despite my re-assurance."* Perth's Jewish parents' and grandparents' demographics remain convinced meat consumption is essential for health, growth, and wellbeing, an opinion supported since early medieval times by chicken soup's significance as a Jewish table icon with curative, healing properties. His friends too have been supportive. *"Some friends make jokes, but they are of a good nature."* In general Ben does not think that veganism has had a huge impact on his social life: *"Usually if I am going out with friends, we find a place that has vegan options."* Yet he further adds that: *"When it comes to meeting new people, I wouldn't necessarily bring up my veganism. The connotation of being vegan very much still exists. Some people are respectful and strongly believe in what I am doing, despite not having the motivation themselves. Some people label me as a 'do-gooder,' someone causing more harm than good . . . but I actually feel that there was a far more negative perception of veganism 3 years ago, when I started this diet to now. There were less restaurants catering for vegans than there are today . . . in Perth there is a vegetarian and vegan kosher restaurant catering to both the Jewish and wider Perth community."* Ben is representative of this increasingly socially-accepted trend toward Jewish values-driven veganism among Jewish youth and young adults.

CONCLUSION

The experiences of, and community attitudes toward, Ben's Jewish val-ues-driven vegan lifestyle illustrate that Jewish ethical meat avoidance is becoming increasingly mainstream, particularly among young adults choosing to participate in a Jewish values-driven vegan vanguard embody-ing a more holistic, integrated spirituality and ethical Jewish dietary choice. Contemporary Jewish thinkers have described how Jewish religious ethical vegetarians are pioneers of a healing world and the vanguard of the mes-sianic era. Ben is such a pioneer, standing firm in his belief that the initial vegan dietary law remains an ultimate and increasingly urgent goal toward which all people, but particularly Jews, should strive.

Suggested Readings

Albo, Joseph. *"Seffer Ha-Ikkarim."* Translated by Isaac Husik. Philadelphia, Jewish Pub-lication Society of America, 1929, https://www.sefaria.org/Sefer_HaIkkarim,_Title.4?ven=Sefer_Ha-ikkarim,_Jewish_Publication_Society_of_America,_1929&lang=bi&with=all&lang2=en.

Australian Bureau of Statistics. *"Regional Population Growth, Australia, 2015–16. Census of Population and Housing."* Perth, ABS Statistical Division, 2017, http://www.abs.gov.au/AUSSTATS/abs@.nsf/DetailsPage/3218.02015-16?OpenDocument.

Australian Bureau of Statistics. *"Community Profile Series: Census of Population and Housing."* Perth, ABS Statistical Division, 2007, http://www.abs.gov.au/AUSS-TATS/abs@.nsf/ViewContent?readform&view=productsbyCatalogue&Action=Expand&Num=2.1.

Cohen, Alfred. S. "Vegetarianism from a Jewish Perspective." *Journal of Halacha and Contemporary Society*, Vol. 1, No. II (Fall 1981): 38–63.

Eisenbud, Daniel.K. "Thousands flock to mass Tel Aviv rally for animal rights." *Jerusalem Post*, September 10, 2017, https://www.jpost.com/israel-news/watch-thousands-flock-to-mass-tel-aviv-rally-for-animal-rights-504657.

Frazin, R. "How Israel Became the Global Center of Veganism." *The Tower Magazine*, Issue 42, September 2016, http://www.thetower.org/article/how-israel-became-the-global-center-of-veganism/.

Graham, David. *"The Jewish Population of Australia: Key findings from the 2011 Census."* New South Wales, Jewish Community Appeal and Monash University Australian Centre for Jewish Civilisation, 2014.

Green, Joe. *"Chalutzim of the Messiah—The Religious Vegetarian Concept as Expounded by Rabbi Kook."* (text of a lecture given in Johannesburg, South Africa).

Hertz, Rabbi Joseph. H. *"The Pentateuch and Haftorahs"* (Second Ed.). London, Soncino Press, 1981

Kalechofsky, Roberta. *"Rabbis and Vegetarianism: An Evolving Tradition."* Marblehead, MA: Micah Publications. 1995.

Klein Leichman, Abigail. "The Halachic case for veganism." *The Jerusalem Post*, December 12, 2015, https://www.jpost.com/Magazine/The-halachic-case-for-veganism-432808.

Kook, Avraham, Isaac. *"A vision of vegetarianism and peace"*. Edited by David Cohen, translated by Jonathan Rubenstein. Jerusalem, Boys Town Press. 1961.

Leibowitz, Nehama. *"New Studies in Bereshit (Genesis)."* Translated by Aryeh Newman. Jerusalem, The World Zionist Organization Department of Torah Education in the Diaspora, 2010.

Maimonides, Moses. *The Guide for the Perplexed*. Translated by Michael Friedländer (ed.). 2nd edition, New York, Dover Publications, 1956.

Roy Morgan Research. *"The slow but steady rise of vegetarianism in Australia."* Finding No. 6923. Press Release August 16, Australia, Roy Morgan. 2016, http://www.roymorgan.com/findings/vegetarianisms-slow-but-steady-rise-in-australia-201608151105.

Safran Foer, Jonathan. *"Eating Animals."* London: Penguin Books. 2009.

Schwartz, Richard. H. *"Judaism and Vegetarianism."* 3rd ed. New York: Lantern Books. 2001

Sears, David. *"The Vision of Eden: Animal Welfare and Vegetarianism in Jewish Law and Mysticism.,* New York, Orot, 2014.

Surkes, Sue. "Sixty senior rabbis call for end to 'evil crime' of live animal shipments." *The Times of Israel.* May 3, 2018, https://www.timesofisrael.com/sixty-senior-rabbis-call-for-end-to-evil-crime-of-live-animal-shipments/.

Wilcox, Christie. "The Social Side of Eating." *Nutritional Wonderland.* August 17, 2009, http://nutritionwonderland.com/2009/08/social-side-eating/.

Zamore, Mary, L. ed. *The Sacred Table: Creating a Jewish Food Ethic*, New York, CCAR Press. 2011.

Notes

1. ABS, *Regional Population Growth*.
2. Graham, *The Jewish Population of Australia*.
3. Roy Morgan, *The slow but steady rise of vegetarianism in Australia*.
4. Genesis 1–29.
5. Hertz, *The Pentateuch and Haftorahs*, 854.
6. Maimonides, *Guide for the Perplexed*, 3:48.
7. Albo, *Sefer ha-Ikkarim*, 3:15.
8. Schwartz, Judaism and Vegetarianism, 15.
9. Genesis 6:12.
10. Genesis 9:3.
11. Genesis 9.1–17.
12. Leibowitz, New Studies in Bereshit (Genesis), 77.
13. Kalechofsky, *Rabbis and Vegetarianism.*
14. Sears, The vision of Eden.
15. Zamore, *The Sacred Table: Creating a Jewish Food Ethic*
16. Schwartz, *Judaism and Vegetarianism*. 1, 12, 16, 19, 188.

17. Kook, *A Vision of Vegetarianism and Peace.*
18. Hertz, *The Pentateuch and Haftorahs,* 5.
19. Cohen, *Vegetarianism from a Jewish Perspective,* 45.
20. Green, *Chalutzim of the Messiah,* 1.
21. Isaiah 11:9.
22. Schwartz, *Judaism and vegetarianism.*
23. Klein Leichman, *The Halachic case.*
24. Frazin, *How Israel Became the Global Center of Veganism.*
25. Eisenbud, *Thousands flock to mass Tel Aviv rally for animal rights.*
26. Surkes, *Sixty senior rabbis call for end to "evil crime" of live animal shipments.*
27. Safran Foer, *Eating Animals,* Wilcox, *The Social Side of Eating.*

CHAPTER 3

AUSTRIA

WIENER SCHNITZEL VERSUS PLANT-BASED FOOD. THE TRANSITION OF MEAT-BASED REGIONAL AUSTRIAN FOOD TO VEGAN PRODUCTS

ELISABETH OBERZAUCHER,
ULRIKE ATZMÜLLER-ZEILINGER,
AND HELMUT JUNGWIRTH

Global attitudes toward nutrition, at least in the minority world, are undergoing a major change. This is also the case in Austria. Young people in particular, who live in cities, are increasingly interested in where their food comes from, as well as in the ethical and health implications of what they actually eat. This may, in part, stem from an accumulation and translation of scientific knowledge about the negative impacts of meat or fat consumption on our health, creating a new food awareness. It may also relate to issues around sustainability, with more public discussion that challenges the proposition that food security can be supported if meat remains a major component of mainstream diets. The way in which animals have been mistreated in the modern food stock industry is now more topical than ever, and people have easy access to graphic depictions of animal cruelty. Anecdotally, it seems that we are now more skeptical of anything to do with food. It would appear that consumers are now questioning the legitimacy of nutrition knowledge especially in the face of numerous food scandals—such as the use of analogue cheese—and the seemingly contradictory and ever-changing dialogue about what constitutes "good" nutrition. Not surprisingly, many people, mostly young, are turning away from dairy and meat toward a diet based solely on plants.[1,2,3,4,5,6,7]

This development is reflected in the growing market in vegan and vegetarian products in Europe.[8,9] In Austria, the number of vegans and vegetarians has more than tripled between 2005 to 2013, according to reports by the Vegan Society of Austria (Vegane Gesellschaft Österreich, www.vegan.at). Vegans make up about 10 percent of that group, resulting in approximately 80,000 Austrians who rely on plant-based food alone.[10,11] Speciality diets, such as the vegan one, have led to new demands and opportunities in terms of food supply. Indeed, the growing number of vegans, vegetarians, and flexitarians (people who are mainly vegetarian, but occasionally eat meat and fish) has driven the success of vegan restaurants, and a substantial change in the assortment of convenience food in supermarkets.[5] Recent research at the University of Graz[12] investigated the availability, labeling, and contents of vegan replacement products for meat, processed meat, or cheese. The study focused on major supermarket chains in Austria that offer the largest variety of products. The study analyzed 184 products originating from seven countries. Many typical Austrian dishes are meat-based, such as Wiener Schnitzel, and all types of sausages. Therefore, it is not surprising that more than 75 percent of the analyzed Austrian products were vegan replacements for meat or processed meat.[13] This has also fueled a territorial battle: there is ongoing discussion as to whether something that does not contain meat can be called "schnitzel." Interestingly, the new demand for vegan products has led to the rehabilitation of other redundant or mis-marketed food products. For example, imitation or analogue cheese had gone out of favor just a few years ago as a food product that pretends to be something it is not, that is, a dairy product, and suffered a major image loss. Now it has resurfaced, re-branded with a completely new image as a vegan cheese that sells for a much higher price under this label.

These analyses show that meat replacement products are an important component of vegan food supply (and perhaps demand) in Austria. It also indicates that many vegans do not change their preference for traditional food and flavors so much as their composition, meaning that meat replacement products enable Austrians to continue enjoying their favorite foods. This might make it easier for some people to change their diet and reduce the animal-based fraction of food contents.

However, meat replacement products are not uniformly embraced by the vegan community. They are highly processed food products, and as such, go against one main driver for people deciding to go on a vegan diet: Many vegans choose to live on a plant-based diet for health reasons. We talked to Ulrike Atzmüller-Zeilinger, who runs a vegan food blog in Austria, about her motivations to go vegan and the challenges this brings about in her everyday life.

Ulrike Atzmüller-Zeilinger is thirty-two years old and consciously made the decision to remove all animal-based ingredients from her diet five years ago, for ethical considerations. Before that, she had been consuming a vegetarian diet for eight or so years. She has a number of food allergies and intolerances, which make it more difficult for her to ensure balanced nutrition. She eats according to plant-based principles, which means all vegetables, fruit, seeds, and grains. However, she tries to avoid wheat wherever possible and anything she is allergic to or that she feels causes intolerances (like hazelnuts) or indigestion (like soy/tofu). She is reluctant to call herself a vegan because there are many different definitions of vegan and prefers instead the notion of what it means to consume a plant-based diet. Her decision to change her diet was motivated by two considerations. First, she was disturbed about the conditions under which animals suffer in the meat industry; not wanting animals to suffer for her benefit was a strong driver. Second, she wanted to leave a smaller ecological footprint and removing animal-based food from her diet seemed to be a good way to do so.

In comparison to her early years as a vegan, she has seemingly settled in to living the plant-based way, with very few challenges or obstacles. In her mind, there is simply no need for supplements or meat substitutes and there is no risk of missing out on certain nutrients. The only supplement she takes and recommends to other vegans is vitamin B12. She notes that most people are ill informed about plant-based nutrition, which for her, is inextricably linked to mis-information: that meat is something humans need, at least from an evolutionary perspective. She is somewhat frustrated that many people construct "going vegan" as unhealthy, where followers have been positioned as pale and very thin. She concedes that removal of animal-based ingredients does not necessarily make for a healthy diet; vegans can eat unhealthy foods too—just as you can in any other nutrition style—sugar and fried foods are not forbidden to vegans.

Public perceptions of someone living on a plant-based diet varies greatly in her view. It depends on how open-minded people are. Some people say it is great to live on a plant-based diet, others just don't understand it and think "vegan" means to go on demonstrations against cattle breeding or to run around naked, covered in fake blood! Therefore, she rationalizes that, sometimes, people treat her differently. Mostly, though, she is met with curiosity and interest, and people ask a lot of questions about what she can and cannot eat.

As families go, Ulrike's family members respond in very different ways. Her sister, who lives on a vegetarian diet, is the one who best understands her, but even her husband, with whom she has been living for twelve years, is not always sure about what Ulrike is "allowed to eat." Family members are not judgmental, but in Ulrike's opinion they often fail to be truly supportive due to their ignorance or incompetence.

Reading vegan blogs and exchanging ideas and experiences with "vegan" friends provides her with information about vegan events and new products. There is quite a large vegan community on Facebook and Instagram, and most vegans are happy to answer any questions regarding their diet. Living plant-based in everyday life is one thing, but at events and family gatherings, it is not always easy to find something suitable among the dishes on offer. Over a period of eight years, Ulrike explained she has learned how to handle this. For example, she always brings something to nibble on when she is unsure of the food environment. Usually there is at least one vegan dish on the menu, and if not, one can always order side dishes and salad. She recalls that even in the smallest rural restaurant you can find something vegan. At her own wedding, and about to marry an avid meat eater, Ulrike and her husband-to-be were adamant that the celebratory food would cater for both of their worlds. A friend of hers, who is a vegan chef, made a small plant-based buffet for her, and a spread of omnivorous bagels was on offer for him and his meat-loving guests.

Ulrike considers herself to be non-judgmental and open-minded toward people who follow different eating regimes. Being married to a meat eater demonstrates that she does not choose her friends (or lovers) by their diet. She considers the choice of nutrition style a very personal decision, which everyone must make wisely for himself or herself. She says that if she wants others to understand why she does not eat certain things, she also has to respect their choices in the same regard. Hosting guests is no problem for her. Most of the time her guests are vegan. But if they are not, she always prepares several small dishes, some with and some without meat or fish. The best thing is to have a BBQ in summer where every diet can be accommodated easily. Also, BBQ guests can bring their own food. She also cooks meat for her husband but does not touch or taste it herself.

Ulrike is happy to assert that a plant-based nutrition style is a common denominator for all people: almost anyone can eat vegan food. While Ulrike likes the idea of offering only vegan food at gatherings in principle, she is a realist and recognizes that this just isn't feasible. Ideally, she likes to include vegan options at every gathering so that non-vegans get to know the vegan diet, in the hope that this may reduce potential prejudice or even encourage uptake of a plant-based diet. While meat replacement products are also something that might help people to move toward a plant-based diet, Ulrike does not necessarily consider them healthy. From her perspective, consuming "pretend" meat products would contradict her identity as a plant-based consumer, as she thinks eating such products is tricking the mind into thinking that the meal consists of animal products, which goes against her idea of animal welfare. In a way, these products could be compared to e-cigarettes— you do not go through withdrawal, so it is quite possible to slip back into being a meat eater. She is convinced that a healthy and fulfilling plant-based diet can well do without these meat replacement products. If fresh produce is prepared in a creative way, any craving can be satisfied without having to fall back on these products. To share these ideas with a wider community, she has started a food blog. Today, Ulrike is Austria's most successful vegan food blogger, and she has published an online cookbook to inspire people to cook plant-based meals more often. Her webpage is at https://cookiesandstyle.at.

Suggested Readings

Gollowitsch, Lisa Marie. "Health aspects of vegan diet." University of Graz (2017). Master thesis.

Hauner, Hans. "Der ultimative Hype". *MMW—Fortschritte der Medizin* 157.10 (October 2015): 40.

Janssen, Meike, Claudia Busch, Manika Rödiger, and Ulrich Hamm. "Motives of consumers following a vegan diet and their attitudes towards animal agriculture." *Appetite* 105 (October 2016): 643–51.

Kerschke-Risch, Pamela. "Vegan diet: Motives, approach and duration. Initial results of a quantitative sociological study." *Ernährungs Umschau* 62 (March 2015): 98–103.

Padinger Florian. "Analysis of vegan instant meals." University of Graz (2017) Master thesis.

Radnitz, Cynthia, Bonnie Beezhold, and Julie DiMatteo. "Investigation of lifestyle choices of individuals following a vegan diet for health and ethical reasons." *Appetite* 90 (July 2015): 31–36.

Schmidt, Julie A., Sabina Rinaldi, Pietro Ferrari, Marion Carayol, David Achaintre, Augustin Scalbert, Amanda J Cross, Marc J Gunter, Georgina K Fensom, Paul N

Appleby, Timothy J Key, and Ruth C Travis. "Metabolic profiles of male meat eaters, fish eaters, vegetarians, and vegans from the EPIC-Oxford cohort." *The American Journal of Clinical Nutrition* 102(6) (December 2015): 1518–26.

Strecker, Till. "Definitions of 'vegan' and 'vegetarian' in accordance with the EU Food Information Regulation," *EC Register of Interest Representatives* 109356110578-03 (September 2015).

Tai Le Lap and Joan Sabaté. "Beyond Meatless, the Health Effects of Vegan Diets: Findings from the Adventist Cohorts." *Nutrients* 6.6 (June 2014): 2131–47.

Notes

1. Till Strecker. "Definitions of 'vegan' and 'vegetarian' in accordance with the EU Food Information Regulation," EC Register of Interest Representatives 109356110578-03 (September 2015).

2. Julie A. Schmidt, Sabina Rinaldi, Pietro Ferrari, Marion Carayol, David Achain-tre, Augustin Scalbert, Amanda J. Cross, Marc J. Gunter, Georgina K. Fensom, Paul N. Appleby, Timothy J. Key, and Ruth C. Travis. "Metabolic profiles of male meat eaters, fish eaters, vegetarians, and vegans from the EPIC-Oxford cohort." *The American Journal of Clinical Nutrition* 102(6) (December 2015): 1518–26.

3. Cynthia Radnitz, Bonnie Beezhold and Julie DiMatteo. "Investigation of life-style choices of individuals following a vegan diet for health and ethical reasons." *Appetite* 90 (July 2015): 31–36.

4. Pamela Kerschke-Risch. "Vegan diet: Motives, approach and duration. Initial results of a quantitative sociological study." Ernährungs Umschau 62 (March 2015): 98–103.

5. Meike Janssen, Claudia Busch, Manika Rödiger and Ulrich Hamm. "Motives of consumers following a vegan diet and their attitudes towards animal agriculture." *Appetite* 105 (October 2016): 643–51.

6. Hans Hauner. "Der ultimative Hype." MMW—Fortschritte der Medizin 157.10 (October 2015): 40.

7. Lap Tai Le and Joan Sabaté. "Beyond Meatless, the Health Effects of Vegan Diets: Findings from the Adventist Cohorts." *Nutrients* 6.6 (June 2014): 2131–2147.

8. Till Strecker. "Definitions of 'vegan' and 'vegetarian' in accordance with the EU Food Information Regulation," EC Register of Interest Representatives 109356110578-03 (September 2015).

9. Meike Janssen, Claudia Busch, Manika Rödiger and Ulrich Hamm. "Motives of consumers following a vegan diet and their attitudes towards animal agriculture." *Appetite* 105 (October 2016): 643–51.

10. Lisa Marie Gollowitsch. "Health aspects of vegan diet." University of Graz. (2017) Master thesis.

11. Florian Padinger. "Analysis of vegan instant meals." University of Graz (2017) Master thesis.

12. Ibid.

13. Ibid.

CHAPTER 4

BELGIUM

EXCEPTIONAL OR COMMON? VEGETARIANISM AND VEGANISM IN BELGIUM

LAURENCE VERHEIJEN
AND SARA ERREYGERS

As of the 27th of April 2018, in Antwerp, Belgium, Domino's Pizza added not one, but three vegan pizzas to their product range. Similar developments are seen among local brands; Ijsboerke, an ice company, and Aoste, a company that produces meat, have launched vegan and veggie versions of their products. In Belgian supermarket chains like Delhaize, Carrefour, and Lidl, the vegan and vegetarian product range is increasing as well.[1] These examples illustrate the advance of vegetarian and plant-based products in Belgium. Does this mean that eating habits are changing in Belgium? To answer that question, we need a deeper look at the Belgian food-culture.

Figures of the northern region of Flanders show that 1 percent of the population is vegan, 3 percent vegetarian, and 8 percent consider themselves flexitarian.[2] For the overall Belgian population, 96 percent consider meat as an important part of a meal because of taste, habit, and perceived nutritional value.[3] One out of four Belgians consumes meat daily.[4] Nevertheless, in all, the consumption of meat per capita in Belgium has decreased 16.7 percent between 2012 and 2016, and the number of animals that are slaughtered per year in Belgium also saw a significant decrease.[5] On average, meat-consumption in Western Europe decreased by 1.4 percent between 2012 and 2016, so Belgium is a striking outlier.[6] The group most responsible for this decline is not the group of vegetarians, but the flexitarians; those who consciously reduce their meat intake.

The group of flexitarians in Belgium is booming.[7] In 2017 a national survey revealed that 44 percent of the Belgians claim to eat less meat in comparison to the year before.[8] For flexitarians, as well as vegetarians, the most important reasons to eat less or no meat are animal welfare, followed by environmental concerns and health in second and third place, respectively.[9] That animal concerns are listed as the first priority is striking. In 2015, environmental concerns were still considered more important than animal welfare.[10] This evolution might be related to the numerous scandals linked to meat that were covered by the media in Belgium in the past years.[11] In March 2017, the media showed undercover images of pig slaughterhouses. In June of that year there was commotion around pictures of industrial-raised chickens, in September the maltreatment of cows was in the news, and in November bad practices in the chicken industry were covered again. More recently, people were confronted with gruesome images of a Spanish pig producer delivering to Belgian supermarkets.[12] This gives us a possible clarification for the discrepancy between Belgium and the rest of Europe in terms of meat reduction. Nadine Lucas, the representative of the organization Animal Rights, claims that every scandal triggers more people to abandon meat or animal-based products as a whole.[13]

Not only do negative events inspire people to change. In Flanders there have been some positive campaigns encouraging people to eat less meat. What the campaigns have in common is that they focus on social relations by creating a supporting community. One of these campaigns is Thursday Veggieday, organized by Eva vzw, a non-profit organization that advocates for a healthy and sustainable lifestyle. The campaign stimulates people to eat vegetarian on Thursdays by emailing recipes and tips each Thursday. It is focused on a very broad audience, as the campaign is not limited to those who already consciously reduce their meat-intake. The campaign has reported some significant results: 43 percent of the people who subscribed indicate that they eat less meat on Thursdays because of the action, 40 percent also eat less meat on other days, and 28 percent has become a vegetarian because of it.[14] Another campaign is Days without Meat, which challenges people not to eat meat for 40 days. In 2017, 114,183 people participated and together they spared 6,456,052 m^2 on their ecological footprint by eating less meat than they would usually do.[15] This year, Days Without Meat was replaced by Try Vegan. The aim of this campaign was to encourage people to eat vegan for a whole month. Participants could subscribe for a daily newsletter and become a member of an online Facebook group to find support and share personal insights. This group had 2,207 members that posted regularly and traded tips and advice.

One of the participants of Try Vegan, Barbara Creemers, was willing to share her experiences, allowing us to gain more insight into the impact of this challenge, the community around it, and by extension, into maintaining a plant-based lifestyle in general. Barbara is a thirty-seven-year-old mother of two young boys (10 and 12 years old) living in Flanders. She describes herself as a "flexanist": she eats plant-based on weekdays, but vegetarian on weekends or on special occasions such as family gatherings or parties. On these social gatherings, she allows herself some "sins." For Barbara, sinning means consuming products that contain dairy or eggs. The main reason for Barbara to become a vegetarian and later on a flexanist is her health; when she consumes meat or dairy, she feels sick. She describes this as an "intolerance." At the time of the interview she was participating in the Try Vegan challenge and was not consuming any animal-derived products. Thus, in the interview Barbara mainly reflected about the period during which she was eating strictly vegan.

One may ask whether there is such a big difference between eating mostly vegan or full-time vegan, as it seems like a minor detail. During the Try Vegan challenge, Barbara has more difficulties with social gatherings than when she is a flexanist. She explained that during the Try Vegan period, she is confronted more regularly with several prejudices when she informs people about her diet, which makes her avoid going to parties or social gatherings at which she knows there will be people who are not open to her lifestyle. One of those prejudices is that she is considered extreme or difficult. Another one that she hears regularly is that "vegans can't eat anything and have to sacrifice a lot." Barbara shared that those prejudices are partly true for her: banning eggs and dairy out of her meals feels indeed like a sacrifice for her, as she likes the taste of it, and sometimes she feels like she is acting extreme. Although Barbara partially agrees with the existing prejudices, she said that she does try to tackle them when people confront her. She addresses these issues in a subtle way, as she does not want to draw attention to herself. Coping with how friends and colleagues perceive her because of her eating habits is the most difficult thing for her about a plant-based lifestyle. This is why she will not talk about her personal lifestyle and choices. She would rather try to "direct the discussion into a broader perspective." This broader perspective consists of lighthearted things such as sharing recipes or discussing alternative food options, and also of profound discussions about the impact of meat on health and environment. For that reason, Barbara likes the recent update of the food pyramid, the official Flemish nutrition guide.[16] Because this official institution now advises to eat mainly plant-based meals, she feels supported in her arguments. It is important to notice that she will only bring up these arguments when she is confronted with prejudices, as openly advocating for a vegan lifestyle is not in her comfort zone. Barbara does not believe in extreme or radical changes, but rather in a steady, personal, and informed growth, and she acts accordingly. She feels that people are not ready for the truth about animal welfare, so she avoids that topic, in order not to be seen as "extreme." This is also why she will not confront people with shocking images or disturbing facts.

In situations where a profound discussion is not appropriate, Barbara is relieved that she can use her health as a valid excuse for not eating meat or consuming dairy. When she states that she feels sick after eating it and makes the comparison with a gluten-intolerant person, people seem to be more likely to accept that it is not completely her "fault" that she is being "difficult," as it is a health issue, rather than a conviction. One of those situations is going out for dinner. Barbara explained that she does not mind eating something different than the people she is out with, but she does mind that she has to specifically ask for it. This makes her stand out from the group, since people have to make an extra effort to meet her needs. For Barbara, asking the cook what broth he used in a soup, is already out of her comfort zone and makes her feel like she is being "extreme." This is the main reason why she will go back to being a flexanist and will not remain a full-time vegan when the Try Vegan challenge is over; it gives her the flexibility to participate in social gatherings, without being demanding. She feels at ease when she does not draw too much attention to herself; she stated that "blending in" is easier for her when eating vegetarian. If finding a suitable dish when meeting with friends or colleagues at a restaurant is difficult, she can go for a vegetarian option, since most restaurants offer that option nowadays. This is, according to Barbara's experience, an improvement compared to approximately ten years ago when vegetarianism was not very common.

However, her problem would not be as prominent if there was a vegan option that she could choose. Barbara explained that she would rather see the vegetarian option that most restaurants have be vegan by default. Thus, when she wants to eat vegan, she would not have to ask beforehand if people could make an exception for her and it would not take an extra effort. The results of the survey by Ivox revealed that there is public support for this idea: 48 percent of the respondents indicated that they think that every restaurant should have a vegan option.[17] When asked what an ideal situation would be for Barbara, she suggested that we could even take it one step further. She proposed that all meals in restaurants should be vegan by default, with the option to add meat or dairy for an additional fee. According to her, that would not only increase our general well-being, as she considers eating vegan to be more healthy and beneficial for the environment, it would also make meat eaters more aware of the actual cost of their meat. Plus, this would accommodate the ongoing trend of Belgian consumers eating less meat. However, this will not happen soon as meat is still important for many Belgians because of taste, habit, and perceived nutritional value.[18]

So far, Barbara talked about interactions with colleagues or friends, but what about closer friends or family? When reflecting about interactions in a more private sphere, Barbara said that her relatives are very understanding. They let her know in advance which food they will prepare. If this does not fit within her plant-based diet, Barbara brings her own food. Her family is even more accommodating, as they are willing to eat plant-based together with Barbara. Her husband and kids eat what she serves and they do not demand her to prepare meat. Barbara's mother even took it one step further and became a vegetarian because of Barbara's influence. The study of Ivox for Eva vzw endorses Barbara's personal experiences. When cooking for other people, 47 percent of the respondents take vegans or vegetarians into consideration, by asking them beforehand about their food restrictions and by providing an alternative. Another finding of that same study was that 43 percent of the respondents indicated that they are willing to eat the same if a family member decides to become vegan or vegetarian.[19]

Even though she is understood and supported by her relatives and close friends, Barbara still seeks for interaction with like-minded people. She thinks the Internet is a great tool for interacting. She explained that the online vegan community is quite large. There are many groups and pages where people exchange tips and practices and provide moral support. During the Try Vegan challenge, there was a Facebook group for the participants. Barbara thinks these groups can be very inspirational and supportive, as long as people do not start preaching a vegan lifestyle, which she thinks happens frequently and often drives a wedge between vegans. Besides those groups, Instagram is a great refuge for her as well. There is an abundance of posts and pictures related to veganism and many like-minded people to be met. Barbara warned that this contributes to a biased view on reality for her, as it seems like the whole world is vegan. She talked about a "reality-check" when she switches from the online world to her "offline" life. This is not surprising, as Barbara lives in Limburg, a rural part of Flanders that she describes as "an ecological desert." The numbers confirm her statement: It is mostly urban areas that are vegan/vegetarian minded. This is illustrated by Brussels, the Belgian (veggie) capital city: 4 percent of the Brussels inhabitants are vegans and 7 percent are vegetarians, which is significantly more than in other parts of Belgium.[20] This difference between rural and urban areas explains why Barbara's colleague, who lives in Ghent, another big city, finds it quite easy to maintain a vegan lifestyle and complete the Try Vegan challenge, while for Barbara it is more difficult. Barbara gave a few examples to illustrate why she feels inspired by green(er) cities such as Antwerp: only one of the five restaurants in her town is prepared to serve vegan or vegetarian meals, while she has the impression that in Antwerp or Ghent you can walk into any restaurant and still have a good chance of finding vegan options. The same goes for supermarkets. Barbara has the feeling that in many supermarkets in Antwerp about three quarter of the products are vegan, while in Limburg it is the other way around. For Barbara this does not necessarily mean that veganism is accepted in bigger cities, but it is easier to blend in, whilst in Limburg she feels like she is extreme.

Being considered extreme or feeling extreme is the common thread running through Barbara's story, while vegetarianism is more accepted and is often even seen as normal. Luckily, this feeling is not as prominent when interacting with her relatives and close friends, as they do not have troubles with Barbara's eating habits and are willing to adapt to her. On top of that, Barbara feels that cities are becoming more accommodating for a plant-based lifestyle. Although vegans are still a vast minority, the range of plant-based products in supermarkets and options in restaurants is increasing, and they are finding a place next to vegetarian and omnivore products. Slowly but steadily, a shift in eating habits seems to be taking place, as 40 percent of the Belgians are planning to eat less meat and fish.[21] The impact of this evolution is noteworthy; Belgium is currently at the top of Europe when it comes to decreasing meat consumption.[22] A fully plant-based society is still a utopia at this point, and may not be what we should strive for, but Barbara hopes that Belgium will continue to evolve to a society where vegans can blend in and are considered normal, so that she should not settle with eating vegetarian to be more or less accepted.

Suggested Readings

Belga. "Belgen eten minder vlees." *Landbouwleven.* February 14, 2018, http://www. landbouwleven.be/2410/article/2018-02-14/belgen-eten-minder-vlees.

Bernburg, Anna. "Bijna helft van de Belgen heeft zijn vleesconsumptie het laatste jaar verminderd." *Eva vzw.* February 13, 2018, http://www.evavzw.be/nieuws/bijna -helftvan-de-belgen-heeft-zijn-vleesconsumptie-het-laatste-jaar-verminderd.

Dagen Zonder Vlees. "DZV Teller dag 40." Accessed August 20, 2018, https://dagen zondervlees.be/.

Flanders' Agricultural Marketing Board. "Wat is gezonde voeding volgens de consument?" Algemeen. Accessed February 10, 2018, https://www.vlam.be/nl/ feitenencijfers/algemeen.

Flanders' Agricultural Marketing Board. "Belg gaat steeds bewuster om met vlees. Hij wisselt vlees vaker af met gevogelte, vis en vegetarisch." Vlees. Accessed February 10, 2018, https://www.vlam.be/nl/feitenencijfers/vlees.

Gezond Leven. "Voedingsdriehoek." September 19, 2017, https://www.gezondleven. be/themas/voeding/voedingsdriehoek.

Mooijman, Ruben. "Belgische vleesconsumptie daalt het snelst." *De Standaard.* November 4, 2017, http://www.standaard.be/cnt/dmf20171103_03168897.

Mechelen, Timon Van. "Van Domino's Pizza tot McDonald's: Iedereen wil een graantje meepikken van de vegan-trend." *Het Laatste Nieuws,* April 27, 2018, https:// www.hln.be/nina/nina-kookt/van-domino-s-pizza-tot-mcdonald-siedereenwil -een-graantje-meepikken-van-de-vegan-trend~acbf813b/.

Statbel. "More bovine animals and less pigs slaughtered." News, last modified March 5, 2018, https://statbel.fgov.be/en/news/more-bovine-animals-and-less -pigs-slaughtered.

Vlaams Infocentrum Land-en Tuinbouw. "44 procent Belgen at vorig jaar minder vlees." Nieuws, April 4, 2018, http://www.vilt.be/44-belgen-zegtminder-vlees-te-eten.

Notes

1. Timon Van Mechelen, "Van Domino's Pizza tot McDonald's: Iedereen wil een graantje meepikken van de vegan-trend." *Het Laatste Nieuws,* April 27, 2018, https://www.hln.be/nina/nina-kookt/van-domino-s-pizza-tot-mcdonald-sieder een-wil-een-graantje-meepikken-van-de-vegan-trend~acbf813b/.

2. Anna Bernburg, "Bijna helft van de Belgen heeft zijn vleesconsumptie het laatste jaar verminderd." *Eva vzw.* February 13, 2018, http://www.evavzw.be/nieuws/ bijna-helft van-de-belgen-heeft-zijn-vleesconsumptie-het-laatste-jaar-verminderd.

3. "Wat is gezonde voeding volgens de consument?" Algemeen, Flanders' Agricultural Marketing Board, 2016, https://www.vlam.be/nl/feitenencijfers/algemeen.

4. "Belg gaat steeds bewuster om met vlees." Vlees, Flanders' Agricultural Marketing Board, 2017, https://www.vlam.be/nl/feitenencijfers/vlees.

5. "More bovine animals and less pigs slaughtered." News, Statbel, last modified March 5, 2018, https://statbel.fgov.be/en/news/more-bovine-animals-and-less -pigsslaughtered.

6. Ruben Mooijman, "Belgische vleesconsumptie daalt het snelst." *De Standaard*, November 4, 2017, http://www.standaard.be/cnt/dmf20171103_03168897.

7. Flanders' Agricultural Marketing Board. "Belg gaat steeds bewuster om met vlees."

8. Anna Bernburg, "Bijna helft van de Belgen heeft zijn vleesconsumptie het laatste jaar verminderd." Eva vzw, February 13, 2018, http://www.evavzw.be/ nieuws/bijna-helft-van-de-belgen-heeft-zijn-vleesconsumptie-het-laatste-jaar -verminderd.

9. Belga, "Belgen eten minder vlees." Landbouwleven. February 14, 2018, http:// www.landbouwleven.be/2410/article/2018-02-14/belgen-eten-minder-vlees.

10. Belga. "Belgen eten minder vlees."

11. Mooijman, "Belgische vleesconsumptie."

12. Mooijman. "Belgische vleesconsumptie."

13. "44 procent Belgen at vorig jaar minder vlees," Nieuws, Vilt, April 4, 2018, http:// www.vilt.be/44-belgen-zegt-minder-vlees-te-eten.

14. Bernburg. "Bijna helft van de Belgen heeft zijn vleesconsumptie het laatste jaarverminderd."

15. DZV Teller dag 40 (2017). Retrieved from https://dagenzondervlees.be/.

16. "Voedingsdriehoek." Gezond Leven, September 19, 2017, https://www .gezondleven.be/themas/voeding/voedingsdriehoek.

17. Bernburg. "Bijna helft van de Belgen heeft zijn vleesconsumptie het laatste jaarverminderd."

18. Flanders' Agricultural Marketing Board, "Gezonde voeding."

19. Bernburg. "Bijna helft van de Belgen heeft zijn vleesconsumptie het laatste jaarverminderd."

20. Bernburg. "Bijna helft van de Belgen heeft zijn vleesconsumptie het laatste jaarverminderd."

21. Bernburg. "Bijna helft van de Belgen heeft zijn vleesconsumptie het laatste jaarverminderd."

22. Mooijman. "Belgische vleesconsumptie."

CHAPTER 5

BRAZIL

BRAZIL AND ITS VEGAN AND VEGETARIAN DIETS

ANTHONIETA LOOMAN MAFRA

INTRODUCTION

Brazil is well known for barbecue meats. The prevalence of Brazilian barbecues both in country and internationally speaks to the deep-rooted cultural appreciation and mastery this country has achieved for its grilled foods. One of the most known Brazilian dishes is called *feijoada*. African slaves who lived in Brazil in the sixteenth century invented it. This national dish is a mix of black beans and pork leftovers (such as ears, tails, and tongues) after the slaves had cooked the best parts of the pig for their lords.

Although food access is better nowadays than in past centuries, it is not hard to find people who consume poor quality, rich in fat and/or nerve meat such as ox's neck. It is due to the limited access to good meat consumption. Some housekeepers, for example, ask their employers for the meat leftovers after they prepare the best part of the beef. Also meat prices differ a lot. While bovine liver and pork intestine are around R$ 10,00/kg, a good piece of beef like a tenderloin is around R$ 33,00/kg. As a country in development, Brazil has a high social inequality (index Gini of 49 percent).[1] Consequently, most of its population belongs to a low socioeconomic status, which makes it more difficult for them to afford good quality and expensive meat. On the other hand, Brazil is a huge country, very diverse in vegetation, offering an ideal setting for vegan and vegetarian diets with a vast possibility to be explored. The numbers indicate that there is a 40 percent growth in the vegan/vegetarian market a year.[2] Taking into consideration that most of the Brazilian population has a low socioeconomic level, it is difficult to invest in a vegan/vegetarian healthy alimentation if you do not have access to information about meals you can cook and different sources to have all nutrients that the human body needs. A good way for the vegan diet to reach a larger number of Brazilians would be to reduce the price of vegan products, as well as increasing their availability, and disseminate knowledge about unconventional food plants (UFP). The UFP would increase the possibility of ingested foods and decrease costs for a healthy vegan diet.

In this chapter, I present first a brief characterization of the growth potential of veganism in Brazil, then I bring reports from two friends: Celso, who has started his diet in the most vegetarian/vegan Brazilian city and moved to Natal, and Paulo, who started his vegan diet already in Natal.

BRAZIL CHARACTERIZATION

Brazil is the fifth largest country in the world and the only one that touches the equator and tropic of Capricorn, which may be observed through Brazilian animal and plant diversity. Despite the diversity, the exploitation of native plants species is very low. Indeed, there are some studies addressing the importance of including UFP in the Brazilian diet.[3,4,5] Kinupp claims that Brazilian natural resources are underutilized and there is no incentive for the consumption of native species. For instance, tropical and subtropical countries have the greatest diversity of vascular plant species,[6] but only three out of twenty fruit species most consumed in Brazil are natives. Pineapple, guava, and passion fruit are the only native fruits most consumed, while apple, coconut, lime, orange, avocado, melon, and watermelon and other nonnative fruits occupy the place of other native fruits that could be more explored as *jaboticaba* and *pitanga*.[7] Furthermore, there are regional vegetables very rich in nutrients, but often considered as weeds, such as beetroot, carrot stems, and sweet potato leafs.[8]

In addition, Brazil is the fifth most populous country in the world, with 207.6 million people.[9] Notwithstanding Brazilian area and population sizes and vegetable diversity, data collected by IBOPE Intelligence pointed out that 12 percent of the Brazilian population is vegetarian. Even though this percentage seems to be very low, the Brazilian Vegetarian Society states that it increased 75 percent from 2012 to 2018 in metropolitan areas, the beef consumption decreased 8 percent from 2014 to 2015, and 63 percent of the population wants to reduce the meat consumption, indicating that the country is moving toward greater vegetarianism-friendly behavior. One support for this prediction is that 55 percent of Brazilians would buy more vegan products if there were some indication on the products' packages about its origin.[10]

In São Paulo, the biggest Brazilian city, with 12.1 million inhabitants, located in the southeast, there are around fifty vegetarian and/or vegan restaurants and lots of restaurants with vegetarian/vegan options. In Natal, a smaller city with 885,180 people, 2,969 km away from São Paulo in northeast Brazil, there are few options of vegan/vegetarian restaurants. Cuisines of both regions are also very distinct. While São Paulo is the richest city in Brazil, in a more developed region, with millions of immigrants, mainly Italians and Japanese (it is home to the largest Japanese colony outside Japan), that influenced a lot of the local gastronomy, northeast Brazil is one of the poorest Brazilian regions. Besides the great concentration of poor people in this region, it has a great coastline, but it suffers from a very harsh drought in its interior. The weather makes it difficult to raise animals, with goat being one of the least difficult animals to raise because it is more resistant. All of this together contributes to gastronomy quite differently from that of São Paulo, with goat meat and stomach and pork intestine as specialties. Let's look at how vegetarians/vegans experience living in both cities.

TWO CITIES, TWO INTERVIEWERS, AND THREE DIFFERENT EXPERIENCES

Celso is a twenty-nine-year-old man and was a meat eater, who loved barbecue, especially chicken hearts. However, at the same time, he used to think about the animals that were dying because of it. He started to modify his diet, cutting out beef, then chicken, and after a while fish, eggs and dairy, even though he still eats butter, cheese, and eggs, when there is no other option available. The whole process lasted a year and a half. He first started cutting out all slaughter animals, and fish was the last one he cut down on, because in general, they are taken out of the natural environment. His reason for adopting the diet is the fact that human beings judge themselves in the right to commercialize lives, "we think our existence is a priority in regards to other species, that our life and culture are worth more." For him, it is understandable that species' life is worth more for that determined species, and "by a cultural inertia, we end up eating meat, but is there a relationship of necessity that justifies the sacrifice of a life or is it just for pleasure?"

Differently from Celso, who modified his diet because of his principles, Paulo began it after witnessing animal suffering. Paulo is thirty-five years old but started to change his diet into the vegan one when he was fourteen years old and saw a chicken being killed and prepared to eat. "I could not eat the chicken. After that, I stopped eating any food prepared with chicken. And when I was 16 years old, also in a farm, I saw a cow being killed, so I stopped eating beef. When I was 18, I stopped eating fish." His transition for a complete vegan diet was five years later, due to a stomach lesion occasioned by a bad alimentation distribution, with excess of ice cream, beer, and coffee, which led him to cut out dairy products and eggs from his diet.

Paulo says that, at the beginning, it was really difficult to follow the diet because of the idea of having to eat a substitute of animal protein and the lack of prepared food to buy, which made him learn how to cook. Currently, his diet is very diverse. He studies about and cultivates UFP, inserting them gradually in his diet that is also very diverse in conventional vegetables, and he is always trying new recipes that he often makes available in his vegan delivery restaurant (only delivery packed lunches). According to Paulo, a meat-eater person ends up being restricted in his/her alimentation, varying around ten types of food during a day, while a healthy vegetarian/vegan can have that amount only in one meal, reaching thirty to fifty food variations in a day.

While Paulo started his vegan life in Natal, Celso started being a vegetarian when he was living in São Paulo. He declared it was not difficult since São Paulo has many vegetarian/vegan restaurants or, at least, plenty of restaurants with vegetarian food options. Now he has moved away to Natal, the same city Paulo lives, and he finds it more difficult to follow the vegetarian diet there because of the scarcity of restaurants with vegetarian options and vegetarian-prepared food at the supermarkets. Therefore, he has to search for places with vegetarian options or eat before leaving home because unlike São Paulo there is no vegetarian/vegan food options everywhere you go. Besides the size difference between both cities, the gastronomy may also be a reason why there are more vegetarian options available. Thinking about the Brazil characterization, we notice that the Northeast has a strong culture of meat consumption, seeming reasonable that most of the restaurants of this region offer meat as the main dish. Celso claims, "The regions customs that involve social meetings and appreciation of certain types of menu (dry meat, shrimps, etc.), make it appears challenging situations in which I have to decide to break the social ritual and ask an alternative food only for me, eat only the side dishes or give my diet away in the light of the occasion." He also relates that the vegetarian culture is stronger in São Paulo. "I felt a *tendency* towards this kind of diet among people of the social circle I was part of. It was way more frequent to find other vegetarians in other common areas (excluding, of course, restaurants that offer vegan/vegetarian menu, where there is a predominance of adepts of these diets). So even in bars and *cafés*, casual domestic meetings, it was often to find that more than one of the presents had a vegan or vegetarian diets. For example, in the apartment I used to live, I shared it with other people and two of them started the vegetarian diet in the same period, without even talking about it." Unlike gastronomy difference, Celso relates that people of São Paulo and Natal deal in the same way with the fact that he is a vegetarian, always respecting his choice and trying to choose the best option available for everyone. "People respect my decision in the same way in both cities, but, in Natal, it is more uncommon to find a vegetarian/ vegan outside of places planned to include this public and those places are few," Celso says.

Celso does not consider himself a vegan because of the lack of greater vegan options. As the lack of supply leads to very high food prices, he thinks it is not worthy investing in these products because the impact is not substantial in nature but the financial impact is too significant on him, not being able to follow the vegan diet. "If the vegan products were more widely distributed, I would have greater access and would not have to decide at times what I would eat between cheese bread or bread and butter on the plate because they were the least harmful products," he said.

Paulo has a different view. He finds it easier than Celso to be a vegan. Maybe it is due to the fact that Paulo has been a vegan for twenty-one years. If compared to Celso's transition, Paulo's was slower which may reflect in the different level of difficulty that each one faces. In addition, Paulo also affirmed that it was really complicated to follow the diet initially, "it takes time to adapt to the new routine." The routine adaptation involves also the social circle.

Paulo and Celso report that friends and family did not take their deci- sion seriously at first, but now they support them. "In the beginning of my transition to the new diet, my friends and family did not really believe that I had made that decision and some of them even asked me if I was going crazy, when they realized that I was serious about my new lifestyle, they respected it. (...) After a while, I could notice them trying to please me if a vegetarian food and always choosing places to go with vegetarian options, without me asking," Celso said. Although Celso's family is omnivore, they always order vegetarian dishes or go to a place which has vegetarian food and, even though Paulo's family was resistant initially because they believed he was going to be anemic (but he never did), after a long time they adhered to the vegetarian diet too. "My parents have 90 percent vegan diet: most part of their diet is vegan but they eat crackers with butter in the mornings, buy any kind of bread, regardless it is made with milk and eggs, and sometimes they eat fish. Now my younger sister is a vegetarian," Paulo related. Paulo and his family take veganism as a "personal revolution," in Paulo's words, so they do not show that their way of living is more important than social interactions, not depriving themselves of going to events such as barbecues. Although Celso had not expressed himself as Paulo did, his idea about being a vegetarian is the same: He does not try to convince people to adhere to the vegetarian diet either, and he goes to any kind of event too, regardless of the kind of food that will be available; the caution both take is to always eat before leaving home. Additionally, they frequently perceive people trying to make food for them. "A friend of mine is not a vegan but, in her wedding, there was a vegan menu available because of me," Paulo gladly stated. Besides that, meat eaters do not eat only meat, so vegans/vegetarians can still eat other food that omnivores eat, so even though they go to a barbecue, there still is food that they can eat if they need something. "I think people do not realize that their food base is vegan, because rice, beans and lettuce and tomatoes is kind of *must* for Brazilian lunch," Paulo said.

Celso noticed that some people seem to think he is engaged in a cause that does not have the possibility of becoming concrete at the population level, that the effort does not generate any substantial result, but Celso says that it does not upset or discourage him because his reason to adhere to the vegetarian diet is a personal cause in which he feels better without contributing to animal cruelty. Similarly, Paulo claimed that most people face the fact he is a vegan "with irony, mistrust and a lot of misinformation because they think you have to eat everything and who does not do it is considered spoiled." Considering that Paulo was raised in Natal, where the most diverse types of meat are eaten and there are a few choices of food, it is understandable why some people share the thinking that if you do not eat something someone is offering, you have the *privilege* to choose your food, meaning that you belong to a higher socioeconomic class, and, consequently, you are *spoiled*. But the scenario has been changed in the last few years. People are trying to find out more about veganism and approaching Paulo because of his "activism in food form," as he said, to ask questions about food preparation and his lifestyle. According to Paulo, from around five years to now, "veganism has come into *fashion* more because of the *fashion* of healthy eating, than through animal and human liberation, which is the real reason for the vegan diet." In spite of the fact that the reason that is propelling veganism is not consistent with its real one, Paulo thinks there is a good side to people's concern about the *fashion* of eating healthy: increased tolerance with the vegan diet and a greater variety of food industry products.

CONCLUSION

Although there are more difficulties to be a vegetarian in Natal than in São Paulo because of the city size, options of food available, and culture, Paulo, who began to be a vegan when living in Natal does not think he has to make a huge effort, differing from Celso. The transition time from an omnivore to a vegetarian/vegan diet seems to be a fact that affects people's experiences: Celso thinks it is more difficult to follow the diet because of the lack of vegetarian/vegan food available but has changed his diet in only one year and a half, eight years less than Paulo, who had enough time to do lots of research about the diet and learn how to cook in order to not have to eat animal-based products. Even though the culture in São Paulo leads people toward the vegan/vegetarian diet, Celso says that people of both cities show same respect to his diet. Similarly, Celso and Paulo do not feel that the diet disturbs their social interactions and believe that people are becoming more tolerant with veganism and informed about vegetarian and vegan diets. They feel comfortable in attending any event since their motivation to the diets is the thinking that *we are what we eat*. Through vegetarian and vegan diets, they demonstrate how engaged they are in the animal well-being, including efforts in having to learn how to cook, always eating before leaving home, or looking for places with vegan/vegetarian options available in order for the liberation of animal exploitation.

Suggested Readings

Barreira, T. F., G. X. Paula Filho, V. C. C. Rodrigues, F. M. C. Andrade, R. H. S. Santos, S. E. Priore, and H. M. Pinheiro-Sant'Ana. "Diversidade e equitabilidade de plantas alimentícias não convencionais na zona rural de Viçosa, Minas Gerais, Brasil" ["Diversity and equivalence of unconventional food plants in rural zone of Viçosa, Minas Gerais, Brazil"]. *Revista Brasileira de Plantas Medicinais* [*Brazilian Journal of Medicinal Plants*] 17 no. 4 (Scielo 2015): 964–74, http://dx.doi.org/10.1590/1983-084X/14_100.

Campos Júnior, Sérgio Darcy Oliveira de, Kerollen Luana Silveira da Rosa and Diego Moreira da Rosa. "PANCs Not Dead: Plantas Alimentícias Não-Convencionais" ["PANCs not dead: Unconventional food plants"]. *Semex em resumo* [*Semex in abstract*] 2, no. 2 (IFRS 2014): 1. https://periodicos.ifrs.edu.br/index.php/SEMEX/article/view/710/603.

Carreiro, Juliana. "Mercado vegano cresce 40% ao ano no Brasil" ["Vegan market grows 40% a year in Brazil"]. *Estadão,* February 6, 2017 http://emais.estadao.com.br/blogs/comida-de-verdade/mercado-vegano-cresce-40-ao-ano-no-brasil/.

Central Intelligence Agency (CIA). "The World Factbook." Accessed October 2, 2018, https://www.cia.gov/library/publications/the-world-factbook/rankorder/2172rank.html.

Instituto Brasileiro de Geografia e Estatística (IBGE) [Brazilian Institute of Geography and Statistics]. "Por cidade e estado" ["For city and state"]. Accessed June 2, 2018, https://www.ibge.gov.br/estatisticas-novoportal/por-cidade-estado-estatisticas .html?t=destaques&c=2408102.

Kelen, Maria Elisa Becker, and Brack, Paulo. "Viveirismo Comunitário—Difundindo o conhecimento sobre as PANCs (plantas alimentícias não convencionais) e a agrobiodiversidade no Brasil" ["Community livelihood—Spreading the knowledge on the PANCs (unconventional food plants) and agrobiodiversity in Brazil"]. *V feira de ensino e popularização da ciência* [*V teaching and popularization science fair*], October 19, 2015, http://www.lume.ufrgs.br/bitstream/handle/10183/134499/FeiraIC2015_44015.pdf?sequence=1.

Kinupp, Valdely Ferreira. "Plantas Alimentícias Não-Convencionais (PANCs): uma Riqueza Negligenciada" ["Unconventional food plants (PANCs): A neglected wealth"]. *Anais da 61ª Reunião Anual da SBPC* [*Annals of the 61st Annual SBPC Meeting*], July 2009, http://www.sbpcnet.org.br/livro/61ra/mesas_redondas/MR_ValdelyKinupp.pdf.

Pensamento Verde [Green Thinking]. "Conheça as principais frutas nativas do Brasil" ["Know the main native fruits of Brazil"]. May 9, 2014, https://www.pensamentoverde.com.br/meio-ambienteconheca-principais-frutas-nativas-brasil/.

Projeto Nutrir [Nourish Project]. "Prática de PANCs veg." ["UFP veg practices"]. Accessed October 16, 2018, https://nutrir-horta-comunitaria4.webnode.com.

Sociedade Vegetariana Brasileira [Brazilian Vegetarian Society]. "Pesquisa do IBOPE aponta crescimento histórico no número de vegetarianos no Brasil. [IBOPE survey shows historical growth in the number of vegetarians in Brazil]." May 20, 2018, https://www.svb.org.br/2469-pesquisa-do-ibope-aponta-crescimento-historico-no-numero-de-vegetarianos-no-brasil.

Notes

1. "The World Factbook," Central Intelligence Agency (CIA), accessed October 2, 2018, https://www.cia.gov/library/publications/the-world-factbook/rankorder/2172rank.html.
2. Juliana Carreiro, "Mercado vegano cresce 40% ao ano no Brasil" ["Vegan market grows 40% a year in Brazil"], Estadão, February 6, 2017, http://emais.estadao.com.br/blogs/comida-de-verdade/mercado-vegano-cresce-40-ao-ano-no-brasil/.
3. T. F. Barreira et al., "Diversidade e equitabilidade de plantas alimentícias não convencionais na zona rural de Viçosa, Minas Gerais, Brasil" ["Diversity and

equivalence of unconventional food plants in rural zone of Viçosa, Minas Gerais, Brazil"], Revista Brasileira de Plantas Medicinais [Brazilian Journal of Medicinal Plants] 17, no. 4 (Scielo 2015): 964, http://dx.doi.org/10.1590/1983-084X/14_100.

4. Sérgio Darcy Oliveira de Campos Júnior, Kerollen Luana Silveira da Rosa and Diego Moreira da Rosa. "PANCs Not Dead: Plantas Alimentícias Não-Convencionais" ["PANCs not dead: unconventional food plants"], Semex em resumo [Semex in abstract] 2, no. 2 (IFRS 2014): 1, https://periodicos.ifrs.edu.br/index.php/SEMEX/article/view/710/603.

5. Maria Elisa Becker Kelen and Paulo Brack, "Viveirismo Comunitário—Difundindo o conhecimento sobre as PANCs (plantas alimentícias não convencionais) e a agrobiodiversidade no Brasil" ["Community livelihood—Spreading the knowledge on the PANCs (unconventional food plants) and agrobiodiversity in Brazil"], V feira de ensino e popularização da ciência [V teaching and popularization science fair], October 19, 2015, http://www.lume.ufrgs.br/bitstream/handle/10183/134499/FeiraIC2015_44015.pdf?sequence=1.

6. Valdely Ferreira Kinupp, "Plantas Alimentícias Não-Convencionais (PANCs): Uma Riqueza Negligenciada" ["Unconventional Food Plants (PANCs): a Neglected Wealth"], Anais da 61a Reunião Anual da SBPC [Annals of the 61st Annual SBPC Meeting], July, 2009, http://www.sbpcnet.org.br/livro/61ra/mesas_redondas/MR_ValdelyKinupp.pdf.

7. "Conheça as principais frutas nativas do Brasil" ["Know the main native fruits of Brazil"], Pensamento Verde [Green Thinking], May 9, 2014, https://www.pensamentoverde.com.br/meio-ambiente/conheca-principais-frutas-nativas-brasil/.

8. "Prática de PANCs veg." ["UFP veg practices"], Projeto Nutrir [Nourish Project], accessed October 16, 2018, https://nutrir-horta-comunitaria4.webnode.com.

9. "Por cidade e estado" ["For city and state"], Instituto Brasileiro de Geografia e Estatística (IBGE) [Brazilian Institute of Geography and Statistics], accessed June 2, 2018, https://www.ibge.gov.br/estatisticas-novoportal/por-cidade-estado-estatisticas.html?t=destaques&c=2408102.

10. "Pesquisa do IBOPE aponta crescimento histórico no número de vegetarianos no Brasil." ["IBOPE survey shows historical growth in the number of vegetarians in Brazil"], Sociedade Vegetariana Brasileira [Brazilian Vegetarian Society], May 20, 2018, https://www.svb.org.br/2469-pesquisa-do-ibope-aponta-crescimento-historico-no-numero-de-vegetarianos-no-brasil.

CHAPTER 6

CANADA

THE CANADIAN CONTEXT ON VEGETARIAN AND VEGAN DIETS

MARYANNE L. FISHER
AND JOANNE C. FISHER

W e are sisters living 6,164 km apart yet within the same country; Joanne lives in Vancouver, British Columbia, located on the southwestern coast of Canada, while Maryanne lives in Halifax, Novia Scotia, on the southeastern coast. It is not surprising that our food experiences are quite divergent, given the geographic distance between us. While Joanne lives in the national hotspot for health consciousness, Maryanne lives in an area that, despite some increased diversity in dining options, is still primarily known for lobster, scallops, fried pepperoni, and oatcakes, and less so for fine dining or vegan opportunities. Here we first present the current state of demographic-related adoption of plant-based diets in Canada, and then review our own experiences with such a diet. Note here that we are using the term "plant-based" in the sense of a diet primarily centered around fruits, vegetables, tubers, whole grains, and legumes, with dairy, eggs, and meat being exclusively minimized.[1] The term vegetarian here implies an absence of any meat, while vegan refers to a diet free of any animal product (e.g., eggs, dairy).

THE CANADIAN FOOD LANDSCAPE

Canada is a vast country, spanning 9.985 million km^2 and home to a population of approximately 36.29 million people. The size is significant and means that the 10 provinces and 3 territories include an incredibly diverse range of views regarding animals, diets, and health. In addition, there are noteworthy differences in access to foods which may impact one's ability to adopt a meat-free or meat-reduced diet. For example, in the northern most communities, such a diet would be nearly impossible, given the harsh growing conditions and a culture that thrives on locally hunted bison and moose.[2]

There is limited data available on current rates of vegetarianism in Canada. However, in 2015, an online poll of 1,507 Canadian adults revealed 33 percent of Canadians (approximately 12 million individuals) were either vegetarian or eating a meat reduced diet.[3,4] Included in these statistics were the 8 percent who identified as vegetarian or mostly vegetarian and 25 percent who indicated they were trying to eat less meat. At a regional level, this poll revealed the province of British Columbia, on the west coast, had the highest rate, with 13 percent of respondents identifying themselves as vegetarian (or mostly vegetarian) and an additional 26 percent indicating they were attempting to eat less meat. In addition, according to that same poll, approximately 12 percent of younger Canadians (aged 18–34) reported they were vegetarian or mostly so, while 33 percent of those aged 55 and older were trying to eat less meat and a further 5 percent reported being vegetarian (or mostly so).

A scan of recipe books from the 1950s through the 1970s clearly indicates that meat is traditionally a staple for the Canadian diet. However, according to the online poll,[5] the consumption per capita of pork and beef declined between 2012 and 2014, and milk consumption has also declined. The primary reason for this decrease has been attributed to the increased popularity of a vegan diet among young Canadians (18 to 24 years). When asked to explain the reasons for decreasing beef consumption, a survey of 504 Canadians over the age of 18 cite financial reasons, health and food safety concerns, environmental reasons, and ethical reasons.[6]

Vancouver, the largest city in British Columbia and the third largest in Canada, is well-known for being a lightning rod for vegetarianism; in 2010, People for the Ethical Treatment of Animals (PETA) labeled it as the most vegetarian friendly city in Canada.[7] In addition to numerous successful plant-based restaurants, the area is home to meat and dairy alternative industries (e.g., Gardein and Daiya) who sell their products across North America. By way of contrast, Halifax, the provincial capital of Nova Scotia and the thirteenth largest city in Canada, has around six vegetarian/vegan restaurants.

Despite some regional variations, the restaurant industry across Canada is noticing an increased demand for plant-based options. Chef Justin Cournoyer, owner of Toronto's Actinolite restaurant, reports that offering vegan dishes is important for business because it is in keeping with the trend toward vegetable-centric cooking.[8] Michael Lyons, owner of Vancouver's Graze restaurant concurs in that meat eaters are now understanding that they may enjoy vegetarian food. Indeed, Lyons believes diners are developing increasingly sophisticated palates such that they view vegan food as a viable choice on their checklist of cuisines.[9]

The political climate of Canada is also changing, such that so-called hard-line vegans are now legally fighting for dietary accommodation to be considered equal with accommodations made for religious purposes.[10] In the province of Ontario, veganism is being considered as a component of a legally-protected creed, with the expectation that "creed" refers to a core belief system. If successful, this change would mean that incarcerated individuals, for example, would be able to request specially prepared meals.

There are also national-level changes that are noteworthy. In 2017, the Canadian Association of Physicians for the Environment wrote to the Minister of Health in response to her drafting a new set of guiding principles for Canada's next food guide. The new draft includes an emphasis on plant-based protein,[11] which is key because the existing guidelines are thought to prevent Canadians from correctly identifying plant-based protein-rich foods.[12] Current Canadian regulations overlook issues such as sustainability, health benefits, or other advantages of adopting a plant-based diet. Consequently, Canadians are not provided with sufficient information to make educated decisions regarding these plant-based sources of protein.

PERSONAL FOOD EXPERIENCES: MARYANNE

I define my diet as vegetarian although I recently added lean chicken on rare occasions. I began exploring vegetarianism at sixteen, while living on my parent's farm. My turn toward vegetarianism was in response to the raising of animals (poultry, cows, pigs) for consumption, and also for health and environmental sustainability reasons. Due to health reasons that developed in my thirties, I turned vegan (no animal products) for two years. Although my health improved, I left this diet because I found it challenging, especially while traveling outside of Canada and outside of large cities. While maintaining a largely vegetarian diet, I still strive to minimize my dairy intake and buy free range eggs.

Approximately six years ago, I met my (now-ex) husband, who was an omnivore with a strong love for meat. Food preparation became easier when we agreed to consume chicken on occasion in shared meals prepared at home. When recipes listed other kinds of meat as an ingredient, two dishes were prepared such that one used a plant-based substitute and the other used the animal product. I was willing (and sufficiently skilled) to cook a minimum number of meat-based dishes, such as casseroles, and there was the expectation that plant-based substitutes would be cooked when others prepared meals I was to share. We also decided that our children would be exposed to both types of diets so as to maximize their food experiences, although given they live with me, they primarily consume a vegetarian diet. My hope is that the diverse range of foods they consume will allow them to travel internationally with ease, and encourage them to develop their own preferences.

In the earlier stages of my vegetarian "journey," the biggest barrier to adopting a vegetarian diet was public awareness. For example, I would attend social gatherings and the host would serve chicken or fish, under the belief that all vegetarians ate some meat. When I did not eat the meat, it became a point of conversation which routinely led to uncomfortable and predictable group discussions about vegetarianism and personal motives, often followed by assumptions about my personality or other beliefs. I found these moments unpleasant, as I felt that I am attending social gatherings for a sense of community, not to feel isolated or individuated. I can recollect several conversations where someone seated beside me at a dinner party inquired about the food I either selected or had been given, leading to questions about my beliefs and health within the span of a few minutes. What compounds my discomfort is that I often did not know these individuals well and engaging in such discussions often felt revealing and judgmental. Today, vegetarianism is not as novel and people are often used to special dietary requirements at social gatherings, although these types of conversations still occur.

Traveling to small, remote locations remains a problem, though, as there are often limited vegetarian selections even at restaurants. I eat poorly at times by primarily consuming items like french fries or deep-fried vegetables in an effort to be able to dine out with others. International travel can pose particular difficulties, as meat may be in dishes that I did not expect. I often travel with a "cheat sheet" of local names for meats, or ask my host or local travel companion to help select an appropriate dish. When traveling with others, I try to be accommodating of their comfort and food needs, and believe that my decisions are not intended to impact on them. Thus, I am willing to eat at a local steakhouse for example, provided that it is understood that I cannot share in any meat-based dishes.

I feel a general sense of tolerance from my friends and family, especially those who live in rural areas where I might be the only vegetarian they have met. I do not often feel acceptance (and certainly not supported) with some individuals; despite the passing of years, there are still conversations around the fact that I am vegetarian and these conversations are marked with disdain. For example, "what are we going to do about the vegetarian?" or "I don't understand why she can't just eat this." I often bring extra food with me (e.g., nuts, fresh fruits, meat substitutes) so that when I stay with family, I have options available and can make the host feel less stressed. People have, on numerous occasions, stated that they do not know what to cook for me, and the solution is often that I bring my own food. I have noticed that if I bring tofu hot dogs and other meat substitutes (e.g., soy burgers), they usually are well received because they are at least somewhat familiar to most individuals. A small number of friends and family members are highly supportive and look at my visit as a way to hone their culinary skills. Some try new recipes ahead of my visits and present me with unusual dishes they have refined. Others, particularly those living in rural locations with minimal experience with vegetarians, cook a meat-based main dish as they typically would and prepare a larger version of a salad or side dish that is plant-based for me to consume.

PERSONAL FOOD EXPERIENCES: JOANNE

I define myself as being both an omnivore and a flexitarian. Like Maryanne, I began to explore vegetarianism at age sixteen. This was the result of two factors; firstly, the ethical dilemma of living on a farm where animals were raised for slaughter, and secondly, a move from central Canada to the country's west coast, where vegetarian food options were more common at the time and remain even more so now. I adopted a vegetarian diet that included both dairy and egg products immediately upon moving to Vancouver. Vegetarian food selections were common and readily available in both restaurants and grocery stores, much more so than in rural southern Ontario. In Vancouver, I shared a large house with a common kitchen with numerous people. I was the only person with any apparent interest in food preparation and cooking, so I organized a system of sharing expenses for food, which I then bought and prepared for everyone. The household then maintained a solely vegetarian diet. It was never discussed, nor were all residents vegetarian; it was simply accepted that as I was a vegetarian, so would be the meals that I prepared. Although anyone was free to use the kitchen as they wished to cook alternative meals (including meat dishes), no one did, as everyone was apparently sufficiently satisfied with a vegetarian menu.

I then met my partner who was mainly a vegetarian but ate meat on certain cultural occasions connected to his German background. Socially, these situations became difficult for me, so I began to incorporate some meat back into my diet in order to avoid friction of refusing meat-based dishes, which could be interpreted as being unappreciative or insulting by my partner. I then began to buy fish on a regular basis as a means of trying to bridge my partner's different food preferences. This worked for some time and also, with Vancouver being a hub for the west coast fishing industry, fresh fish was readily available.

However, I once again began to question the ethics of eating meat. My social circle included a number of vegans, who were completely against the consumption and use of animal products, whether it be for food or clothing (leather, wool) and I noticed that these views seemed to be becoming more widespread and that they appealed to me as well. I decided to adopt a vegan diet, with the exception of eggs from my own backyard organic hens. I fluctuated between a vegan and vegetarian diet for about seven years, until I experienced a major health event which required me to make changes once again, which included adding meat back into my diet for protein. I now regard myself as both an omnivore, relying primarily on poultry and fish for animal protein as I view them as more sustainable options. However, I also regard myself as a flexitarian, as I am perfectly comfortable with a vegetarian meal with friends on occasion.

Socially, I view vegetarian food choices which are "safe, go-to" options that generally please everyone when entertaining. The only difficulty I experience with vegetarianism now is I prefer to avoid wheat. I find it difficult to digest, despite confirmation that my intolerance is not celiac-based and also prefer grains of lower value on the glycemic index for general health reasons (e.g., lentils, brown rice, amaranth pasta).[13] When I cook for friends, it is generally an assortment of vegetarian dishes, with a fish or poultry dish on the side so all eating preferences can be easily addressed with a minimum of questions to my guests so that everyone feels welcome.

CONCLUSION

The Canadian food landscape suggests that there is an increasing departure from a meat-based diet to one that is more inclusive of plant-based options. There are various reasons for this shift, which seems to be led by younger generations, and is echoing through the country to the point where it is becoming a political issue. The increased social acceptance of alternative diets is also evident in the number of restaurants that are providing plant-based options. We have recounted our social and familial experiences with embracing vegetarian and vegan diets. Our experiences are similar, despite living in two highly distinct regions in Canada. Both of us have experienced fluidity in our eating styles; we have shifted between being vegan, vegetarian, omnivore, and flexitarian to accommodate changes in our lives, such as aging, health issues, social or romantic relationships, and relocating to different regions. For us, the moral decisions surrounding food choices are present but have taken a back seat to more immediate concerns that we have faced in our daily lives.

Suggested Readings

Atkinson, Fiona S., Kaye Foster-Powell, and Jennie C. Brand-Miller. "International tables of glycemic index and glycemic load values: 2008." Diabetes care (2008), https://doi.org/10.2337/dc08-1239.

Canadian Association of Physicians for the Environment (CAPE). "Letter to the Honourable Dr. Jane Philpott, Minister of Health." Accessed November 23, 2017, https://cape.ca/letter-to-minister-philpott-re-canadas-food-guide-aug-2017/.

Csanady, Ashley. "Is being a vegan a human right? Advocates claim protection under new Ontario policy, but that wasn't the point." Accessed November 23, 2017. http://nationalpost.com/news/canada/is-being-a-vegan-a-human-right-advocates-claim-protection-under-new-ontario-policy-but-that-wasnt-the-point.

Fricker, Peter. "How Vancouver became a vegetarian paradise." Accessed November 23, 2017, http://www.huffingtonpost.ca/peter-fricker/vancouver-vegetarian-food_b_12753706.html.

Imatome-Yun, Naomi. "Plant-based primer: The beginner's guide to starting a plant-based diet" (2017). Accessed July 25, 2018, https://www.forksoverknives.com/plant-based-primer-beginners-guide-starting-plant-based-diet/#gs.Y2irIgA.

Lam, Amy. "Why vegetarianism dies up north." The Walrus. Accessed November 24, 2017, https://thewalrus.ca/why-vegetarianism-dies-up-north/.

Marinangeli, Christopher P. F., Samara Foisy, Anna K. Shoveller, Cara Porter, Kathy Musa-Veloso, John L. Sievenpiper, and David J. A. Jenkins. "An Appetite for Modernizing the Regulatory Framework for Protein Content Claims in Canada." Nutrients 9, no. 9 (2017): 921.

Pippus, Anna. "Almost 12 million Canadians now vegetarian or trying to eat less meat." Accessed November 23, 2017, http://www.vancouverhumanesociety.bc.ca/almost-12-million-canadians-now-vegetarian-or-trying-to-eat-less-meat/.

"Statista." Accessed November 23, 2017, https://www.statista.com/topics/3262/vegan
-vegetarian-diets-in-canada/.

Tancock, Kat. "Vegan cuisine moves into the mainstream – and it's actually delicious."
The Globe and Mail. Accessed 13, 2017, https://www.theglobeandmail.com/
life/food-and-wine/food-trends/vegan-cuisine-moves-into-the-mainstream/
article22430440/.

Notes

1. Naomi Imatome-Yun, "Plant-based primer: The beginner's guide to starting a plant-based diet." Accessed July 25, 2018, https://www.forksoverknives.com/plant-based-primer-beginners-guide-starting-plant-based-diet/#gs.Y2irIgA.

2. Amy Lam, "Why vegetarianism dies up north." *The Walrus*. Accessed November 24, 2017, https://thewalrus.ca/why-vegetarianism-dies-up-north/.

3. Anna Pippus, "Almost 12 million Canadians now vegetarian or trying to eat less meat." Accessed November 23, 2017., http://www.vancouverhumanesociety.bc.ca/almost-12-million-canadians-now-vegetarian-or-trying-to-eat-less-meat/.

4. "Statista." Accessed November 23, 2017, https://www.statista.com/topics/3262/vegan-vegetarian-diets-in-canada/.

5. Ibid.

6. Ibid.

7. Peter Fricker, "How Vancouver became a vegetarian paradise." Accessed November 23, 2017, http://www.huffingtonpost.ca/peter-fricker/vancouver-vegetarian-food_b_12753706.html.

8. Kat Tancock, "Vegan cuisine moves into the mainstream—and it's actually delicious." *The Globe and Mail*. Accessed 13, 2017, https://www.theglobeandmail.com/life/food-and-wine/food-trends/vegan-cuisine-moves-into-the-mainstream/article22430440/.

9. Tancock, "Vegan cuisine moves into the mainstream—and it's actually delicious."

10. Ashley Csanady, "Is being a vegan a human right? Advocates claim protection under new Ontario policy, but that wasn't the point." Accessed November 23, 2017, http://nationalpost.com/news/canada/is-being-a-vegan-a-human-right-advocates-claim-protection-under-new-ontario-policy-but-that-wasnt-the-point.

11. Canadian Association of Physicians for the Environment (CAPE). "Letter to the Honourable Dr. Jane Philpott, Minister of Health." Accessed November 23, 2017, https://cape.ca/letter-to-minister-philpott-re-canadas-food-guide-aug-2017/.

12. Christopher Marinangeli et al., "An Appetite for Modernizing the Regulatory Framework for Protein Content Claims in Canada." *Nutrients* 9, no. 9 (2017): 921.

13. Fiona Atkinson, et al., "International tables of glycemic index and glycemic load values: 2008." Diabetes care (2008).

CHAPTER 7

FINLAND

THE UNSELFISH VEGAN

MARI NIVA, ANNUKKA VAINIO, AND PIIA JALLINOJA

Finland is a Nordic welfare state with a population of 5.5 million in 2018. For most Finns, healthiness, pleasure, price, and convenience are the most important factors influencing their food choices.[1] The production and consumption of animal protein is high, particularly for milk products.[2] Meat consumption has increased during the past decades and in 2016, it was around 78 kg of meat per capita each year, which was somewhat below the average for the European Union of 86 kg.[3]

Finland is also known as a country with public health campaigns since the 1970s focusing on cardiovascular diseases and the need to reduce the consumption of saturated fat. Such campaigns have been successful in replacing animal fats with vegetable oils and spreads among the majority,[4] and increasing consumption of vegetables.[5] Recently, the advice from nutritionists and public health researchers has been contested in the public sphere,[6] and diets that challenge the national nutritional recommendations, such as low-carbohydrate, gluten-free, paleo, fasting day, or "clean eating," have gained wide media publicity. Food and nutrition as well as food policies arouse huge interest in the news media and on social media channels. In contrast to many other diets, the discourses related to vegetarianism and veganism are not restricted to personal well-being or public health but expand to the realms of sustainability and animal rights, and they are also today well accepted in Finnish Nutrition Recommendations.[7]

THE PREVALENCE OF DIFFERENT FORMS OF VEGETARIAN/VEGAN DIETS IN FINLAND

Although vegan and vegetarian diets are currently topical, vegetarianism is not a recent phenomenon in Finland. The year 1894 may be considered as a milestone in vegetarianism in Finland, since that year saw the founding of the first Finnish vegetarian restaurant and the publication of the first vegetarian cookbook.[8] The first vegetarian societies were founded in 1907 and 1913. After World War II, vegetarianism became more marginalized and only started to attract new consumer groups in the 1970s, reflecting the increased societal interest in environmental issues, the peace movement, and Eastern philosophies.[9] In the 1990s, the vegan movement was a part of the "fourth wave" of environmental protests, characterized by ecocentrism and postmaterialistic values.[10]

During the 2010s, the interest in veganism and plant-based diets has again increased in Finland. This change is characterized by the increasing popularity of vegan pledges and festivals, development and marketing of new vegan products, social media activity around veganism, and celebrities reporting their veganism in the media.[11] For instance, Meatless October, organized since 2013 by an animal rights organization (urging people not to eat meat for a month), and Vegan Challenge initiated by two TV celebrities in 2014 (encouraging people to try a vegan January), attract thousands of participants every year.[12] Retail trade actors also report rapidly rising sales of vegan products.[13]

Despite increasing interest, vegetarianism and veganism are still not very widespread in Finland. Finnish household expenditure surveys indicate that in 2006, the proportion of households not consuming meat was 6 percent.[14] Health surveys carried out by the National Institute for Health and Welfare in 2014 show that 4 percent of Finns identified as vegetarian.[15] In Finland, vegetarians are typically women, have a high level of education, and live in single households.[16] Adolescent girls, especially, have reported vegetarianism.[17,18]

A FINNISH VEGAN NARRATIVE

The narrative described here about becoming and living as a vegan is based on an interview conducted in February 2018. Our interviewee was a man in his thirties working in the creative industries. He lived in an urban, previously working class but now gentrified area popular among students and young professionals in the capital city of Helsinki. His work included traveling and he sometimes spent periods of time outside the city. But when he was at home, he cooked for himself from scratch, avoided processed foods, and prepared large amounts, even for the whole week. Let's call him Mikael (which is not his real name).

BECOMING A VEGETARIAN AND THEN A VEGAN

Mikael told us that his path to becoming a vegan started around five years ago, when he one day realized that he didn't eat much meat at all. "The process started on the quiet," when he began to think about his eating, which he hadn't really done before. Gradually he and his girlfriend stopped eating meat at home altogether and only had meat dishes when eating in restaurants. They also took part in a Meatless October pledge. Two and a half years later he decided that he could as well be vegetarian. After a year had passed he thought, "well this was really easy," and he "just decided that now, for the next year, I'll be vegan." He laughingly explained that it was only after this decision that he started to learn about the meat and dairy industries: "For a while, I felt quite bad when I realized how much I had consumed milk products when I was vegetarian." Similar to other vegans, he accessed information from vegan online discussion forums and vegan websites.[19]

Mikael described how his journey toward vegetarianism resulted from a process during which he had already been reducing his meat consumption. Later, the realization that he was "almost" vegetarian made him decide that he could be that "officially." He said, "health was my first interest, and when I studied [vegetarianism] I found that often it means eating a plant-based diet. The ecology and ethics have come only after I turned vegan, [...] and now they are the most important things. So I selfishly ended up vegan and then unselfishly stayed vegan." This account illustrates how the socially constructed idea of veganism as "ecological and ethical" may be gradually incorporated during the vegan journey, although the initial motivations for veganism may lie elsewhere, e.g., health-related.

Mikael's story thus seems to give support to research findings suggesting that both self-focused motives such as health, and other-oriented motives, such as environment or animal rights, play a role in the adoption of plant-based diets.[20,21,22] Mikael's experiences also support research that has highlighted the dynamic nature of reasons to become vegetarian or vegan.[23]

And similar to other findings,[24] Mikael's transition was a gradual process, starting from a more or less conscious reduction of meat eating, then shifting to vegetarianism and, finally, veganism. Mikael's story is also in line with the finding that "ethical" vegetarians tend to be stricter in avoiding a wider range of animal products compared to "health" vegetarians.[25,26]

EXPERIENCED DIFFICULTIES IN ADOPTING A VEGAN DIET

In the Finnish cultural context, a range of factors may function as barriers to adopting a plant-based diet. These include enjoying the eating of meat, daily routines, health beliefs, and difficulties in preparing plant foods,[27] as well as habits, lack of knowledge, and disinterest.[28] Economic reasons[29] or limited supply[30] of pulses seem to be somewhat less prominent in hindering consumers from increasing pulse consumption. As compared to those who follow an omnivorous diet, consumers of a plant-based diet report fewer barriers[31] to increasing plant-based foods in their diet, perhaps because vegans or vegetarians often hold a wider range of motives supporting a plant-based diet than omnivores do.[32]

Since Mikael was a vegan at the time of the interview, he had probably already overcome the barriers mentioned above. Some of the barriers reported in earlier studies probably were not that significant to him in the first place, such as enjoying meat. When asked whether he had faced difficulties in adopting a vegan diet, Mikael said, "surprisingly few [. . .] I can eat really simple food, I feel great if I have steamed broccoli and beans." Recently he had become interested in how to replace animal-based ingredients, for instance in baking. Outside home, veganism is "really easy these days," particularly in Helsinki, where practically all restaurants have at least one vegetarian option, which is usually easy to "veganise." However, he noted that in the countryside it is sometimes different. For instance, when he's working in the countryside, usually a catering company provides food for the whole crew, and sometimes there are misunderstandings about what foods a vegan diet allows and what foods are not eaten. But during his year as a vegan, "people's consciousness has increased amazingly."

When traveling abroad, things are more complicated, he said, if there is no shared language with the staff. In uncertain situations abroad he didn't want to "make a big fuss about it" but "took the risk" and ate what was offered. He explained, however, that he would not knowingly eat anything non-vegan.

DEVELOPING A VEGAN IDENTITY
IN AN OMNIVOROUS WORLD

Mikael agreed with the phrase "you are what you eat," since "eating is such a big part of us," and it affects not only health but also the environment and the animals. But he acknowledged that not everyone thinks the same way, which may create conflicts. People have got used to vegetarians, but he felt that veganism is still seen as a form of extremism. This perspective is reflected in the literature, where many vegans, reportedly, have negative experiences about how people react to their diet and challenge their vegan identity.[33,34,35,36]

In Mikael's case, however, very few people had ridiculed his veganism. Rather, people tended to show interest and curiosity. He noted that people often see (his) veganism merely as a diet and a health issue rather than as "a way of life and a moral disposition." So far, however, he had not started to "educate" people about the ethical and environmental aspects of veganism. Apparently health issues was a safer ground on which vegans and omnivores could engage in a discourse and reach an agreement about the importance of eating vegetables. By concentrating on health, one avoids the inescapably moral tone underlying the questions of animal rights and suffering and the impact of animal-derived foods on the environment.[37,38]

NEGOTIATING VEGANISM IN FAMILY CONTEXTS

Eating in the Nordic countries has recently become somewhat more individualized, that is, less patterned around socially shared norms, conventions, and practices,[39] increasing the public acceptance of various dietary regimes, such as veganism. However, those who perceive eating as a communal activity may be prone to stigmatize vegans, although the evidence is not very strong.[40] Indeed, many studies both internationally and in Finland have suggested that vegetarians and vegans feel that social situations make it challenging to follow a vegetarian or vegan diet: many vegans/vegetarians feel their diet is depicted in mainstream culture as deviant and even unpatriotic, and they have experiences of relatives, friends, and even strangers dismissively commenting on their diet.[41,42,43]

Mikael, however, had few negative experiences about social encounters involving eating, and he acknowledged that he was "lucky, since I have people around me who understand" as well as having close relatives who were vegans or vegetarians. When asked whether he felt his family supported him being vegan he gave a little laugh and said, "well they don't question it, and that's really all the support I need." At the same time, however, he admitted that with his "hard core meat eater" relatives "there's been a bit of argument, but [. . .] we see each other so rarely that I try to avoid conflicts, and I don't want to ruin the atmosphere."

When asked how he and his social circles deal with situations in which people have different interests and diets, Mikael explained that they usually have a variety of foods so that everyone can eat according to their palate. In his opinion, if there was only one dish available, it would have to be vegan, and the meat eaters "could heat their sausage in the microwave." If he invited people to his home, he would expect them to eat vegan food, as he was not prepared to cook meat dishes for his guests. He also noted that in Finland "food-related allergies are taken into account when preparing meals to others, and the needs of vegans could be taken into account the same way." Indeed, many types of food allergies are more common in Northern Europe than other parts of Europe,[44,45] and therefore Finns are relatively used to taking into account different needs for special diets in social settings.

Mikael avoids situations where conflicts may arise. He explained that his "social groups have changed during the turn to vegetarian and vegan diet," and that nowadays he preferred to seek the company of people whose values were similar to his own. He also searches for support from like-minded people on social media. He mentioned that "in social media groups one learns how to discuss about veganism and how to deal with the feelings of anger," and that "the aggression is not always personal but is a part of the meat eater's information processing [. . .] the negative attitude is often just ignorance and is resolved with discussion."

During his time as a vegan, Mikael had become convinced that the world is increasingly going to be vegan. For him, the spread of veganism was a global-scale phenomenon. "The increase has been wild, if you think of the number of vegans and vegetarians in the world. [. . .] And everything that's on offer at the shops." He believed that even his parents would be vegan one day: "I just see it as inevitable."

This work has been funded by the Academy of Finland, grants No. 296883 and No. 315898.

Suggested Readings

Books or articles for further reading about vegetarian diets in Finland are marked with *.

Breshanan, Mary, Lie Zuangh, and Xun Zhu. "Why is the vegan line in the dining hall always the shortest? Understanding vegan stigma," *Stigma & Health* 1, no. 1 (2015): 3–15.

Dairy Nutrition Council. "Consumption of milk around the world," accessed April 30, 2018, http://www.maitojaterveys.fi/maitotietoa/maitovalmisteiden-kulutus/maidon-kulutus-maailmalla-2015.html.

*Elorinne, Anna-Liisa, Mari Kantola, Sari Voutilainen, and Juha Laakso. "Veganism as a choice: Experiences and food strategies in transitioning to a vegan diet," in *Food Futures: Ethics, Science and Culture*, ed. I. Anna S. Olsson, Sofia M. Araújo and Vieira, M. Fátima (Wageningen: Wageningen Academic Publishers, 2016), 421–26.

Fox, Nick and Katie Ward. "Health, Ethics and Environment: A qualitative study of vegetarian motivations," *Appetite* 50 (2008): 422–29.

Greenebaum, Jessica B. "Managing Impressions: "Face-saving" strategies of vegetarians and vegans," *Humanity and Society* 36, no. 4 (2012): 309–25.

Helldán, Anni and Satu Helakorpi. "Health behaviour and health among the Finnish adult population," Spring 2014 (Helsinki: National Institute for Health and Welfare, 2015).

Holm, Lotte, Drude Lauridsen, Thomas Bøker Lund, Jukka Gronow, Mari Niva, and Johanna Mäkelä. "Changes in the social context and conduct of eating in four Nordic countries between 1997 and 2012," *Appetite* 103 (August 2016): 358–68.

Jallinoja, Piia, Nina Kahma, Satu Helakorpi, Mari Niva, and Mikko Jauho. "Dietary fat choices in Finland, long-term trends and short-term changes 1978–2014," *Research on Finnish Society* 8 (2015): 73–77.

Jallinoja, Piia, Mikko Jauho, and Johanna Mäkelä. "Newspaper debates on milk fats and vegetable oils in Finland, 1978–2013: An analysis of conflicts over risks, expertise, evidence and pleasure," *Appetite* 105 (October 2016): 274–82.

*Jallinoja, Piia, Mari Niva, and Terhi Latvala. "Future of sustainable eating? Examining the potential for expanding bean eating in a meat-eating culture," *Futures* 83 (October 2016): 4–14.

*Jallinoja, Piia, Markus Vinnari, and Mari Niva. "Veganism and plant-based eating: Analysis of interplay between discursive strategies and lifestyle political consumerism," in *The Oxford Handbook of Political Consumerism*, ed. Mikael Bostrom, Michele Micheletti and Peter Oosterveer (The Oxford University Press, online publication, August 2018).

Keskinen, Jonnamaria. "Sometimes My Mother Still Serves Me Sausages"—Vegetarians' Experiences in Surrounding Community (Master's Thesis, in Finnish, University of Helsinki, 2017).

KESKO. "Kasvipohjaisten tuotteiden myynti kasvaa edelleen voimakkaasti—vegehylly löytyy jo 200 K-ruokakaupasta (The sales of plant-based products still increases strongly—veggie shelves can be found already in 200 K-grocery stores, published June 9, 2017)," accessed September 13, 2018, https://www.kesko.fi/media/uutiset-ja-tiedotteet/uutiset/2017/kasvispohjaisten-tuotteiden-myynti-kasvaa-edelleen-voimakkaasti--vegehylly-loytyy-jo-200-k-ruokakaupasta/.

Konttinen, Esa. "Four Waves of Environmental Protest," in All Shades of Green. *The Environmentalization of Finnish Society*, ed. Esa Konttinen, Tapio Litmanen, Matti

Nieminen and Marja Ylönen (Jyväskylä: University of Jyväskylä SoPhi, 1999), 20–46.

Konttinen, Hanna, Sirpa Sarlio-Lähteenkorva, Karri Silventoinen, Satu Männistö, and Ari Haukkala. "Socio-economic disparities in the consumption of vegetables, fruit and energy-dense foods: The role of motive priorities," *Public Health Nutrition* 16, no. 5 (2013): 873–82.

Meat Information Society. "Lihankulutus Euroopassa (Meat consumption in Europe)," accessed April 30, 2018, http://www.lihatiedotus.fi/liha-tilastoissa/lihankulutus -euroopassa.html.

*Mäkiniemi, Jaana-Piia and Annukka Vainio. "Barriers to climate-friendly food choices among young adults in Finland," *Appetite* 74, no. 1 (2014): 12–19.

McDonald, Barbara. "Once You Know Something, You Can't Not Know It." An Empirical Look at Becoming Vegan," *Society and Animals* 8, no. 1 (2000): 1–23.

National Nutrition Council, Finnish nutrition recommendations (Helsinki: Evira, 2014).

*Niva, Mari, Annukka Vainio, and Piia Jallinoja. "Barriers to increasing plant protein consumption in Western populations," in *Vegetarian and Plant-based Diets in Health and Disease Prevention*, ed. Francois Mariotti (London: Academic Press, Elsevier, 2017), 157–74.

Nwaru, Bright I., Lennart Hickstein, Sukhmeet S. Panesar, G. Roberts, A. Muraro, and Aziz Sheikh. "Prevalence of common food allergies in Europe: A systematic review and meta-analysis," *Allergy* 69, no. 8 (2014): 992–1007.

Parviainen, Heli, Anna-Liisa Elorinne, Pertti Väisänen, and Arja Rimpelä. "Consumption of special diets among adolescents from 1999 to 2013," *International Journal of Consumer Studies* 41, no. 2 (2017): 216–24.

*Pohjolainen, Pasi, Markus Vinnari, and Pekka Jokinen. "Consumers' Perceived Barriers to Following a Plant-Based Diet," *British Food Journal* 117, no. 3 (2015): 1150–67.

Potts, Annie and Mandala White. "New Zealand Vegetarians: At Odds With Their Nation," *Society and Animals* 16, no. 4 (2015): 336–53.

Rozin, Paul, Maureen Markwith, and Caryn Stoess. "Moralization and Becoming a Vegetarian: The Transformation of Preferences into Values and the Recruitment of Disgust," *Psychological Science* 8, no. 2 (1997): 67–73.

Roos, Eva, Kirsi Talala, Mikko Laaksonen, Satu Helakorpi, Ossi Rahkonen, Antti Uutela, et al. "Trends of socioeconomic differences in daily vegetable consumption, 1979–2002" *European Journal of Clinical Nutrition* 62, no. 7 (2016): 823–33.

Ruby, Matthew B. "Vegetarianism. A blossoming field of study," *Appetite* 58, no. 1 (2012): 141–50.

Steinke, Mathias, Alessandro Fiocchi, Veronika Kirchlechner, Barbara Ballmer-Weber, Knut Brockow, Claudia Hischenhuber, et al. "Perceived Food Allergy in Children in 10 European Nations," *Allergy and Immunology* 143, no. 4 (2007): 290–95.

*Vainio, Annukka, Mari Niva, Piia Jallinoja, and Terhi Latvala. "From beef to beans: Eating motives and the replacement of animal proteins with plant proteins among Finnish consumers," *Appetite* 106 (November 2016): 92–100.

*Vinnari, Markus, Jukka Montonen, Tommi Härkänen, and Satu Männistö. "Identifying vegetarians and their food consumption according to self-identification and operationalized definition in Finland," *Public Health Nutrition* 12, no. 4 (April 2009): 481–88.

*Vinnari, Markus Pekka Mustonen, and Pekka Räsänen. "Tracking down trends in non-meat consumption in Finnish households, 1966–2006," *British Food Journal* 112, no. 8 (2010): 836–52.

Vornanen, Jukka. "Lihaton lautanen (Meatless plate)," in *Lihansyöjien maa* (The Land of Meat-Eaters), ed. Taru Anttonen and Jukka Vornanen (Helsinki: Into, 2016), 261–312.

Notes

1. Hanna Konttinen, et al., "Socio-economic disparities in the consumption of veg-etables, fruit and energy-dense foods: The role of motive priorities," *Public Health Nutrition* 16, no. 5 (2013): 876.
2. Dairy Nutrition Council, "Consumption of milk around the world," accessed April 30, 2018, http://www.maitojaterveys.fi/maitotietoa/maitovalmisteiden-kulutus/maidon-kulutus-maailmalla-2015.html.
3. Meat Information Society, "Meat consumption in Europe," accessed April 30, 2018, http://www.lihatiedotus.fi/liha-tilastoissa/lihankulutus-euroopassa.html.
4. Piia Jallinoja, et al., "Dietary fat choices in Finland, long-term trends and short-term changes 1978–2014," *Research on Finnish Society* 8 (2015): 76.
5. Eva Roos, et al., "Trends of socioeconomic differences in daily vegetable consump-tion, 1979–2002" *European Journal of Clinical Nutrition* 62, no. 7 (2016): 823.
6. Piia Jallinoja, et al., "Newspaper debates on milk fats and vegetable oils in Finland, 1978–2013: An analysis of conflicts over risks, expertise, evidence and pleasure," *Appetite* 105 (October 2016): 280.
7. National Nutrition Council, *Finnish Nutrition Recommendations* (Helsinki: Evira, 2014), 32, 40–42.
8. Jukka Vornanen, "Lihaton lautanen (Meatless plate)," *Lihansyöjien maa* (The Land of Meat-Eaters), ed. Taru Anttonen and Jukka Vornanen (Helsinki: Into, 2016), 268.
9. Ibid, 273.
10. Esa Konttinen, "Four Waves of Environmental Protest," in All Shades of Green. *The Environmentalization of Finnish Society*, ed. Esa Konttinen, et al. (Jyväskylä: University of Jyväskylä SoPhi, 1999), 34–39.
11. Piia Jallinoja, et al., "Veganism and plant-based eating: Analysis of interplay between discursive strategies and lifestyle political consumerism," *The Oxford Handbook of Political Consumerism*, ed. Mikael Bostrom, et al. (The Oxford Univer-sity Press, online publication, August 2018), 15.
12. Ibid, 11–12.
13. KESKO, "Kasvipohjaisten tuotteiden myynti kasvaa edelleen voimakkaasti—vegehylly löytyy jo 200 K-ruokakaupasta (The sales of plant-based products still increases strongly—veggie shelves can be found already in 200 K-grocery stores, published June 9, 2017)," accessed September 13, 2018, https://www.kesko.fi/

media/uutiset-ja-tiedotteet/uutiset/2017/kasvispohjaisten-tuotteiden-myynti -kasvaa-edelleen-voimakkaasti--vegehylly-loytyy-jo-200-k-ruokakaupasta/.

14. Markus Vinnari, et al., "Tracking down trends in non-meat consumption in Finnish households, 1966–2006," *British Food Journal* 112, no. 8 (2010): 847.

15. Anni Helldán and Satu Helakorpi, "Health behaviour and health among the Finnish adult population," Spring 2014 (Helsinki: National Institute for Health and Welfare, 2015), 153.

16. Markus Vinnari, et al., "Identifying vegetarians and their food consumption according to self-identification and operationalized definition in Finland," *Public Health Nutrition* 12, no. 4 (April 2009): 483.

17. Anni Helldán and Satu Helakorpi, "Health behaviour and health among the Finnish adult population," Spring 2014 (Helsinki: National Institute for Health and Welfare, 2015), 153.

18. Heli Parviainen, et al., "Consumption of special diets among adolescents from 1999 to 2013," *International Journal of Consumer Studies* 41, no. 2 (2017): 219.

19. Anna-Liisa Elorinne, et al., "Veganism as a choice: Experiences and food strategies in transitioning to a vegan diet," in *Food Futures: Ethics, Science and Culture*, ed. I. Anna S. Olsson, et al. (Wageningen: Wageningen Academic Publishers, 2016), 422.

20. Piia Jallinoja, et al., "Veganism and plant-based eating: Analysis of interplay between discursive strategies and lifestyle political consumerism," *in The Oxford Handbook of Political Consumerism*, ed. Mikael Bostrom, et al. (The Oxford University Press, online publication August 2018), 17–18.

21. Anna-Liisa Elorinne, et al., "Veganism as a choice: Experiences and food strategies in transitioning to a vegan diet," *Food Futures: Ethics, Science and Culture*, ed. I. Anna S. Olsson, et al. (Wageningen: Wageningen Academic Publishers, 2016), 423.

22. Annukka Vainio, et al., "From beef to beans: Eating motives and the replacement of animal proteins with plant proteins among Finnish consumers," *Appetite* 106 (November 2016): 97.

23. Nick Fox and Katie Ward, "Health, ethics and environment: A qualitative study of vegetarian motivations," *Appetite* 50 (2008): 428.

24. Anna-Liisa Elorinne, et al., "Veganism as a choice: Experiences and food Sstrategies in transitioning to a vegan diet," *Food Futures: Ethics, Science and Culture*, ed. I. Anna S. Olsson, et al. (Wageningen: Wageningen Academic Publishers, 2016), 422.

25. Matthew B. Ruby, "Vegetarianism. A blossoming field of study," *Appetite* 58, no. 1 (2012): 144.

26. Paul Rozin, et al., "Moralization and becoming a vegetarian: The transformation of preferences into values and the recruitment of disgust," *Psychological Science* 8, no. 2 (1997): 70.

27. Pasi Pohjolainen, et al., "Consumers' perceived barriers to following a plant-based diet," *British Food Journal* 117, no. 3 (2015): 1158.

28. Mari Niva, et al., "Barriers to increasing plant protein consumption in Western populations," *Vegetarian and Plant-based Diets in Health and Disease Prevention*, ed. Francois Mariotti (London: Academic Press, Elsevier, 2017),161.

29. Annukka Vainio, et al., "From beef to beans: Eating motives and the replacement of animal proteins with plant proteins among Finnish consumers," *Appetite* 106 (November 2016): 98.

30. Piia Jallinoja, et al., "Future of sustainable eating? Examining the potential for expanding bean eating in a meat-eating culture," *Futures* 83 (October 2016): 9.

31. Jaana-Piia Mäkiniemi and Annukka Vainio, "Barriers to climate-friendly food choices among young adults in Finland," *Appetite* 74, no. 1 (2014): 15.

32. Annukka Vainio, et al., "From beef to beans: Eating motives and the replacement of animal proteins with plant proteins among Finnish consumers," *Appetite* 106 (November 2016): 98.

33. Annie Potts and Mandala White, "New Zealand vegetarians: At odds with their nation," *Society and Animals* 16, no. 4 (2015): 347.

34. Jessica B. Greenebaum, "Managing impressions: 'Face-saving' strategies of vegetarians and vegans," *Humanity and Society* 36, no. 4 (2012): 314.

35. Mary Breshanan, et al., "Why is the vegan line in the dining hall always the shortest? Understanding vegan stigma," *Stigma & Health* 1, no. 1 (2015): 13.

36. Barbara McDonald, "'Once you know something, you can't not know it.' An empirical look at becoming vegan," *Society and Animals* 8, no. 1 (2000): 12.

37. Piia Jallinoja, et al., "Veganism and plant-based eating: Analysis of interplay between discursive strategies and lifestyle political consumerism," *The Oxford Handbook of Political Consumerism*, ed. Mikael Bostrom, et al. (The Oxford University Press, online publication August 2018), 17.

38. Jessica B. Greenebaum, "Managing Impressions: 'Face-saving' strategies of vegetarians and vegans," *Humanity and Society* 36, no. 4 (2012): 319–20.

39. Lotte Holm, et al., "Changes in the social context and conduct of eating in four Nordic countries between 1997 and 2012," *Appetite* 103 (August 2016): 367.

40. Mary Breshanan, et al., "Why is the vegan line in the dining hall always the shortest? Understanding vegan stigma," *Stigma & Health* 1, no. 1 (2015): 8.

41. Annie Potts and Mandala White, "New Zealand vegetarians: At odds with their nation," *Society and Animals* 16, no. 4 (2015): 347.

42. Barbara McDonald, "'Once you know something, you can't not know it.' An empirical look at becoming vegan," *Society and Animals* 8, no. 1 (2000): 12.

43. Jonnamaria Keskinen, "Sometimes My Mother Still Serves Me Sausages"—Vegetarians' Experiences in Surrounding Community (Master's Thesis, in Finnish, University of Helsinki, 2017), 41, 45.

44. Bright Nwaru, et al., "Prevalence of common food allergies in Europe: A systematic review and meta-analysis," *Allergy* 69, no. 8 (2014): 992.

45. Mathias Steinke, et al., "Perceived food allergy in children in 10 European nations," *Allergy and Immunology* 143, no. 4 (2007): 290.

CHAPTER 8

GERMANY

I EAT HONEY ALSO— SOMETIMES . . . MARITA'S* STORY ABOUT HER VEGAN DIET

PAMELA KERSCHKE-RISCH

At present there are contrasting global trends in relation to the consumption of meat. For one thing, the worldwide demand for meat and animal products is increasing, while on the other hand, Western societies in particular are experiencing a remarkable growth in the number of vegetarians as well as vegans.[1,2] In Germany, changes in public opinion regarding food, especially meat production and factory farming, are evident in an increasing interest in political discussions over animal welfare, resulting in the use of special labels on the packaging of meat and meat products in supermarkets for human consumption that support the well-being of animals.[3] The actual percentage of vegetarians and vegans living in Germany can only be estimated, but there are indications that the number has grown steadily since the turn of the millennium.[4,5] The last reliable figures

---

* Real name withheld

date back to the "National Verzehrsstudie II" from 2007, which stated that only 0.1 percent followed a vegan diet, whereas the number of vegetarians was significantly higher.[6] Optimistic estimates currently suggest that 1.6 percent vegans and nearly 10 percent vegetarians are living in Germany.[7,8] The most important motives for eliminating animal products from the diet include concerns about factory farming, climate change, and health issues.[9] There is also significant variation in regional distribution of vegetarians and vegans in Germany. Most people who identify as vegetarian or vegan live in cities with more than 100,000 inhabitants.[10] Moreover, most vegans are aged eighteen to twenty-nine years, have a high level of education, and around 80 percent are female.[11]

Marita, the subject of this chapter, is typical of many German vegans—female, young, well-educated, and living in a large modern city. This 26-year-old student lives in Hamburg, the second-largest city in Germany with around 1.8 million inhabitants. The city offers a high standard of living for its citizens along with the associated high cost of living. As a result, there is a wide range of diverse foods available, including a broad selection of vegetarian and vegan food that can be bought even in discount supermarkets. Marita's cultural milieu is dominated by young critical students with whom alternative ways of living are popular—and a meat-free diet is widely accepted even if it is not a role model for others. A vegetarian diet is already present in most parts of Germany, while veganism is also increasingly accepted, as reflected by the growing number of animal-free meals offered in the city's universities' canteens, as well as in many restaurants in Hamburg. The same is true for coffee shops, almost all of which offer vegan milk alternatives.

MARITA'S DIET

Marita described her diet by saying that she eats no animal products, with the exception of honey. As she explained, she does not buy honey, but if honey happens to be present in a food product she would not refuse it. Asked if she would define her diet as vegan, she answered: "for convenience only . . . perhaps I would say, I'm vegan, I don't know, usually I explain it in this way: 'I don't eat no animal products,' so." Upon request, she recounted how she became a vegan: she grew up in a family where great importance was placed on eating healthy food. She illustrates this in the following examples: Even during her childhood, meat was rarely served, and fast food was not allowed at all. That her parents were very health-oriented is indicated with the example of soft drinks: they explicitly prohibited their daughter from consuming Cola and justified this with the false assertion that it was forbidden by law up to the age of twelve, similar to age limits on restrictions for watching films. If she was taking part in children's birthday parties where Cola was served, she was really frightened, because she thought that she was watching others committing a criminal act; this made a permanent impression on her.

Having been a vegetarian and giving up eating meat previously, Marita has in the meantime become a vegan and has been living as such for about six years. Although she recalls the decisive reason for her final resolution to become a vegetarian, namely a film documentary about abattoirs, she does not know the exact date. This fairly long process could explain why she does not remember the exact moment of beginning her vegan diet. As she explained, it was at no time difficult or even a heavy step to give up eating any animal products—indeed, quite the contrary. She explained that a doctor gave her advice to remove animal products from her diet. As at this time she only consumed very limited milk products and had already eliminated all eggs, omitting "the last mozzarella pearl" was not significant to her. Interestingly, only at the end of the interview did Marita conclude that her diet had been *vegan* for a long time without her realizing this. Marita called this process "downstream," explaining as follows: "I didn't say, ok, I will now start a vegan diet and have to respect this and that or so, but I just did the things and then noticed, ok, what does that mean specifically? . . . and what do the others do and then *this* somehow has found this name or so. . . ." This process is consistent with McDonald's assertion that the decision to convert to veganism was often seen as a logical and inevitable fit with an individual's beliefs and principles.[12]

BARRIERS IN THE ADOPTION OF A VEGETARIAN DIET

Marita reported that it had become much easier to follow her diet over the last few years and emphasized that she had not experienced any nutrient deficiencies. On the other hand, she felt that others treat her in a special manner, and that she causes inconvenience when going out to eat with others. When she is invited to someone's home to eat, hosts may be very well meaning but not very familiar with the vegan diet, and therefore often mix together ingredients of animal origin that Marita would never consume under any circumstances. Convenience foods also pose problems, as they often contain non-vegan ingredients or additives that she would prefer not to consume.

YOU ARE WHAT YOU EAT?

When presented with this statement, Marita responded that she was not familiar with this figure of speech and had never heard someone use it in her sphere. She explained that only a few people are aware of her diet, because to her it is simply one detail alongside other aspects of her personality. Nevertheless, Marita accepted that consumer decisions can reveal aspects about one's identity: "yeah, and through your consumer decisions you can reflect your personality or, or transport it so that it is outwardly visible—or somehow so, and that you, well! as an acting subject you can definitely make an impact somehow." Despite this, she did not appear to be aware that being a vegan and acting as a vegan, including her consumption of food products, reflects her identity. She partly tries to view this from a political perspective. "A little bit this is also . . . this is political. I would at least interpret it in that way." On the other hand, Marita is worried that she might be "put in a box" if she attempts to defend her position regarding her choice of eating habits, because despite indicating previously that her decision to become vegan was motivated by health reasons, in reality her dietary choices are more driven by animal welfare concerns.

In answering questions posed by people she does not know well about her motives for living as a vegan, Marita appeared to be overeager to create irrefutable arguments. Instead of revealing her real motivation, namely animal welfare, Marita tries to reason with political justification, thinking that this is a more convincing and superior argument. In this context, she mentions violation of human dignity, as for example corporations or industry exploiting humans as well as inhumane working conditions. This justification is based on her experience that discussions, especially if they drift into philosophical areas, could be problematic for her because she could not respond with compelling arguments in a timely way. It thus becomes clear that in her subjective perception, the majority of people are of the opinion that animals are of lesser value than humans. Marita's reasoning suggests that despite the relatively supportive conditions for following an animal-free diet in Germany, vegans are still a minority who feel the need to justify their choices. This notwithstanding, Marita emphasized that if people feel offended by her diet, she does not care, because she has no important social ties to them.

MEAT OR NOT: IDENTITY FORMATION THROUGH ONE'S CHOICE OF DIET

Marita can be characterized as a person who is strongly convinced about her own way of eating, because she believes that she is doing the right thing in political terms. Therefore, she enjoys her status as an individual who may be seen as morally superior by others. Marita's comments suggest that she savors what she imagines to be her "exotic" status and is not afraid of being isolated in some cases. Actually, the opposite may be true of her, as she sees herself as a type of fighter who is not searching for a community of like-minded people. Although observing that she exchanged recipes with other vegans, Marita also emphasized that she is not interested in establishing contact with them. As she explained, she has no need for emotional support to adhere to a diet that she chose as a result of her own conviction.

She also observed that sometimes people feel sorry for her, as they perceive she cannot enjoy the food that they see as being superior to a vegan diet. However, to her it is not a problem if she is invited to social events that do not include vegan options on the menu. As she noted:

> If there is a wedding buffet or so, then I can nevertheless eat the cauliflower, if it is not buttered. . . . For me it's enough to have the side dishes (laughs). So . . . vegetables with potatoes and sauce or so, which is also vegan . . . in case of doubt. That I even find a super meal and if I can't have a cutlet with it or a surrogate cutlet—that's nothing to me! I don't feel as if this is a bad or second-class meal or so. (Marita)

In contrast to these relatively relaxed views, Marita's opinion about sharing meals with passionate meat eaters was unambiguous: Because of the fact that meat is not an essential but even possibly a harmful part of nutrition, the meat eaters should forgo meat on this occasion.

SOCIAL RELATIONS

Instead of suffering from rejection by others, Marita experiences quite the opposite; namely, admiration regarding her perseverance. She does not feel that she has to sacrifice anything. Even her mother, who took her daughter's diet as an incentive, supports her by cooking vegan meals. At Christmas, Marita's family supports her by giving presents of vegan food stuffs, especially certain vegetable sandwich spreads as well as sweets. Since her mother is aware of the cost of vegan specialties, she gives her products from health food shops as a means of indirect financial support.

Her friends neither support nor hinder her from following the vegan diet. However, many of her friends are vegetarians, and therefore presumably share similar diets. This likely also explains why, when asked if she feels the need to look for a community with similar values and opinions regarding her diet, Marita explained that she does not feel the necessity to come together with like-minded people. Moreover, as many of her friends share her vegetarian or vegan lifestyle, there is less likelihood of any conflict arising within her social group in relation to her dietary choices.

CONCLUSION

Consistent with other studies,[13,14] Marita stopped eating meat about eighteen months before converting to veganism. Having adhered to the rules of her vegan diet for six years, it is obvious that she is not following a fashionable trend, and her strong convictions suggest she will maintain this diet in the future. To her, being vegan is an important part of her identity, because she does not act out of external or societal pressure.

As Marita's experiences suggest, relatively supportive conditions exist for individuals who choose to follow a vegan lifestyle in Germany. Marita has had positive experiences through her family socialization and receives support from her mother and her social group. The main challenges she experiences relate to higher prices for prepared vegan products and her worry about having a balanced diet in stressful situations. She appears motivated by well thought out arguments promoting veganism that she describes as political, although on closer inspection they reflect a complex interaction of health consciousness, animal welfare, *and* political beliefs. However, in no respect would Marita describe herself as radical or even a militant animal liberationist.

Small exceptions to her rules are consistent with her understanding of being vegan, as for example eating a little bit of a cream sauce prepared by her Granny are tolerable. Moreover, in her opinion if someone is addicted to cheese, but otherwise follows the vegan diet, this is fine. As she explained: "vegan is not a name which can be damaged by [eating] cheese." She further qualified her view on this by adding: "as said before—I eat honey also ...sometimes."

Individuals' motives for adopting vegetarian or vegan diets indicate that animal welfare, health, and environmental concerns are of the upmost importance; this is also true for Marita.[15] As such, Marita can be characterized as a typical representative of the urban middle-class, health-conscious and with internalized post-material values. Vegetarians are, however, far from a homogenous group[16] and the same is presumably true for vegans. Marita's example indicates that her understanding of being vegan cannot be reduced to her diet. Instead, it has to be seen as a combination of identity, morals, and ethics; a dynamic previously highlighted by Greenebaum.[17]

As more people shift to a vegetarian or vegan diet, and they become accepted as a normal way of eating, there will be an expansion in the availability and diversity of animal-free products. In part, this will probably be driven through the inclusion of vegan product lines within a mainstream food industry[18] agilely responding to market changes. In this respect, Marita's ideas of making a political statement by refusing animal products are unlikely to cause significant or long-term economic harm to big food companies. Arguably, the social, environmental, and health implications of vegetarianism and veganism will be more profound, both in Germany and internationally.

Notes

1. World Health Organization, "3. Global and regional food consumption patterns and trends," 2016, accessed April 29, 2018, http://www.who.int/nutrition/topics/3_foodconsumption/en/index4.html.

2. Pamela Kerschke-Risch, "Vegans and omnivores: Differences in attitudes and preferences concerning food," in *Food Futures. Ethics, Science & Culture*, ed. Anna I. Olsson, Sofia M. Araújo, and M. Fátima Vieira (Wageningen: Wageningen Academic Publishers, 2016), 415–20.

3. BMEL/Bundesministerium für Ernährung und Landwirtschaft (Federal Ministry of Food and Agriculture), "Das staatliche Tierwohllabel: Kriterien und Anforderungen" (2018), accessed April 29, 2018, https://www.bmel.de/DE/Tier/Tierwohl/_texte/Einfuehrung-Tierwohllabel.html;nn=6260024.

4. Pamela Kerschke-Risch, "Vegan diet: Motives, approach and duration. Initial results of a quantitative sociological study," *Ernaehrungs Umschau* 62, no. 6 (2015): 98–103. DOI: 10.4455/eu.2015.016.

5. Claus Leitzmann, "Vegetarian nutrition: Past, present, future," *The American Journal of Clinical Nutrition* 100, Supplement no. 1 (2016): 4965–5025.

6. Max Rubner Institut, (ed), "Nationale Verzehrstudie II, Ergebnisbericht, Teil 1," 2008, accessed April 28, 2018, https://www.mri.bund.de/fileadmin/MRI/Institute/EV/NVS_II_Abschlussbericht_Teil_1_mit_Ergaenzungsbericht.pdf.

7. VEBU, 2018, "Anzahl der Vegetarier und Veganer in Deutschland," accessed April 28, 2018, https://vebu.de/veggie-fakten/entwicklung-in-zahlen/anzahl-veganer-und-vegetarier-in-deutschland/.

8. Skopos market research, "1,3 Millionen Deutsche leben vegan," 15.11.2016, accessed April 28, 2018, https://www.skopos.de/news/13-millionen-deutsche-leben-vegan.html.

9. Kerschke-Risch, "Vegan Diet," 98–103.

10. VEBU, "Vegetarier und Veganer in Deutschland."

11. Gert B. M. Mensink, Clarissa Lage Barbosa, and Anna-Kristin Brettschneider, "Verbreitung der vegetarischen Ernährungsweise in Deutschland," *Journal of Health Monitoring* 1, no. 2 (2016): 2–15. DOI 10.17886/RKI-GBE-2016-033.

12. Barbara McDonald, "Once you know something, you can't not know it. An empirical look at becoming vegan," *Society & Animals* 8, no. 1 (2000): 1–23.

13. Kerschke-Risch, "Vegan Diet," 98–103.

14. Rachel M. MacNair, "McDonald's 'Empirical Look at Becoming Vegan'. Commentary," *Society & Animals* 9, no. 1 (2001): 63–69.

15. Kerschke-Risch, "Vegan Diet," 98–103.

16. Daniel L. Rosenfeld and Anthony L. Burrow, "The unified model of vegetarian identity: A conceptual framework for understanding plant-based food choices," *Appetite* 112, no. 1 (May 2017): 78–95.

17. Jessica Greenebaum, "Veganism, Identity and the Quest for Authenticity," *Food, Culture and Society* 15, no. 1 (March 2012): 129–44.

18. "3 Trends Driving Disruptions in the Food Industry," accessed August 24, 2018, https://www.industryleadersmagazine.com/3-trends-driving-disruptions-food-industry/.

CHAPTER 9

IRELAND

MEAT AVOIDANCE DIETS IN IRELAND: HOW FOOD CHOICES INFLUENCE THE WAY WE ARE PERCEIVED BY OTHERS AND THE WAYS IN WHICH WE INTERACT WITH OTHERS

MAEVE HENCHION

Meat is central to the Irish economy and society. Beef production, for example, is one of the largest agricultural sectors, and it is practiced by the majority of farmers. Furthermore, similar to many cultures today, wealth in the past was traditionally measured by the number of cattle one owned. Indeed, there is a famous legend, *Táin Bó Cúailnge*, about a war involving a queen from one region trying to steal a bull from another region. While wealth in Ireland is no longer based on the number of cattle one owns, meat remains a key component of social events. Meat consumption totaled 76 kg/capita in 2015, a decline of 6 kg/capita since 2005. However,

111

it increased to 90 kg/year in 2016, following an upswing in the economy, highlighting a link between economic prosperity and meat consumption.

Despite the continuing importance of meat in Ireland, dietary patterns are changing due to lifestyle decisions linked to health, environmental, and ethical motivations, an increasing prevalence of food allergies and intolerances, as well as changing socio-demographics. In line with other developed countries, there is a trend toward plant-based foods, and increased support from both public health promotions and the media toward a reduction in the consumption of animal-based products. This is reflected in a growth in flexitarianism, but is not yet reflected in meat consumption levels.

There are no official statistics for the number of vegetarians and vegans in Ireland; however, a 2017 survey found that 1 in 20 (5 percent) follows a "mainly vegetarian diet."[1] The same report indicates that this figure ranged from 3 percent to 6 percent between 2003 and 2017 with no consistent trend, either upwards or downwards on an annual basis during this period. An indication of the number of vegans may be deduced from the membership of various vegan Facebook groups—estimated at 6,000[2] (Cleary, 2017). Vegans and vegetarians tend to be predominantly female.

The story of meat reduction in Ireland told below, draws on interviews with three individuals who have either reduced or eliminated animal-based products from their diets, as well as observation of online and mainstream media and secondary sources. The three individuals who were interviewed are:

- "Anna," a female in her twenties, single, no children, in full-time education, and currently a vegetarian.
- "Jim," a male in his forties, married, with children, professional and currently a vegetarian (who eats small amounts of fish on a very infrequent basis), semi-professional athlete in the past.
- "Sineád," a female in her fifties, single, no children, self-employed and currently a vegan.

Their *current* status in terms of dietary patterns is emphasized here as this can be somewhat dynamic as discussed below. Their stories start with the decision to avoid eating meat including the influence of others, both positively and negatively on this decision. However, as will become clear, this decision is not always easy to follow through on. Thus the chapter continues by outlining the factors that supported or hindered these individuals in maintaining their dietary choices over time. Some final comments are made on the extent to which Ireland is a country that makes it easy to sustain a vegan or vegetarian diet.

MAKING THE DECISION

Motivations for becoming vegan seem to be slightly different to becoming a vegetarian, even though individuals may transition between the two dietary patterns. For Sinéad, her primary motivation in becoming vegetarian, and subsequently a vegan, was compassion for animals. A lack of trust in the food industry was also a factor. She says "*compassion for animals is the 1st. It is the principle of rearing animals for food. They are deformed with the breeding. Slaughtering is involved. Finance is involved . . . health doesn't really come into it. If I wanted to be healthy I'd probably eat organic chicken once or twice a week and organic fish once a week. One of my big gripes is the food industry; the information they put out is blurred and confused, even about taking supplements.*" As with Sinéad, Anna also indicated that compassion for animals was the primary motive for her. Interestingly, both Anna and Sinéad seemed to indicate that care for the environment may not be a very strong motivation for vegans. On the contrary, knowledge that some vegan consumption patterns may not be environmentally friendly can be disregarded and thus not influence behavior. Sinéad states that "*cows' milk may be better for the environment than soy or almond . . . almond uses a lot of water*" while Anna believes that a "*vegan diet is probably less environmentally friendly than a vegetarian diet.*" Sinéad, who has many vegetarians and vegans in her family and social circles, says that the vegetarians she knows are primarily vegetarians for ethical reasons, but she has an aunt who is vegetarian for health reasons. Thus, it seems that vegans may be primarily motivated by animal welfare considerations, while motives for meat reducers/vegetarians can be more complex and additionally include health and environmental motivations (as reflected in public health messages and the promotional campaigns of companies producing food products for such market segments).

If anyone reduces their meat intake, s/he is still a meat eater. However, if one eliminates it, one is recategorized in terms of dietary practices. Hence making the decision to avoid meat is deliberate and conscious and is likely to have implications in other areas of one's life. There is limited evidence that significant members of their social circle influenced this decision for the three individuals interviewed. Rather, it seemed to be a rational choice between alternatives that one makes over time as a result of personal observation, and consideration of and reflection on various factors within one's enviroment. Anna and Sinéad did not identify a single individual who influenced their decision. This is not always the case, however. Jim, for example, decided to become a vegetarian because his girlfriend at the time was one. Thus what sociologists call "habitus,"[3] the deeply ingrained habits, skills, and dispositions people have as a result of life experiences, seemed to have limited influence on his decision. It may be that vegetarians and vegans are able to move beyond ingrained dietary habits and strive to obtain the necessary knowledge and skills to forge new dietary habits and lifestyles.

Once a decision is made, many others (from family members to professionals and others within one's broader social circle) may cause meat avoiders to "defend" their decision. In relation to Jim, he was an elite athlete when he decided to become a vegetarian. His parents and coaches were concerned about him having an adequate nutrient intake. "*It would have been one of the things that people* [coaches and my parents] *would have said to me at the time 'where are you going to get your protein from.'?*" They did not see how being a vegetarian could "*fit with the lifestyle of being an athlete.*" However, Jim was confident in his knowledge about food and nutrition and feels that his level of performance in athletics while being a vegetarian reassured his coaches and parents: "*I did make a world cross country team while I was a vegetarian so maybe that demonstrated to people that it really didn't make any difference.*" Others, while not directly challenging Jim's dietary choices, were nevertheless confused or curious. For example, his grandmother was confused on being told he was a vegetarian: "*She wouldn't understand. She said 'you wouldn't have a bit of meat at all?'... The whole concept of not eating meat didn't occur to her because it didn't happen in her generation.*" Furthermore, a number of years after Jim had made his decision, one of his children's friends asked "*Were you born that way?*" indicating that being a vegetarian was seen to be unusual.

Sinéad described similar experiences of being expected to defend her decision to avoid meat and has evolved her response to such confrontations over the years: "*When I meet people they come up with the same jokes, they can be mocking 'how do you know that carrots don't have feelings?' I don't take it anymore. I hand it back to them. Let them handle it. I think it is a defensive thing. They are not looking at what they are doing. People say 'but I grew up in a meat-eating culture...' and I say 'so did I'... If they don't confront me I don't bring it up. However I don't try to make them comfortable if they bring it up. If they confront I defend. It is a confrontation. It is not inquisitorial. Some people think vegans have a 'self-indulgent lifestyle' whereas I think they are outward looking and caring. They are denying themselves the pleasure of meat, which is a pleasure.*"

While Anna has similar experiences, she is more forgiving of others' positions. For example, she finds that it can be difficult for non-vegan/vegetarian family members or friends to support the decision for practical reasons and due to a lack of knowledge. She reports that it is difficult to ask someone to find tofu for you if they are shopping, as they won't know what it looks like. Anna also indicated that gendered norms may make it more difficult for males than females to avoid meat. As she explained, her father and brother were more interested in reducing meat than her mother and sister, but they may *"feel under pressure to be like a man."* Her brother had tried to pursue a vegetarian diet but was not really supported to do so at home and so did not continue. However, in contrast, and in more recent years she says that her father felt he could justify his decision to reduce his meat intake by positioning himself as *"being in solidarity with the vegan"* and that he appreciates the option to consume good vegetarian meals when his daughter is around.

Discussions with Anna in particular highlight that the decision to reduce/avoid meat was not a once-off decision. She tried three times to be a vegan but reverted to being a vegetarian each time. She attributed her success to being a vegan at one particular phase to sharing a house with a chef and the resulting knowledge and support this provided to her. Her housemate shared ideas and recipes which made it easier for Anna to maintain a varied, healthy, and enjoyable diet. He also identified ways of being vegan at a lower cost through, for example, making her own plant-based milks. She also emphasized the importance of social media groups, in both becoming and remaining a vegan, for the knowledge they provide. She identified organizations and websites that provide useful resources for vegans in terms of recipes, sourcing food, and dealing with social situations.

Anna also spoke about the struggle of balancing an aspiration to be the best one can be physically and mentally, with ethical principles. For example, recently she was disappointed with her academic performance and tried to evaluate why this was so. She decided that it was due to her diet and is conscious of the impact of diet on energy and mood. Reluctantly she decided to reintroduce some animal-based (non-meat) foods to her diet to help improve her academic performance, describing this as *"a transgression of personal ethics that sometimes proves very difficult to avoid."* Despite this, Anna foresees a time when her lifestyle will allow her to become a vegan again.

MAINTAINING DIETARY PREFERENCES

Discussions with the three interviewees reflect the three categories of factors that are generally considered to influence food choices: the food, the enviroment, and the individual.[4] They also provide evidence that the influence of factors relating to the food and to the enviroment is dependent on the individual, that is, the impact may be different for different individuals.[5]

In other words, people make decisions based on how they perceive the food environment and food attributes, with different individuals having different perspectives on similar social situations.

Eating at home is relatively easy for these interviewees. However eating out, an increasingly important social situation, can be a challenge. From these interviewees, it is clear that this can be a process of negotiation for the meat avoider; both a negotiation within themselves in terms of the extent to which they want to maintain their dietary boundaries and a negotiation with others in terms of what is available. The negotiation process and outcome varies depending on whether eating out with friends/family or for professional/work reasons, and whether it is in a restaurant context or in someone's home. It also depends on the individual, that is, the impact of the environment varies for individuals, with the three inteviewees adopting different strategies to maintain their dietary preferences in such social contexts. When dining out, Jim tends to frequent maintream restaurants as there are very few vegetarians in his social circle and because "*I'm not the type of person who imposes their views on others.*" Sinéad and Anna however, who both have a broader circle of vegan/vegetarian friends, will frequent vegan/ vegetarian restaurants. However, if invited to a mainstream restaurant, they will take the precaution of phoning the restaurant in advance if possible to ensure that they can cater to their dietary preferences. Sinéad reports that it is more challenging to dine out as a vegan than as a vegetarian: "*becoming vegetarian wasn't difficult. Being vegan is only difficult if eating out.*"

As a result of their social networks, the impact of dining out is therefore different for Jim than for Anna or Sinéad. As Jim highlights, eating in regular restaurants means his choices are more limited: "*I'm always the first person to choose what . . . [laugh] what I want . . . because I've got two options maybe on the menu and everyone else has 12 or 13 . . . so I'm sitting there . . . starving while I wait for everyone else to pick what they want on the menu.*" However, he does not find this challenging: "*I'm so long a vegetarian* [15 years] *it's not an issue any more. People know.*" While he states that eating out in a work context "*can be a bit boring,*" eating a wide variety of foods makes it a little easier for Jim to manage social dining. He says that there is "*usually enough choice not to make any real difference*" and "*I like lots of different types of food, I eat food from many different cultures. I just don't eat the bits with meat in it. It can be difficult if you have a limited palate of food . . . I eat lots and lots of different types of food. There's always something I can eat . . . and basically I am always hungry.*"

While Sinéad's extended family contains several vegans and quite a few vegetarians, she also finds she has to prepare in advance for social occasions.

She recently declined a dinner invitation to a restaurant, explaining *"it was too difficult because I was vegan."* However, she did not want to offend her hosts either, so she declined, offering instead to *"meet them for a drink later."* She knew from experience that the restaurant to which she was invited did not cater to vegans, and she didn't want her hosts paying a lot of money for what would be, for her, a poor quality meal. Other tactics Sinéad uses include pretending to have eaten in advance if vegan menu options are not available. Anna also highlighted her disappointment at the level of knowledge, and care, of some chefs with regards to catering for vegans. *"I asked and they said it was vegan friendly. And I'd ask them how the cheese was vegan and they'd say, well I suppose it isn't."*

Being invited to dine with others in their homes can be somewhat challenging for each of the interviewees, depending on the context. Anna takes care to ensure others are aware of her dietary choices in advance (she spoke about making *"soft reminders"* to relatives about her dietary choices), but takes practical steps to ensure that this does not cause stress for others by offering to bring a dish with her. For example, she recently brought brown bread and hummus when invited to dine with her boyfriend's family. She is also sensitive to the dietary choices of others and ensures the dish she brings is not the main dish. For Sinéad, dining with other family members tends to be relaxed because of the informal dining approach in her family: *"I was at my sister's yesterday. We are very casual in the family. She had a vegan meal for me from the freezer. Often I would bring something I can eat when visiting others."* In other contexts, she would opt for a very plain dish *"I'd ask them to do potatoes without butter for me."* Jim's experiences of eating at other people's homes led him to observe that *"you are only catered for as an afterthought really."* However, he also suggested that a lack of knowledge, as opposed to lack of consideration, influenced what others offer to vegetarians or vegans. When he invited his vegetarian girlfriend to his home fifteen or so years ago, his mother made an effort to welcome her but offered her salami pizza thinking it was vegetarian.

The interviewees highlight that dietary preferences resulting from ethical motivations can result in social pressures, and that other reasons for limiting dietary choices (e.g., health) may be more acceptable and thus result in less social pressure. Anna feels she has to compromise her dietary preferences in certain social occasions. She gave an example of being offered a pasta dish which included cheese at her boyfriend's family's house. She ate it as she did not wish to make a fuss, but felt sick afterwards. She spoke about feeling guilty for asking her boyfriend to tell his family that she was vegetarian and felt it was somewhat unfair that he had to deal with her "*issues.*" She believes that it is more acceptable to say something makes you sick than say you are avoiding a certain food for ethical reasons. Sinéad has similar experiences when traveling abroad: "*when I have traveled I have found that poor people feel they are not offering a guest a proper meal if there is no meat in it, so I used to tell them that I was allergic to meat.*"

Although both vegetarian and vegan diets are characterized by removing meat from the diet, the more restrictive elements of a vegan diet may present challenges even to long-term vegetarians. For example, Sinéad, a vegetarian for forty years but a vegan for 2.5 years, highlighted the difference between being a vegetarian and vegan and the importance of knowledge to be able to act on such food preferences. She says "*it was like starting from scratch becoming a vegan.*" She took a course in macrobiotics when she became a vegan to ensure she had adequate nutrition knowledge. She also highlighted the impact of age on what being a vegan might look like in practice; being a young vegan may mean a relatively unhealthy diet, while older vegans who have an increased focus on health may need more knowledge to be (healthy) vegans. Income can also be a factor due to the price of vegan products. She says: "*I said I'd do it for a year and see. There was no point in doing it for a month because you wouldn't have learned what you can substitute for another thing. It is not so difficult then because when you know where you can get soy for example you can always get it there (unless they stop stocking it). I did a macrobiotic course because while my nephews and nieces are vegan they are not necessarily healthy vegans. They are young so they can eat anything. . . . I didn't want tins and packets of food. I was used to eating yoghurt and eggs and cheese. So I was conscious of what I was going to replace them with. Being a healthy vegan is more expensive than being a healthy vegetarian. Vegan quorn is about twice the price of vegetarian quorn.*"

FINAL COMMENTS

It is becoming easier to adopt vegan and vegetarian food lifestyles in Ireland. This is for several reasons, with changes right across the supply chain from primary producer, to manufacturer to retailer and food service operator. For example, there are increased opportunities to source vegan-certified ingredients and vegan alternatives to most meats, and convenience vegan products are available in mainstream retailers. Furthermore, many restaurants offer high quality vegetarian options across the spectrum from fast food to high end, and cookery courses, as well as vegetarian recipes provided in mainstream media, facilitate such behavior. There is also evidence of social norming with many "firsts" including a mainstream culinary award for a vegetarian restaurant and a mainstream food product award for a vegan product. There is a more positive framing of such dietary choices as a result of the growth in plant-based diets, that is, these food choices are good for you and for animals and the environment. To quote the Irish Vegan Society: *It seems that Ireland now has the "vegetarian thing" completely down, and is slowly coming to grips with the concept of being vegan. . . . Dublin* [the capital city] [has] . . . *a growing vegan community and some wonderful vegan friendly restaurants, eateries, and health-food shops. Outside the cities, things are more challenging. Although many cafes across the nation now offer a choice of soy milk and many restaurants (even if they don't appear to be too vegan friendly at first glance) are actually more than happy to accommodate vegan diners, it will prove handy to pre-plan your vegan meals.*[6]

The trend for centennials (anyone born after 1997) toward a flexitarian diet, meaning they might eat vegan Monday to Friday and then indulge at weekends, may jar with some vegans. *"Why would you do that* [be a part-time vegan]"? asked vegan Bronwyn Slater, bewildered by the idea when interviewed by *The Irish Times* in 2017. *"There is, in her world, no such thing as being a little bit vegan"* (Cleary, 2017, p. 10). This indicates that meat avoiders are far from being a homogenous group. The flexitarian of today, who is consciously reducing their meat consumption, and possibly in the process of making it easier to be a vegan/vegetarian by "mainstreaming" meat avoidance, may be quite different to "traditional" vegans and vegetarians.

Suggested Readings

Bord Bia. "Periscope 2017: Irish and British Consumers and their Food. Accessed June 15, 2018, https://www.bordbia.ie/industry/manufacturers/insight/publications/bbreports/PERIscope6/PERIscope2017/Bord%20Bia%20Periscope%202017%20-%20Irish%20and%20British%20Full%20Report.pdf.

Bourdieu, Pierre. "Distinction: A social critique of the judgment of taste (R. Nice, Trans.)," (1984).

Randall, Elizabeth and Diva Sanjur. "Food preferences—their conceptualization and relationship to consumption." *Ecology of food and nutrition* 11, no. 3 (1981): 151-61.

Rozin, Paul. "Food and eating." In *Handbook of cultural psychology*, edited by Shinobu Kitayama & Dov Cohen, 391–16. New York: Guilford Press, 2007.

Notes

1.   Bia Bord, "Periscope 2017: Irish and British Consumers and their Food. Accessed 15 June 2018, https://www.bordbia.ie/industry/manufacturers/insight/publications/bbreports/PERIscope6/PERIscope2017/Bord%20Bia%20

Periscope%202017%20-%20Irish%20and%20British%20Full%20Report.pdf.

2. Cleary, C. (2017). Vegan, *The Irish Times Magazine*, November 18th, 8–11.

3. Pierre Bourdieu, "Distinction: A social critique of the judgment of taste (R. Nice, Trans.)," (1984).

4. Elizabeth Randall and Diva Sanjur, "Food preferences—their conceptualization and relationship to consumption." *Ecology of food and nutrition* 11, no. 3 (1981): 151.

5. Paul Rozin, "Food and eating." In *Handbook of cultural psychology*, edited by Shinobu Kitayama and Dov Cohen, 391–416. New York: Guilford Press, 2007.

6. "Is Ireland Vegan Friendly?" Accessed October 29, 2018, https://veganinireland.com/is-ireland-vegan-friendly.

CHAPTER 10

ISRAEL

THE ISRAELI CONTEXT ON VEGETARIAN AND VEGAN DIETS

SIGAL TIFFERET

INTRODUCTION

Israel is the home of 8.8 million citizens (74 percent Jews, 21 percent Arabs),[1] situated by the Mediterranean Sea. Accordingly, Israelis (Arabs and Jews) eat a Mediterranean diet, consuming fruits and vegetables at high rates,[2] with 80 percent reporting eating vegetables and fruits every day.[3] Israeli youths, as well, consume about seven servings of fruit and vegetables per day.[4] Nevertheless, Israelis also eat meat at higher rates than the OECD average.[5] They hardly eat pork, but they do eat about twenty kg beef and fifty-seven kg poultry per capita yearly.[6]

Vegetable-based diets are on the rise in Israel. In 2010, only 2.6 percent of the Israeli population defined themselves as vegetarian or vegan in the national survey of the Central Bureau of Statistics.[7] By 2014, this figure increased to 4.7 percent vegetarians and 1.7 percent vegans.[8] Another national survey conducted by the Israeli Ministry of Health reported that

8.5 percent of the population define themselves as vegetarian or vegan.[9] In school-aged children, rates are similar, with 7.6 percent reporting not eating meat and poultry.[10] In addition to vegans and vegetarians, many are flexitarians. Half of the population report eating only small quantities of meat,[11] 23 percent report eating less meat than in the previous year, and 13 percent report they are considering converting to vegetarianism/veganism in the near future.[12]

The leading reasons for choosing a vegetable-based diet in adults are ideological (39 percent), taste preferences (36 percent), and health (17 percent).[13] Vegetarianism and veganism are more prevalent in the Jewish population (10 percent) than among Arab Israelis (4.3 percent).[14] Other demographics related to a vegetable-based diet are young age, education, and female gender.[15] Meat is perceived as masculine for both Arab[16] and Jewish[17] Israelis.

PLANT-BASED CULINARY ACTIVITIES IN ISRAEL

Israeli ethical veganism was linked, in the past to the human-rights movement and the Palestinian struggle. Today, however, with the rise of vegetarianism, this link has weakened.[18] One of the triggers for the surge in plant-based diets was the vegan activist Gary Yourofsky. Yourofsky's You-Tube video "The most important talk you will ever hear"[19] spread virally in Israel, and later he visited Israel in a highly media-covered tour. Yourofsky, a Jew, uses Holocaust terminology when describing the use of animals in the food and fashion industries. This terminology may have struck a sensitive chord in the hearts of Israelis. Today, Israel is considered as one of the leading vegetarian countries[20] and Tel Aviv has been named the vegan capital of the world by the *Independent*,[21] with 400 vegan and vegetarian restaurants.

Another cultural drive of vegetarianism comes from the Jewish religion. Some claim that Jewish believers should be active vegetarians as a practice of Jewish values such as righteousness, sustainability, health, atonement, and compassion.[22] For the religious, vegetarianism has practical benefits, as well. Kosher-keeping Jews are prohibited from eating milk and meat together. This prohibition requires waiting six hours between eating meat and dairy. For the same reason, most religious Jews keep separate dishes and even sinks for meat and dairy. A vegetarian diet is an easy way to adhere to the kosher laws since there would be no need for separate dishes and sinks nor a need to wait between meals.[23]

PERSONAL FOOD EXPERIENCE: HADAR

Hadar is a secular Jewish twenty-two-year-old young woman. She lives with her extended family in a Moshav (a cooperative agricultural community) in the center of Israel. As part of her mandatory army service, she serves as a welfare NCO, helping soldiers with their personal and socio-economic problems. Hadar is a vegan, who does not eat meat, poultry, fish, dairy, or egg products. Also, she does not purchase leather or fur items. This is her story.

"When I was nine, we visited the US, and in one of the parks, I saw a whole pig grilled on a skew. Since then I stopped eating meat. At the start, I still ate fish from time to time, but gradually I stopped that as well. When I was 16, I became a vegan. After seven years of being a vegetarian, it felt natural to become a vegan. I also went to see Gary Yourofsky when he gave a talk in Israel, in order to become a vegan. The transformation to a vegan lifestyle was easier for me than for others, since I was already used to not eating meat. My main motivation was ideological, not to hurt animals. Later, an ecological perspective was also added.

"Although I don't eat commercial eggs or products with eggs, I do eat eggs from our family hens. We grow about 20 hens in our backyard on a large piece of land and not in cages. I know they are treated well, they get good food and a good life. They are not butchered, chicks are not killed, and their lives are not interfered with too much. My parents love them and care for them, and they are part of our home environment. They are not there just to lay eggs.

"There are some difficulties in being a vegan. I don't think I eat healthy, as much as I want to, it's a bit difficult because of the army, and because I don't prepare my meals. I try to eat legumes and nuts, but I usually eat mostly carbs and vegetables. Everyone around me eats normal, and it's hard for me to find what to eat. Not eating cheese is still difficult for me. And having to check everything, look, read the ingredients, ask the waiter. Eggs and dairy can pop up in unexpected places. Eating in the army is not simple. It's difficult when you go out to places like a pizzeria, that by definition don't support vegans. It's especially hard that I need to look out for myself. When I'm not with my family and people are less supportive of vegans, I need to remind them I am vegan. Sometimes people prepare only a little vegan food, and others forget that and eat it, and then I don't have anything to eat. It's hard for me to remind people that they should keep me in mind and keep some food for me."

One source of support for Hadar is Israeli vegan groups on Facebook: The group "Vegans eating out" is very active. One of the most active groups I am in. People ask: "Where can I eat in Zichron Yaacov?" or "I want to impress my friends and show them that vegan food can be delicious, where should I go?" People get answers straight away, everyone wants to help out.

Hadar mentions the difficulties in keeping a healthy vegan diet while serving in the army. It is worth noting that the Israeli Defense Forces (IDF) recognize the rights of vegan soldiers, providing them with non-animal made shoes and berets and including vegetable-based proteins in the meals. In the past, they also gave a small allowance for food purchases, but this was canceled in 2017. Hadar also mentions the need to check labels. However, as a Jewish state, Israeli food products are marked as meat-based (Bsari), milk-based (Halavi), or neither meat nor milk (Parve). These markings facilitate plant-based diets since consumers can easily identify vegetarian and vegan options.

"Being a vegan is one of the things that define me. I am Hadar; I am a Welfare NCO; I am a vegan. It characterizes me. It is part of my identity. As a vegan, people see me differently. They think I'm a leftist, nicer than others, perhaps too nice, that I love animals, gentle. They automatically ask me if I'm a 'Tivo-nazi' (Nazi-vegan), which means that I preach for veganism, that I'm very extreme, I protest, I go naked into cages. They think I am a moral person, and they expect me to be moral because I am a vegan. A soldier I helped wrote me: 'You are amazing, and you are also a vegan, which says something about you.' What she meant was that vegans are giving people, who help others and see others beyond their self-interest."

Viewing a vegan as a liberal left-wing is understandable since they follow the similar ideology of human and animal rights. Today, however, with the growing number of vegetarians and vegans in Israel, this link is no longer as strong as it was before.[24] As Hadar words it: People are cautious around me. Once, in the army, someone asked me if it would be OK for her to peel a hard-boiled egg next to me. Or people ask me if it is OK that they cook meat next to me. That's the nice side. But some people tease me about not being able to eat things. Someone that I just casually met told me, 'I could never be with a vegan girlfriend. It's too hard.' But aside from that, I feel that many times people pick a place to go out so that I can eat there as well. People who know me make sure I have things to eat or think about me and organize something. Two soldiers in my base were just released, and they had a Prisat Shihrur (farewell meal). They weren't my best friends, but without even telling me, they brought me a lot of vegetables and told me they thought about me and brought me vegetables. They didn't know that I could eat the other snacks they brought.

This cautious behavior, described by Hadar, sounds similar to the religious sensitivity that many secular Jews hold toward religious friends, whose feelings they don't want to hurt. It is possible that non-vegetarians view vegetarians as religious, in a sense, and act toward them with caution, as they would act toward others who adhere to religious beliefs. As Hadar words it: I feel that others support me. My dad always tells me, "enough with the nonsense, eat like a human being!" But he always prepares vegan food for me and thinks about me when he is shopping. There are a few people who would like me to stop, who's life would be simpler if I stopped, but most people are very accepting, supportive, and helpful.

People still don't know vegans well enough, and they don't know what they can eat. They always think I don't have anything to eat, and that it is tough to get along as a vegan. Part of my dialogue with people who don't know me is to explain what veganism is, and why it's important, and why I won't eat the cow, although it is already dead and in the freezer. I take on myself the role of quiet explanation, not through protests. It's important to me that when people ask me questions, I really explain and show them that it's not terrible or difficult. I don't have to preach to turn people into vegans. I don't look at their plates and tell them they're murderers. This way, people listen more, and they don't leave with negative feelings toward veganism and vegans.

CONCLUSION

Vegetarianism and veganism are popular in Israel and seem to be on the rise. They are related to ideology, religion, and geography. In her story, Hadar explains the difficulties in eating well as a vegan in the army, and as a young person going out with friends. She also describes the support and good intentions of family, friends, and acquaintances. It seems that the growing number of vegans and vegetarians may drive an increase in their culinary options and promote greater sensitivity and awareness among other Israelis.

Suggested Readings

Aharoni, Efrat. "Survey: 25% of Israelis eat less meat, 10% have become vegetarians." *Globes*, 2014, https://www.globes.co.il/news/article.aspx?did=1000906210.

Aviely, Nir. *Food and Power: A Culinary Ethnography of Israel*. Oakland: University of California Press, 2018.

Central Bureau of Statistics. "Press Release: Israel Population." Jerusalem, 2017.

Diemling, Maria. "The politics of food: Kashrut, food choices and social justice (Tikkun Olam)." *Jewish Culture and History* 16, no. 2 (2015): 178–95, doi:10.1080/14621 69X.2015.1069468.

Dovrin, Nurit and Yigal Eisenman. "Central Bureau of Statistics: Press Release." *Central Bureau of Statistics.* Jerusalem, 2016, http://www.cbs.gov.il/reader/newhodaot/hodaa_template.html?hodaa=201715328.

Gvion, Liora. "Cooking, food, and masculinity: Palestinian men in Israeli society." *Men and Masculinities* 14, no. 4 (2011): 408–29, doi:10.1177/1097184X11411269.

Israel Center for Disease Control. The Ministry of Health. "Mabat Youth." Tel Hashomer, 2017, https://www.health.gov.il/PublicationsFiles/mabat_youth_2015_2016_Full.pdf.

Israeli Portal for Agriculture. "Volcani Center survey: 80% of the Israelis consume vegetables and fruits daily." *Israeli Portal for Agriculture, Nature and Environment,* 2015, http://israel.agrisupportonline.com/news/csv/csvread.pl?show=5838&mytemplate=tp2.

Kishik, Yael. "Is everyone vegan? How many Israelis stopped consuming animal-based products?" *Mako,* 2014, https://www.mako.co.il/weekend-surveys/Article-9f352f-f4e5cd541006.htm.

OECD. "Health at a Glance 2015: OECD Indicators." Paris, 2015, doi:10.1787/19991312.

———. "Meat consumption." *OECD,* 2017, https://data.oecd.org/agroutput/meat-consumption.htm.

Phull, Jasmine. "How Tel Aviv became the vegan capital of the world | The Independent." *Independent,* 2017, https://www.independent.co.uk/travel/middle-east/vegan-food-tel-aviv-best-restaurants-israel-vegetarian-friendly-port-capital-meshek-barzilay-orna-a8036081.html.

Sawe, Benjamin Elisha. "Countries with the highest rates of vegetarianism—World Atlas.Com." *WorldAtlas,* 2017, https://www.worldatlas.com/articles/countries-with-the-highest-rates-of-vegetarianism.html.

Teschner, Naama. "Megamat Tzimchonut Ve'Tivonut Be'Israel Uva'Olam [Trend in Vegetarianism and Veganism in Israel and the World]." Jerusalem, 2014, doi:10.11844/cjcb.2016.03.0353.

Weiss, Brian. "The planet-saving mitzvah: Why Jews should consider vegetarianism." *Tikkun* 24, no. 4 (2009): 29–73.

Weiss, Erica. "'There are no chickens in suicide vests': The decoupling of human rights and animal rights in Israel." *Journal of the Royal Anthropological Institute* 22, no. 3 (2016): 688–706, doi:10.1111/1467-9655.12453.

Yourofsky, Gary. "The Most Important Talk You Will Ever Hear," 2011, https://youtu.be/omweihtaYwI.

Notes

1. Central Bureau of Statistics, "Press Release: Israel Population" (Jerusalem, 2017).
2. OECD, "Health at a Glance 2015: OECD Indicators" (Paris, 2015), doi: 10.1787/19991312.

3. Israeli Portal for Agriculture, "Volcani Center survey: 80% of the Israelis consume vegetables and fruits daily," *Israeli Portal for Agriculture, Nature and Environment*, 2015, http://israel.agrisupportonline.com/news/csv/csvread.pl?show=5838&mytemplate=tp2.

4. Israel Center for Disease Control. The Ministry of Health, "Mabat Youth" (Tel Hashomer, 2017), https://www.health.gov.il/PublicationsFiles/mabat_youth_2015_2016_Full.pdf.

5. OECD, "Meat consumption," *OECD*, 2017, https://data.oecd.org/agroutput/meat-consumption.htm.

6. Ibid.

7. Naama Teschner, "Megamat Tzimchonut Ve'Tivonut Be'Israel Uva'Olam [Trend in Vegetarianism and Veganism in Israel and the World]" (Jerusalem, 2014), doi:10.11844/cjcb.2016.03.0353.

8. Nurit Dovrin and Yigal Eisenman, "Central Bureau of Statistics: Press Release," *Central Bureau of Statistics* (Jerusalem, 2016), http://www.cbs.gov.il/reader/newhodaot/hodaa_template.html?hodaa=201715328.

9. Teschner, "Megamat Tzimchonut Ve'Tivonut Be'Israel Uva'Olam [Trend in Vegetarianism and Veganism in Israel and the World]."

10. Israel Center for Disease Control. The Ministry of Health, "Mabat Youth."

11. Yael Kishik, "Is everyone vegan? How many Israelis stopped consuming animal-based products?," *Mako*, 2014, https://www.mako.co.il/weekend-surveys/Article-9f352ff4e5cd541006.htm.

12. Efrat Aharoni, "Survey: 25% of Israelis eat less meat, 10% have become vegetarians," *Globes*, 2014, https://www.globes.co.il/news/article.aspx?did=1000906210.

13. Teschner, "Megamat Tzimchonut Ve'Tivonut Be'Israel Uva'Olam [Trend in Vegetarianism and Veganism in Israel and the World]."

14. Ibid.

15. Ibid.; Dovrin and Eisenman, "Central Bureau of Statistics: Press Release"; Kishik, "Is everyone vegan? How many Israelis stopped consuming animal-based products?"

16. Liora Gvion, "Cooking, food, and masculinity: Palestinian men in Israeli society," *Men and Masculinities* 14, no. 4 (2011): 408–29, doi:10.1177/1097184X11411269.

17. Nir Avieli, *Food and Power: A Culinary Ethnography of Israel* (Oakland: University of California Press, 2018).

18. Erica Weiss, "'There are no chickens in suicide vests': The decoupling of human rights and animal rights in Israel," *Journal of the Royal Anthropological Institute* 22, no. 3 (2016): 688–706, doi:10.1111/1467-9655.12453.

19. Gary Yourofsky, "The Most Important Talk You Will Ever Hear," 2011, https://youtu.be/omweihtaYwI.

20. Benjamin Elisha Sawe, "Countries With the Highest Rates of Vegetarianism—WorldAtlas.Com," *WorldAtlas*, 2017, https://www.worldatlas.com/articles/countries-with-the-highest-rates-of-vegetarianism.html.

21. Jasmine Phull, "How Tel Aviv became the vegan capital of the world | The Independent," *Independent*, 2017, https://www.independent.co.uk/travel/middle-east/vegan-food-tel-aviv-best-restaurants-israel-vegetarian-friendly-port-capital-meshek-barzilay-orna-a8036081.html.

22. Brian Weiss, "The Planet-Saving Mitzvah: Why Jews Should Consider Vegetarianism," *Tikkun* 24, no. 4 (2009): 29–73; Maria Diemling, "The Politics of Food: Kashrut, Food Choices and Social Justice (Tikkun Olam)," *Jewish Culture and History* 16, no. 2 (2015): 178–95, doi:10.1080/1462169X.2015.1069468.

23. Weiss, "The Planet-Saving Mitzvah: Why Jews Should Consider Vegetarianism"; Diemling, "The Politics of Food: Kashrut, Food Choices and Social Justice (Tikkun Olam)."

24. Weiss, "'There Are No Chickens in Suicide Vests': The Decoupling of Human Rights and Animal Rights in Israel."

CHAPTER 11

ITALY

FOND OF VEG-FOOD: TRADITION, TRANSITION, TRANSFORMATION

ALESSANDRA MICALIZZI

VEGETARIANISM IN ITALY

The Mediterranean diet is well known all over the world, both because of its health benefits, and the focus on conviviality and the joys of eating together.[1] Italians, with their deep affinity for food and culinary traditions, have contributed to this recognition. In Italy, dining with family or friends is a deeply entrenched social practice; culture and identity are passed on through cooking and the practice of sharing food with others.[2] Even though Italians are known as food and cooking enthusiasts loyal to traditions, the social changes in the past fifty years have generated a slow reduction of time spent every day on cooking and eating together. At the same time, the food chain has undergone a process of industrialization (both for vegetables and animals) along with a reduction in the quality of the products offered to consumers.

The introduction and expansion of industrialized food chains has also led to a new attitude: Italians are now paying more attention to the types of food they consume. A new kind of food consciousness or a scrutinizing of food that was once unnecessary is now evident in Italy. For example, Italians are now reading food labels and information about origins and ingredients. This new awareness is somewhat reflected in a new market or explicit branding of organic produce, whereas once the notion of organic or wholesome Italian foods would have once been presumed or implicit in its production and preparation. This is demonstrated by the 20 percent growth in what we now know as the "organic produce" market, a sub-market of which is "organic veg" food, such as cereals, vegetables and cheese that occupy 68 percent of the parent market.[3]

The Mediterranean pyramid puts red meat at the top (for least consumption) and other animal proteins (such as cheese) in the middle (for moderate consumption), leaving a large space for vegetarian dishes at the bottom (greatest consumption). However, most regional recipes which are part of the Italian culinary tradition, combine meat and vegetables, using animal protein and their derivatives as the main ingredients. Despite these strong cultural traditions, the numbers of Italians (partially) opting for a vegetarian diet, mainly driven by health reasons, has increased over recent years. According to the Eurispes Report, in 2016, 40 percent of the Italian population reported eating vegetarian foods, even though only 6 percent identified as vegetarians. The population of vegans in the same period was around 1 percent.[4] Similar to other countries, vegetarians and vegans in Italy seem mostly driven by animal rights, and respect for all forms of life.[5] The numbers of vegetarians and vegans do fluctuate, however. In 2017 veganism had grown while vegetarianism had declined, and the last Eurispes[6] report indicates the inverse: the number of vegetarians is growing again, while the number of vegans is declining. Analysts have tried to explain these fluctuations by the fact that perhaps a strict vegan diet is too difficult to maintain in the Italian culinary context, forcing vegans to return to former vegetarian or omnivore eating habits. We further explore this in this chapter by interviewing several Italian vegetarians and vegans.

VEGETARIANS AND VEGANS INTERVIEWED AND THEIR MOTIVATIONS

In total, six narrative interviews were conducted with four vegans and two vegetarians. All were asked about their motives to become vegetarian or vegan, and how this choice affected their social lives; what helped and what has been an obstacle in them keeping to their decision. The people interviewed were Giuseppe, twenty-four years old and vegan since 2015, after six years of a vegetarian diet. Giuseppe is a student and lives with his family. Eleonora, forty-three years old, also vegan since 2012, is a housewife with three children (eight, five, and three years old) who all follow an exclusively vegan diet. Next are Sauro, fifty years old, vegan since 1989, and Renata, fifty-six years old, and vegan since 1999. Sauro and Renata are a couple and the founders of AssoVegan and VeganOK, a brand that labels the quality of foods that respect vegan values. The vegetarians interviewed were Serena, thirty-five years old. Serena is a communications strategist, married and the mother of a two-year-old child. Mara, thirty-eight years old, a vegetarian since 1991, works as a secretary in a public institution, is married and has an eight-year-old child.

All the interviewees follow a plant-based diet, although the vegetarians also allow eggs, milk, and dairy products. All of them viewed the vegetarian diet as a period of transition toward veganism, and their motives were deeply rooted in animal concerns and ecological considerations. They explained that, for them, being vegetarian or vegan is not as simple as just eating plant-based, it is also mandatory that their foods have been grown and produced following ethical practices. They all pay attention to the origins of food, using labels like *veganOK*. All of them also talked about current debates on the spread of soya plantations in regions where it is not in line with the ecosystem. They express a more proactive attitude to being informed and looking for scientific information, at least more so than their omnivore counterparts. The respect of a general and natural equilibrium is the main motivation expressed by interviewees: for them, it is more important to be part of a global project that includes all forms of life, rather than be driven by the health consequences of a plant-based diet. Their ethical motivations also translates into other lifestyle changes, including making ethical choices about clothes, accessories, shoes, and so on. They describe themselves as promoters of a new way of life that needs to be increasingly shared with and explained to Italians. In their perceptions, omnivorous people are full of prejudices due to disinformation and psychological barriers.

EXPERIENCE, KNOWLEDGE, AND READY-MEALS AS SOLUTIONS TO SOCIAL STIGMA

The levels of knowledge about and experience with vegetarian foods varied across the six people interviewed, and they can be grouped in two categories based on their years of experience. The senior vegetarians, who were older and had more years of experience, showed great creativity in cooking tasty and balanced recipes. The junior vegetarians, in contrast, expressed more difficulties in organizing their meals according to a vegetarian diet, made more use of ready-meals and had to make more compromises. Ready-meals, for instance, were not their preference; they enjoyed cooking their own meals more, but they made life easier. In their eyes, the ready-meals looked a lot like omnivorous food in shape, appearance, and sometimes also in taste. These looking-like-omnivorous-food ready-meals were considered not only as a practical solution that allowed them to save time but also, and above all, these meals reduced the impact of their food choice on their social life. In their consumption of these meals, they felt less conspicuous in convivial situations.

TRANSITION AND DOMESTIC IMPACT

All people interviewed remember what triggered their transition to a vegetarian diet. These "transitions" are described as clear and sudden points in their life, linked with a specific episode: meeting someone who is already vegetarian or vegan, or seeing documentaries on cruelty to animals. Or, as in the case of Mara (vegetarian since 1991), following the vegetarian footsteps of a favorite celebrity, in her case a singer. All the interviewees perfectly remember the day, or time period when they transitioned from an omnivorous to a vegetarian diet, because this transition was triggered by a specific event with an important emotive impact. Their transition can be regarded as a flashbulb memory[7]; they hold an exceptionally vivid snapshot of the moment they became vegetarian and the (emotional) consequences that came along with this transition. Their transition clearly became part of their biography: "I remember the exact moment that I decided never to eat meat again or any kind of food coming from the exploitation of animals. We were sitting at the table, we were watching the news when the anchorman started to talk about the fur industry and some actions by animalists against it (. . .)" (Sauro, fifty, vegan). From a narrative perspective, it is a *turning point* that marks their life.[8]

The interviewees declared that once their choice to be vegetarian was made, this had a significant impact on their family's cooking and eating habits, causing, in some cases, the conversion of other family members (especially the partner). In these cases, where others turned vegetarian too, we can talk about, on the one hand, the *beginner or the influence* who starts a vegetarian diet first and introduces novel cooking and eating habits to other people, and, on the other hand, the *follower, often also becoming the mediator*, a member of the influencer's first circle of relations that mediates the relations with other omnivorous members. Having such a supporting partner appears to be important in the first stage of the transition process, when some interviewees experienced resistance within their immediate social context.

Transitioning to a vegetarian diet not only raised the question of whether other adult family members would also change their diet, but also led to dilemmas for the interviewees about how their choices affected the ones they cared for: their children. In Eleonora's family, for example, the parents decided to also let their three sons (three-, five-, and eight-years old) follow an exclusive plant-based diet, both at home and at school. This decision led to major resistance, especially at first. In their case, a personal choice became a cultural and social battle to increase awareness about the importance of healthy food from an early stage of life. In Eleonora's experience, the strong educational power of this choice was clear: her children did not ask for junk food or snacks, either when they were alone or with other children of their own age. They were and still are proud of being vegans, even though the decision was made for them by their parents.

Other members of the household may also have to adjust to changes to their diet based on the decision of other adults. Pets, for example, do not choose themselves what to eat, and in the case of Sauro and Renata their five dogs all followed a vegan diet: "In general, pet food is the result of an artificial diet. Dogs don't naturally eat meat or fish. This is why, with the approval of our vet, we only choose vegetarian pet food. Our dogs love it!" Sauro and Renata's decision is not exceptional; it has been documented more broadly that vegetarians and vegans do not like to feed their pets animal-based diets, and opt for vegetarian alternatives, even though some acknowledge that some pets may feel better when being fed an animal-based diet.[9]

REACTIONS OUTSIDE THE HOME CONTEXT

The senior vegetarians interviewed specified that the transition toward vegetarian diets is simpler today, as the food market is more organized and offers more choices. Vegetarian foods have become more accessible in food chains, including supermarkets and fast food outlets. In addition, more information about vegetarian diets is available today, and there seems to be increasing awareness and tolerance about this topic. The opinions about vegan diets are also changing in the perception of the senior vegetarian interviewees. There are also more and more restaurants that offer vegan alternatives, and the food industry is using this new trend to develop specific lines of products, which are also appreciated by omnivores. In spite of these changes, however, the junior vegetarians interviewed pointed out that they still experience what they call "relational barriers." These refer to conflicts both inside and outside the family boundaries: "it was hard to explain my choice to my father. For him, it is inconceivable to eat only plant-based food, especially for a sportsman. He said it was stupid and unhealthy. . . . Nowadays, even though he hasn't accepted it yet, he respects my diet" (Giuseppe, twenty-four, vegan). As compared to family members, some friends were perceived as even less understanding, especially at the beginning: "I prefer not to say that I'm vegetarian unless someone asks me. When I meet someone new, I know that he/she will start thinking I'm naïve or choosy. Sometimes I feel like I am the problem" (Serena thirty-five, vegetarian). In several of these cases, interviewees felt misunderstood: "I hear some people call me a "grass-eater" . . . they think that my diet is unhealthy. Instead, from the beginning, I started to feel better: lighter and with more energy" (Eleonora, forty-three, vegan).

Discomfort, resistance, and prejudices are not only present between vegetarians and omnivores, but between vegetarians and vegans as well. Vegetarians look at the vegan diet in an aspirational way: it is as though the vegetarian diet is chosen as an intermediate phase which they find difficult to abandon. This situation generates a sense of guilt. In line with the research by Fox and Ward,[10] Serena confessed: "I would like to be vegan but it's hard especially when you have to share your choice with others. I'm a little bit disappointed because some vegans consider me hypocritical and inconsistent. I know perfectly well that the Vegan community blames vegetarians, considering them more inconsistent than omnivores." Vegans—more than vegetarians—underlined the importance of coherence in the respect of the principle of equality among living species. Being vegan means more than choosing a plant-based diet. It involves several aspects of everyday life such as mobility, choices of clothes, use of water, etc. Their behavior becomes a way to show that the conversion is possible and easy, at least to them. Not giving up and perseverance is fundamental to "evangelizing": the tiniest exception is not forgiven.

Interviewees further report that they are repeatedly asked to be flexible, or lenient about their dietary principles by their omnivore friends and family members. This happens especially in the context of official dinners and convivial situations such as Christmas, ceremonies, important lunches, etc. While some of their friends or relatives will prepare separate vegetarian dishes, this is not always the case. Then vegetarians need to think of a plan B: eating only what is in line with their diet; communicating their limitations beforehand or, in the worst scenario, taking something from home. In any case, all people interviewed refused to be lenient about their dietary principles, which they regarded very highly. While not giving in to any request to be flexible does make them feel uncomfortable or bad, this does not necessarily translate to how they self-identify. As Sauro said: "It is important to say I'm vegan; however I don't consider it a divisive label."

To end this part with a positive note, the interviewees also felt lucky to be Italian as they perceive the Italian cuisine to be vegetarian friendly: "The Mediterranean diet is one of the richest in vegetarian dishes. If you just think of tomato pasta, one of our typical dishes, you can understand how cooking vegetarian meals is really simple and practical, without going mad" (Sauro, fifty, vegan).

CONCLUSION

When I started this research, I realized I had a lot of prejudices against vegetarian people. I thought they were part of a close community, choosy, with an extreme ideology, made up mainly of women. On the other hand, thanks to the scenarios, data, and interviews, I discovered a heterogeneous group of people who are open-minded, tolerant, well informed, and strongly motivated. They go into depth, consulting scientific sources, going beyond the mainstream information. They perceive themselves as pioneers, evangelizers, promoters of a new way of life and style of diet that is more possible and practical than omnivores may believe.

In Italy the general trend is positive: the number of vegetarians is growing year by year and the food market is showing greater sensitivity toward the need of this "sub-culture." The strong call to action of veg people is clear and solicits our responsibility: "Above all, those who have children have to understand the urgency to make an ethical choice: it is correct for the animals and for the future of our planet" (Renata, fifty-six, vegan). It is possible to respect *tradition* and to be a part of a *transition*, in order to generate a *transformation*.

Suggested Readings

Brown R., Kulik J., "Flashbulb memories," *Cognition*, vol 5, n.1, (1977), p. 73–99.

Douglas M., *Antropologia e Simbolismo. Cibo e denaro nella vita sociale*, Bologna: Il Mulino, 1987.

Fox N., Ward K., "Health, ethics and environment: A qualitative study of vegetarian motivations," *Appetite 50*, (2008): 422–29.

Jedlowski P., *Un giorno dopo l'altro. La vita quotidiana tra esperienza e routine*, Bologna: il Mulino, 2005.

Mannucci E. J., *La cena di Pitagora. Storia del vegetarianismo dall'antica Grecia a Internet*, Roma: Carocci Editore, 2011.

Niola M., *Homo dieteticus. Viaggio nelle tribù alimentari*, Bologna: il Mulino, 2015.

Phull, Surinder, Wendy Wills, and Angela Dickinson. "The Mediterranean diet: Socio-cultural relevance for contemporary health promotion." *The Open Public Health Journal* 8 (2015): 35–40.

Roby R., "Vegetarianism: A blossoming field of study," *Appetite*, 58 (2012): 141–50.

Rosenfield D. L., Burrow A. L., "The unified model of vegetarian identity: A conceptual framework for understanding plant-based food choices," *Appetite* 112 (2017): 78–95.

Rothgerber, Hank. "A meaty matter. Pet diet and the vegetarian's dilemma." *Appetite*, 68 (2013): 76–82.

Notes

1. Surinder Phull, Wendy Wills, and Angela Dickinson, "The Mediterranean diet: Socio-cultural relevance for contemporary health promotion." *The Open Public Health Journal* 8 (2015): 35.

2. Mary Douglas, *Antropologia e Simbolismo. Cibo e denaro nella vita sociale* (Bologna: Il Mulino, 1987).

3. "Bio in cifre," *Sinab Report 2017*, October 23, 2017, http://www.sinab.it/bionovita/bio-cifre-2017-aggiornamento-al-23-ottobre.

4. "Vegetariani e vegani. Quanti sono in Italia?" *Universefood*, February 6, 2017 http://www.universofood.net/2017/02/06/vegetariani-e-vegani-quanti-in-italia/.

5. "Vegetariani e vegani. Quanti sono in Italia,?" Universefood, February 6, 2017, http://www.universofood.net/2017/02/06/vegetariani-e-vegani-quanti-in-italia/.

6. "Eurispes Rapporto Italia 2018," *Eurispes*, Janurry 30, 2018, http://www.eurispes.eu/content/eurispes-rapporto-italia-2018-vegani-e-vegetariani-sono-il-7-della-popolazione-dai-18-anni.

7. Rogers Brown and James Kulik, "Flashbulb memories," *Cognition*, vol. 5 no.1 (1977), p. 73–99.

8. Paolo Jedlowski, *Un giorno dopo l'altro. La vita quotidiana tra esperienza e routine*, Bologna: il Mulino, 2005.

9. Hank Rothgerber, "A meaty matter. Pet diet and the vegetarian's dilemma." *Appetite*, 68 (2013): 76.

10. Nick Fox, Katie Ward, "Health, ethics and environment: A qualitative study of vegetarian motivations, *Appetite*, 50 (2008): 422–29.

CHAPTER 12

THE NETHERLANDS

VEGETARIANISM IN THE DUTCH POLDER

HANS DAGEVOS

Much has changed in the research domain of vegetarianism since the pioneering studies in the early 1990s.[1] More recently, there has been increased attention to vegetarianism.[2] Despite this, statistics and information on vegetarianism and its development as a notable trend in contemporary food consumer culture are still hard to find and as yet not given rigorous scientific attention in the Netherlands. Against this backdrop, it is not surprising that there is still conjecture about the number of vegetarians in the Netherlands. It has been estimated that around 4.5 percent of the Dutch population is vegetarian, with 4 percent taken as a lower limit and 5 percent an upper limit.[3] This means in absolute numbers that approximately 750,000 vegetarians live in the Netherlands, among which an estimated 10 percent are vegans. There is also limited evidence about the socio-demographics of vegetarians, although a 2004 study by Hoek and colleagues[4] with a small group (N = 63) of vegetarians indicated an over-representation of women and a high percentage of higher educated people who live in more urbanized residential areas.

To bring these "shaky" statistics to life, in this chapter we will consider vegetarianism in the Dutch polder, starting with a review of vegetarianism in the nineteenth and twentieth centuries and moving forward to consider the situation now before previewing the future.

DUTCH GROUND FOR VEGETARIANISM

Vegetarianism has deep historical roots in Dutch ground. In his volumi-nous vegetarian history of the Netherlands, Dirk-Jan Verdonk eloquently explains how vegetarianism has been part of the Dutch food culture for many years.[5] First accounts of vegetarianism were reported at the end of the nineteenth century, and it appears to have been popular during the inter-war years. The vegetarian heyday of the 1920s and 1930s came to an end with World War II, and the second half of the twentieth century in the Netherlands was primarily characterized by an increase in the level of meat consumption, resulting in it almost doubling between the mid-twentieth century and recent times (from less than 20 kilos per person to more than 38 kilos now). However, vegetarianism remained and found new breeding ground in the 1970s and 1980s. The intervening years have seen various vegetarian products mainstreamed into the regular diet of many Dutch consumers. As Verdonk's research highlighted, both vegetarians and veg-etarian consumer practices and products are in various ways neither recent nor exotic aspects of contemporary Dutch food culture.

The ideological basis for vegetarianism is also reflected through the Dutch political party, Party for the Animals. This party opposes (large-scale) livestock farming and (excessive) meat eating. In addition, several environmental or animal welfare-oriented and vegetarian NGOs with shared values encourage ideas promoting a more animal-friendly and less meat-centered future. Noticeable too is a national campaign called "The week without meat," held for the first time in March 2018. This initiative was endorsed by several well-known Dutch citizens and supported by mul-tiple restaurants, retailers, and food companies. Also involved were the food service sector and the so-called Green Protein Alliance—a collaboration of diverse members interested in contributing to the common goal of accel-erating a shift in the type of protein consumed to such an extent that by 2025, 50 percent of protein consumed by Dutch people will be plant-based (coming from a current level of around 40 percent), and rising to 60 percent by 2030.

In addition to these more high-profile activities, all kinds of separate meatless food festivals or vegetarian food outlets, ranging from restaurants and cafés to food trucks and food stalls, take part in promoting vegetarian or vegan choices, and consequently contribute to making the meatless option on the menu increasingly a normal part of Dutch catering. Likewise, the chefs organized in Dutch cuisine add to this process of gradually changing the default option of meat as the main part of a meal. Although the associated chefs do not advocate vegetarianism as such, one of their major principles relates to fostering a dietary shift to more plant-based food choices by offering delicious non- and low-meat dishes.

In a similar vein, the Dutch Health Council is one of the first public health authorities to address the environmental sustainability of meat consumption and takes this into account in formulating the national dietary recommendations.[6] It is no exaggeration to say that this was as much a landmark in relation to consumer choice in the Dutch context, as was the United Nation's study *Livestock's Long Shadow*[7] on a global scale, in relation to meat production and its consequences. Such activities indicate that interest in the "meat issue" is well established in the Netherlands and is further confirmed both in reports of various government-related research institutes and academic publications written by Dutch scholars during the past decade.

FLEXITARIANISM AND VEGETARIANISM

The ongoing media coverage that "meat issues" receive in traditional media (papers, television, magazines, radio) as well as online and social media, could be considered as a parallel phenomenon to the increasing public awareness of vegetarianism in the Netherlands. Together, these have created a shift in public attitude, if not necessarily toward abstaining from eating meat, at least toward reconsidering meat as the "main" food that will and should stay forever and for everyone at the top of the food hierarchy.[8]

An even more practical and tangible contribution to the notion of the meat-free meal as "normal" is provided by the increasing availability of meat substitutes. Plant-based meat alternatives are slowly but gradually penetrating the Dutch food market.[9] The product quality and variety of meat replacements are improving constantly—"tofu times are over," so to speak—and they are becoming more available and accessible to consumers. The prevalence and quality of such products enhance consumer familiarity and help to make the meat-free choice an easier choice.

Vegetarians are not automatically the target for manufacturers of meat substitutes, with the larger consumer segment of flexitarians most responsible for the greater volume of sales. Whatever their differences in design, definitions, and approach, empirical studies that have been conducted in the Netherlands in recent years all subscribe to the conclusion that flexitarians not only exist in Dutch society but also form a substantial group within the contemporary Dutch population.[10] Of course, definition is important here. In contrast to the (Anglo-Saxon) perspective on the term that defines a flexitarian—similar to the definition of a semivegetarian, as a person who is vegetarian but occasionally eats meat—in the Netherlands it is more common to define a flexitarian the other way around: a person who eats meat but abstains from eating meat occasionally, regularly, or often. The latter directly refers to different forms of flexitarianism: from light to medium and heavy.[11] As such, flexitarianism, or so-called reducetarianism, to put it in Brian Kateman's terms,[12] is not automatically a forerunner of vegetarianism. Similarly, a vegetarian food style is also not a precondition to become a fully-fledged vegan. As Daniel Rosenfeld and Anthony Burrow observed: "every vegan is a vegetarian, but not every vegetarian is a vegan."[13] According to the most widely used definition in the Netherlands, a flexitarian diet includes the eating of meat. Most restrictive is a flexitarian diet that includes eating meat at dinner only once or twice a week ("heavy flexitarianism"). Empirical evidence shows that at least 10 percent to over 15 percent of the Dutch population belong to this segment. When the "medium" flexitarians, who limit their meat consumption to three or four days weekly, are added to the "heavies," at least 40 percent to over 50 percent of the Dutch are dedicated followers of this dietary pattern.

Even if the above-sketched "flexitarian tide" may not imply that the Dutch polder will be flooded with vegetarianism, I was interested in finding out if my vegan discussion partners felt personally and socially strengthened by this flexitarian movement. The following section outlines my discussion with two people who practice vegetarian or vegan diets.

VEGANS FOREVER

On being asked abut the impact of the "flexitarian tide," my two interviewees, Zayd Abdulla and Loan van Hoeven, declared "yes." Both enthusiastically confirmed that recent developments in the Netherlands, in which flexitarianism and vegetarianism have become mainstream among consumers, while simultaneously a growing range of good and tasty plant-based food options in supermarkets, snackbars, and restaurants has become available, are encouraging and enjoyable. In practice, these developments also make adopting and sustaining a vegetarian life easier. Both interviewees feel content and "safe" with these circumstances, and because they have been vegetarians for a long time, they are able to remember previous years when the socio-cultural atmosphere and food supply was less supportive of their choices.

Zayd Abdulla, fifty-four years of age, and Loan van Hoeven, thirty years old (in 2018), have been vegans for many years, and prior to that were vegetarian for an even longer period of time. Zayd and Loan share a number of similar experiences in their personal journeys toward a plant-based diet. Although they weren't brought up as vegetarians, both became vegetarian at a young age. Zayd decided at the age of fourteen to give up eating meat, following his elder brother's example, and, as he put it, "a year of reflection." Loan was even younger than Zayd: She became a vegetarian when she was nine years old. Loan remembers vividly: "I couldn't stand the idea of eating chicken after I was given four hens as pets. At that time, I saw the frozen chicken in the supermarket's freezer and became a vegetarian—although I doubt if I knew that word at that time. Anyhow, I told my parents—of whom my father was particularly a meat lover at that time—I was not going to eat meat from now on. My parents agreed under the condition that I would eat fish sticks once a week. The first week I ate the fish fingers with distaste, the second week I sat—in resolute rejection—for more than two hours at the dinner table before my parents gave up. I was taken seriously, and have never eaten a piece of animal flesh since then."

Another similarity in the stories of Zayd and Loan is that although the "de-meatification of their diet" was permanent, they didn't ban all animal-based foods from their diets immediately; both continued to consume eggs and dairy products. After his decision to lead a meat-free life, it took Zayd about thirty-six years to become a vegan in 2014. In reflecting on why he continued to eat eggs and dairy products long after eliminating meat from his diet, Zayd explained that while he knew these products were indirectly related to animal welfare, "apparently I didn't really want to acknowledge this and see it as real in its consequences for my own behaviour." Looking back, it strikes him how long it took him before he was ready to act according to his knowledge.

In Loan's situation, it took around fifteen years to shift from vegetarianism to veganism. For Loan, omnivores' remarks about her vegetarian food style triggered this transition. Teasing remarks that she was not a real vegetarian as long as she was eating cheese and eggs, and wearing leather shoes—reactions that will sound familiar to many vegetarians—made Loan think in the course of time: "actually, they are right." As a result, she gradually eliminated eggs from her diet and ceased wearing leather products and eventually also gave up her favorite cheese and chocolate. In practice, the latter was helped with the welcome market introduction of tasty vegan cheese and chocolate alternatives. As a result, Loan has been a "real" vegan for more than six years.

Vegetarians' motivations traditionally attract scholarly attention,[14] and for Zayd and Loan the key motive is animal welfare. As they explained, avoiding animal suffering and distancing themselves from a food system that kills animals for human consumption are the main ethical motives for them to adopt a plant-based diet. Signficantly, both were keen to emphasize that while concerns relating to health and environmental sustainability—two other important categories that are often cited as important reasons to become vegetarian—are also important to them, they are not the key decisive factors driving them to become and remain vegan.

EATING ANIMALS

Neither Loan nor Zayd consider themselves as activist vegans trying to persuade other people to forego animal products, or confront others with their meat-eating practices. Probably for this reason, neither interviewee recognizes themselves as the type of stereotypical vegetarian who easily arouses irritation in non-vegetarians by accusing them of acting immorally in eating animal products.[15] Nor are they aware whether other people characterize their personality more positively because of their veganism, as suggested by a recent study of Christina Hartmann and colleagues.[16] Hartmann and colleagues' research indicated that consumers of vegetarian products were perceived as more health conscious, environmentally friendly, animal loving or braver than the personality evaluation of people who consume meat products.

All this doesn't imply that Loan and Zayd always feel comfortable in every social situation. Loan, for instance, feels repulsed by people eating half a chicken—her favorite animal—and she has sad memories of a situation where she was in the company of people who all had half a chicken on their plate. Zayd also admits that he doesn't feel at ease in a setting in which he is surrounded by table companions eating animals; that is, having dinner with "omnies" is alright for about an hour, but beyond that period of time Zayd starts feeling awkward. The contrast between his eating habits and sense of morality, and his companions' practices begins to feel oppressive, and the corny jokes about the duck on the plate that will not fly high anymore are no longer funny. "At these moments and in such situations I can feel lonely and isolated," Zayd explains. This sense of isolation was also recognized by Loan, who explains that in most social situations, being vegan is self-evident and not something that has to be discussed, let alone defended. However, in social settings where her identity as a vegan is explicitly recognized, difficult personal or social situations can arise.

Because both interviewees do not want to be a moralist or a militant, they guess that perhaps they subconsciously try to avoid these uneasy aspects of social life. However, both also realize that sometimes more deliberate thoughts and actions are involved in social interactions. Zayd recognizes that on rare occasions when he knows that "meat is involved," he will avoid certain social obligations or consciously cut social encounters short. Loan says that at times she declines an invitation for a barbecue or dislikes the idea of dining out, for instance, in Greece, because "it is unpleasant to me to be confronted with all the meat and fish presented as delicacies."[17]

More frequently, the interviewees will intentionally seek out social eating opportunities that align with their principles. As Zayd explains: "Lately, various passionate and animal-conscious people in the catering industry have started vegan eating houses in different Dutch cities. A couple of my fellow vegans and I follow this development and visit the (new) vegan hotspots to enjoy the food on the menu and each other's company."

The fact that both their partners as well as many friends of Zayd and Loan are vegan or vegetarian is no coincidence; this is something they both realize and appreciate. Loan remembers:

> In the beginning, my partner still ate meat on and off and it was not nice for me to watch this. I'm so happy that my beloved one is now almost as much a vegan as I am. I believe I would have serious difficulties with loving a meat-loving partner. I'm afraid I could not manage to quarrel about meat time and again. I mean, you can avoid a barbecue at someone else's place, but you cannot avoid your partner eating meat at the dining table in our own home. (Loan)

The value in having a supportive, like-minded partner and social network was highlighted by Rosenfeld and Burrow, who observed that "a scarcity of nearby vegetarians can prevent an individual from receiving social support or developing feelings of social belongingness in food-related contexts."[18] In other words, a social network that supports one's vegetarian diet is critical.[19,20] On a more subtle level, Loan and Zayd believe that overt social support from (significant) others is not necessarily needed; simply taking a plant-based diet for granted and quietly respecting a veggie identity can suffice.

Zayd also notes with respect to fellow vegetarians and vegans that he is fully aware of the fact that the vegan social group is not uniform. He states that particularly in social media (Facebook groups and the like) it is evident that controversy and animosity exist among herbivores. Vegetarians and vegans are just ordinary people: they differ and can be intolerant to vegetarians and vegans of different beliefs.

Finally, although Loan and Zayd have no inclination to be moral crusaders, this does not mean they are not committed to the principles underpinning their decision to be a vegan. While they both agree with being polite and tolerant as much as possible to omnivores, they reject the idea that you should eat, for instance, egg-based lasagne out of politeness to the host.[21] For Zayd and Loan, to do so would be a betrayal of their personal identity and a denial of their belief in the ethical value of avoiding consuming anything of animal origin.

IS THE FUTURE OF FOOD CONSUMPTION VEGETARIAN?

Three decades have passed since Paul Amato and Sonia Partridge wrote in *The New Vegetarians:*

> Of course, it is unlikely that the majority of the people in the West will become strict vegetarians in the next few years. Nevertheless, a change in dietary habits is already occurring within the broad majority. It is not difficult to imagine that in 50 years' time, most people will be semivegetarians, eating meat occasionally, but living primarily on plant foods.[22]

While the trend toward flexitarian is hard to ignore in the Netherlands, the emergence of flexitarianism as an acceptable and attainable food style does not necessarily precede vegetarianism or veganism. It is important to remember that eating meat is still central to Dutch food culture and the food habits of most Dutch people. We should recognize that the social context not only shapes and supports meat reduction practices but also constrains and counteracts these—both mentally and materially. Zayd is fully aware of the structural conditions which make it difficult for meat rejection to thrive, and, by implication, doubtful if he will ever see a vegan society become real. Loan, for her part, conjectures that it is probably wise to postpone a vegan revolution a few decades and exchange the Amato and Partridge time frame with that of Simon Amstell's 2017 mockumentary, *Carnage*, taking 2067 as the year in which the vegetarian future will become everyday reality.

Suggested Readings

Amato, Paul R., and Sonia A. Partridge. *The New Vegetarians: Promoting Health and Protecting Life*. New York: Plenum Press, 1989.

Anderson, Eric C., Jolie Wormwood, Lisa Feldman Barrett, and Karin S. Quigley. "Vegetarians' and omnivores' affective and physiological responses to images of food." *Food Quality and Preference*, 71 (2019): 96–105.

Beardsworth, Alan, and Teresa Keil. *Sociology on the Menu: An Invitation to the Study of Food and Society*. London: Routledge, 1997.

Cooney, Nick. *Veganomics: The Surprising Science on What Motivates Vegetarians from the Breakfast Table to the Bedroom*. New York: Lantern Books, 2014.

Cramwinckel, Florien M., "The Social Dynamics of Morality." PhD diss., Utrecht University, 2016.

Dagevos, Hans, and Jantine Voordouw. "Sustainability and meat consumption: Is reduction realistic?" *Sustainability: Science, Practice, and Policy*, 9 (2013): 60–69.

Dagevos, Hans. "Exploring flexitarianism: Meat reduction in a meat-centred food culture." In *Impact of Meat Consumption on Health and Environmental Sustainability*, edited by Talia Raphaely, and Dora Marinova, 233–43. Hershey, PA: IGI Global, 2016.

Dagevos, Hans, and Machiel J. Reinders. "Flexitarianism and social marketing: Reflections on eating meat in moderation." In *Handbook of Research on Social Marketing and Its Influence on Animal Origin Food Product Consumption*, edited by Diana Bogueva, Dora Marinova, and Talia Raphaely, 105–20. Hershey, PA: IGI Global, 2018.

De Waart, Sytske. "Factsheet Consumptiecijfers en Aantal Vegetariërs" [Consumption figures and amount of vegetarians], 2018.

Hartmann, Christina, Matthew B. Ruby, Philomene Schmidt, and Michael Siegrist. "Brave, health-conscious, and environmentally-friendly: Positive impressions of insect food product consumers." *Food Quality and Preference*, 68 (2018): 64–71.

Health Council of the Netherlands. Guidelines for a Healthy Diet: The Ecological Perspective. The Hague: Health Council of the Netherlands, 2011.

Hoek, Annet C., Pieternel A. Luning, Annette Stafleu, and Cees de Graaf. "Food-related lifestyle and health attitudes of Dutch vegetarians, non-vegetarian consumers of meat substitutes, and meat consumers." *Appetite*, 42 (2004): 265–72.

Kateman, Brian, ed. *The Reducetarian Solution: How the Surprisingly Simple Act of Reducing the Amount of Meat in Your Diet Can Transform Your Health and the Planet*. New York: TarcherPerigee, 2017.

Leenaert, Tobias, *How to Create a Vegan World: A Pragmatic Approach*. New York: Lantern Books, 2017.

Rosenfeld, Daniel L., and Anthony L. Burrow. "The unified model of vegetarian identity: A conceptual framework for understanding plant-based food choices." *Appetite*, 112 (2017a): 78–95.

Rosenfeld, Daniel L., and Anthony L. Burrow. "Vegetarian on purpose: Understanding
the motivations of plant-based dieters." *Appetite* 116 (2017b): 456–63.

Rothgeber, Hank. "Attitudes toward meat and plants in vegetarians." In *Vegetarian and
Plant-Based Diets in Health and Disease Prevention*, edited by François Mariotti,
11–35. London: Academic Press, 2017.

Ruby, Matthew B. "Vegetarianism: A blossoming field of study." *Appetite* 58 (2012):
141–50.

Steinfeld, Henning, Pierre Gerber, Tom Wassenaar, Vincent Castel, Mauricio Rosales,
and Cees de Haan. *Livestock's Long Shadow: Environmental Issues and Options*.
Rome: Food and Agriculture Organization of the United Nations, 2006.

Twigg, Julia. "Vegetarianism and the meanings of meat." In *The Sociology of Food and
Eating*, edited by Anne Murcott, 18–30. Aldershot: Gower, 1983.

Verain, Muriel, Hans Dagevos, and Gerrit Antonides. "Flexitarianism: A range of sustainable food styles." In *Handbook of Research on Sustainable Consumption*, edited
by Lucia A. Reisch, and John Thøgersen, 209–23. Cheltenham: Edward Elgar
Publishing, 2015.

Verdonk, Dirk-Jan. *Het Dierloze Gerecht: Een Vegetarische Geschiedenis van Nederland*
[Animals to order: A vegetarian history of the Netherlands]. Amsterdam: Boom,
2009.

Notes

1. See, e.g., Beardsworth and Keil, *Sociology on the Menu*, 218–41.
2. See, e.g., recent issues of the journal *Appetite* to find newly-published studies.
3. De Waart, "Factsheet Consumptiecijfers."
4. Hoek, Luning, Stafleu, and De Graaf, "Food-related lifestyle and health attitudes."
5. Verdonk, *Het Dierloze Gerecht*.
6. Health Council *of the Netherlands, Guidelines for a Healthy Diet*.
7. Steinfeld, et al., *Livestock's Long Shadow*.
8. See Dagevos and Voordouw, "Sustainability and meat consumption," and Twigg, "Vegetarianism and the meanings of meat."
9. The annual sales of plant-based meat substitutes in the Netherlands have more than tripled since the beginning of this century to a total turnover of 83 million euros in 2017, and a prognosis of accelerating growth in the coming years into the direction of a 100 million euro market around 2020.
10. Dagevos and Voordouw, "Sustainability and meat consumption," and De Waart, "Factsheet Consumptiecijfers."
11. See Dagevos and Voordouw, "Sustainability and meat consumption," Dagevos, and Reinders, "Flexitarianism and social marketing," and Verain, Dagevos, and Antonides, "Flexitarianism."
12. Kateman, *The Reducetarian Solution*.

13. Rosenfeld and Burrow, "The unified model of vegetarian identity," 79. See Rothgeber, "Attitudes toward meat and plants in vegetarians," 21–22, for distinctions between vegetarians and vegans.

14. See, e.g., for recent studies Rosenfeld and Burrow, "The unified model of vegetarian identity," and Rosenfeld and Burrow, "Vegetarian on purpose."

15. See Cramwinckel, "The Social Dynamics of Morality," 33–59, and Leenaert, *How to Create a Vegan World*, 71, 101, 128–30, 165.

16. Hartmann, Ruby, Schmidt, and Siegrist, "Brave, health-conscious, and environmentally-friendly."

17. For a recent study on this issue, see Anderson, Wormwood, Feldman Barrett, and Quigley, "Vegetarians' and omnivores' affective and physiological responses to images of food." See also Cooney, *Veganomics*, 37–39.

18. Rosenfeld and Burrow, "The unified model of vegetarian identity," 80.

19. Ruby, "Vegetarianism," 143.

20. Amato and Partridge, *The New Vegetarians*, 175–204, 252–54.

21. Leenaert, *How to Create a Vegan World*, 149–50.

22. Amato and Partridge, *The New Vegetarians*, 260.

CHAPTER 13

SOUTH AFRICA

VEGAN AND VEGETARIAN COMMUNITIES IN SOUTH AFRICA

YANDISA NGQANGASHE

This chapter presents personal experiences of four South African vegetarians and vegans taking into account the diversity of the South African community. To contextualize these experiences, we first describe the meaning of food in South Africa and factors that may influence food choice. This discussion is then followed by the narration of interviews from four participants who represent three of the major ethnic groups in South Africa (Black, Indian, and White).

FOOD IN SOUTH AFRICA

Over the past century, South Africa has undergone various nutritional transitions. First, there was a shift from the traditional African diet that was mainly plant based with occasional meat consumption to more Westernized diets.[1] This pattern was previously observed more in urban areas. However, with increasing urbanization, even the people in rural areas have begun to adopt diets that entail frequent meat consumption.[2] Vegetarian or vegan lifestyles are an under-researched subject in South Africa. Although there are no empirical studies on the prevalence of these lifestyles in South Africa, the vegan societies have observed upward trends in membership.[3]

The predominance of meat as a staple food is a common denominator in the diverse South African community. Apart from meat being a staple food, slaughtering and meat consumption are an important part of some African and Indian traditions and customs. We therefore anticipate that the social implications may be different for those who routinely practice these customs, compared to those who do not. There is an ongoing debate on how cultural practices intersect with ethics and morality in a society that recognizes both human and animal rights.[4] These are the sensitivities both animal rights activists and vegan/vegetarian communities have to navigate in a plural society like South Africa.

Apart from the ethnic and cultural diversity, South Africa is also an economically diverse country with extremes of poverty and affluence co-existing.[5] Therefore, food and lifestyle have different meanings depending on the socioeconomic strata of the South African society. The general perception is that vegetarianism or veganism for animal rights mainly appeals to the privileged elite, while disadvantaged groups are more likely persuaded by perceived dangers of eating meat on their health or religious convictions. Moreover, it may be that animal rights activism is an afterthought for underprivileged communities, who have to deal with more pressing socioeconomic, gender, and racial inclusion issues. Furthermore, for most disadvantaged communities, meat is associated with affluence, and for a long time, eating meat was a luxury and represented superior social standing. Thus, in a developing country like South Africa, peoples' diets are also an indication of social mobility; going from never being able to afford meat to being able to eat meat with every meal is a reflection of one's financial prosperity. These aspirational associations can result in people being reluctant to consider reverting to diets that remind them of their poorer years.

Previous research has drawn attention to how social structure, macroeconomic, and psychological factors inform meat consumption.[6] These factors are particularly evident in the context of the cultural and social diversity in South Africa, where ethnic and class differences are likely to play a significant role in the demographics of vegetarian and vegan lifestyles. With that said, South Africa is a dynamic and constantly evolving country and the observed diversity may also underpin cultural exchange that could, in turn, influence diets. Below, we attempt to capture this diversity by interviewing vegetarians and vegans from the major ethnic groups in South Africa.

NISHA, A THIRTY-YEAR-OLD HINDU VEGETARIAN

Nisha is thirty-year-old Indian female. She is a vegetarian (i.e., she does not eat meat and also tries to reduce her consumption of other animal products). For Nisha, becoming a vegetarian was a moral decision she made when she turned nineteen and was in response to the increasing discomfort she felt with the way animals are treated, whether through factory farms or in captivity. Due to her predominantly Hindu family, her dietary change was easily accepted. Although the rest of her family eats meat, extended family such as cousins or aunts are also vegetarian. This makes life easier at family gatherings. This indicates that although religion is not a primary reason for her lifestyle choices, it nevertheless provides a conducive environment for her vegetarian lifestyle.

Unlike her home environment, Nisha reported challenges to her vegetarian lifestyle in her workplace, such as being the object of snide comments from colleagues. However, she explained that as a vegetarian, she feels she attracts less judgment than if she were a vegan. One of her bosses is also vegetarian, and Nisha feels this makes situations at work a little better during lunch, or when work gatherings are organized, as she has an "ally." This highlights the importance of having fellow vegetarians or vegans in the same social environment.

Although her friends are not vegetarian or vegan, Nisha reported that all her friends accept and understand her choices and are not in any way judgmental. However, she is also conscious to conduct herself in a way that is not abrasive or challenging. For example, she does not "call people out" for eating meat and does not bring up her lifestyle choices if they were not part of the conversations. Nisha's active "management" of her behavior therefore suggests that the way vegetarians or vegans present themselves or engage in social situations is important to their social acceptance.

As an advocate for racially inclusive and diverse societies, Nisha struggles with identifying with the affluence and elitism that characterize the vegan and vegetarian communities in South Africa. She expressed the need for the vegan community to diversify so she, as a person of color, can participate without feeling like a "sell-out": "LOL funny how a movement founded on animal rights has so many class differences and how the elite [are] hijacking it . . . this discourages others from wanting to pursue a meat free life." One study in the United States documents that it is not uncommon for intentional lifestyles such as vegan or vegetarian to exclude certain race and social classes.[7] Nisha also attributes the lack of low-cost fast food outlets for vegetarians or vegans to the elitist nature of the movement. According to Nisha, this appeal of veganism to the upper-middle class has resulted in a niche market for this population, leading to expensive vegan food. These costs are off-putting for "ordinary man" and creates a vicious cycle of exclusion: "Obviously one group dominates the movement, there is very little consideration of how other groups practice veganism/vegetarianism while still retaining their identity."

THABO, A THIRTY-YEAR-OLD ADVENTIST VEGETARIAN

Thabo is a thirty-year old black male, who became a vegetarian for health and religious reasons. He is an Adventist and his church advocates for vegetarian and vegan lifestyles. There is ample literature on the health outcomes of Adventist members, with much of the research indicating that reducing the consumption of animal products does indeed reduce health risks.[8] At home, he observed no barriers because his mother is also a vegetarian and they are a small family who provide support and understanding. His family also practices Adventism, and therefore they do not engage in cultural practices that involve slaughtering meat. Thus, even though vegetarianism or veganism would present challenges to a typical African man his age, his family's religion is protective in this regard.

In contrast, his friends or the people he prefers socializing with outside of his family are not vegetarians or Adventists. Due to this, he faces social exclusion; he reported that very few of his friends accept his lifestyle. Most people in his friendship circles question his lifestyle and hardly cater his needs. Sometimes he does not get invited to BBQs (Braais) and sometimes opts not to attend gatherings to avoid explaining: "People don't invite me to Braais because I'm a vegetarian, they give lame excuses like 'you don't eat meat so what will you do at the Braai. "Sometimes I choose not to attend to avoid having to explain myself." BBQs (Braai) is a big part of South African culture and a way people relax or spend time with each other and so exclusion from these social occasions can be unpleasant and distressing. In general, he feels his lifestyle is more understood by educated and upper-middle-class people compared to poor rural people to whom he must always explain his lifestyle. This highlights the associations between a vegetarian and vegan lifestyle and affluence, and shows how different social classes have different meanings for food.

MEGAN, A THIRTY-ONE-YEAR-OLD
WHITE FEMALE VEGETARIAN

Megan is a thirty-one-year-old white female and has not consumed meat in twenty-one years. She was a vegetarian for ten years and then became vegan eleven years ago. Her veganism is rooted in ethical abolitionism meaning she opposes all animal use by human beings. Megan also refers to herself as a non-intersectional vegan and perceives being a vegan as more activism than lifestyle. "My reasons are completely ethical and moral, I am an ethical abolitionist non intersectional vegan. I am completely against the exploitation, suffering, cruelty and murder of animals who are sentient beings."

Megan reported that as soon as people find out she is a vegan, they make rude and cruel jokes about the death of animals. She feels that most vegans complain about this behavior. Her veganism has had an immense impact on her social life, such that there is a rift between her and her family due to her lifestyle and that she hardly sees them. She also reports to have very few friends and does not accept any invitations to places where there will be meat. In general, she is misanthropic due to how humans treat animals. In her case, her lifestyle and activism has had huge implications on her social interactions, as she generally avoids humans. When she is with people, she always does some activism explaining animal rights, and referring them to documents. Her social life and activism are therefore in a way intertwined. She reports that she has no support systems as she has no vegan friends or family: "I have very few friends and seldom see my family because of my journey. I'm mostly misanthropic due to the cruelty that most humans pay for . . . I avoid them whenever I can and when I do interact with humans I do some activism and point out the cruelty of a non-vegan diet." She is, however, part of a very active online community from which she gets and gives major support. Despite this, she feels she would like to have a stronger support system of vegan people offline as well. In terms of the environment, she found that South Africa was conducive for her lifestyle and activism. There are adequate restaurants and there are always vegetables on the menu. Her stance is clear, as she will not sit at a table where animal cruelty is being practiced.

MPHO, A THIRTY-FOUR-YEAR-OLD
BLACK FEMALE VEGETARIAN

Mpho is a thirty-four-year-old black female who has been a vegetarian since she was a teen, primarily for health reasons. She specifically mentioned that religion and animal rights were not her reasons, she just felt that being vegetarian was healthier. Mpho's father was vegetarian but Mpho did not attribute her lifestyle choice to her father's influence. However, studies show that teens with vegetarian parents are more likely to identify as vegetarians.[9] She feels that people find the idea of being a vegetarian strange, but in her family it is a norm because her father was a vegetarian, and she and her sister are also vegetarians. Her mother only eats chicken, and thus, meat consumption is not central to her family's diet. This is not a norm for most Xhosa families, especially given cultural practices around weddings where certain parts of an animal are to be consumed by the bride as a sacred part of an induction process into marriage life and welcoming to the new family. Mpho married into a non-vegetarian family and she was therefore expected to follow these practices to induct her as a new wife. This would have implications for any vegetarian marrying into a Xhosa family; however, in her case this was not an issue. Her lifestyle was communicated to the new family prior to the wedding day, and everyone agreed to accommodate her by modifying the process: "We spoke to my husband's family in advance, they were very understanding . . . they still slaughtered the animal and I went through all the processes except that I did not eat the meat."

Mpho finds people express curiosity over the reasons for her vegetarian lifestyle and sometimes assume that meat makes her sick. Upon finding out that meat does not make her sick, there is a tendency to convince her to eat it. When it comes to friends, she felt like they all accepted her lifestyle, and she occasionally suggests restaurants that have more vegetarian options when they go out to eat. Her social interactions are generally not affected by her lifestyle. She reported that most times when she gets invited to BBQs she packs her own food so that the hosts do not feel like they have to accommodate her. On the other hand, when she hosts BBQs, she does make sure that there is meat for non-vegetarians: "I'm easy going . . . most times I go to Braais I pack my own vegetarian foods so people don't have to accommodate me. I also host Braais even though I don't eat meat and I make sure there is meat for people that are not vegetarians."

DISCUSSION

In this chapter, four South Africans shared their experiences of following vegetarian or vegan lifestyles. Although the participants come from different cultural backgrounds, they are all middle class and reside in urban areas. This may be an indication that most people who are likely to identify as vegan or vegetarian come from more affluent communities. However, there may be vegetarians or vegans from rural areas or lower socioeconomic status communities where excluding meat from one's diet is not viewed as a lifestyle, and these individuals do not identify as vegetarians or vegans. Although some complained about the lack of suitable meat-free meals on restaurant menus, there are still basic options, especially in urban areas. Therefore, although South Africa is a meat-eating country it is still a conducive environment to lead vegan or vegetarian lifestyles, as a result of the great cultural diversity of the population. Two of the interviewees showed appreciation for cities with high numbers of Indian people, reflecting that these offer better vegetarian food options. In this context, vegan or vegetarian lifestyles may offer opportunities for cultural exchange and bridge gaps between different ethnic groups. The interviewees presented different reasons for being vegetarian or vegan; some were more personal (health and religion) while others were more (ethical). This aligns with previous research, which has identified a dichotomy of personal versus moral reasons people choose vegetarian or vegan lifestyles.[10] These were the factors also observed to influence the maintenance of vegetarian or vegan lifestyles.

Across the individual respondents, having other vegetarians in their social environment helps with normalizing their lifestyles. However, Megan, whose veganism is central to her identity and influences her attitudes and behavior, appeared to have the most limited social interactions. Her social isolation is perhaps not surprising, given that, as Fischler notes, people socialize and form identities through the consumption of food.[11] In contrast, the vegetarians expressed flexibility and reflected more of a lifestyle approach to their diet. The vegetarian interviewees tend to adjust themselves to fit with meat eaters, such as by avoiding references to the vegetarian lifestyle in conversations or by taking their own food to BBQs to receive less backlash from society.

In conclusion, based on these four interviews, the social implications for leading vegan or vegetarian lifestyles vary depending on religion, cultural practices, social environment, and how the vegetarians or vegans present themselves. Pro-vegan and pro-vegetarian religious beliefs and the presence of allies in social environments normalize the lifestyle and increase acceptance. There is an intersection between identity and food choice from race to animal rights activism. There is a difference in how the society receives veganism versus vegetarianism as a lifestyle or as activism. Elements of elitism and exclusivity dominate the vegan and vegetarian communities.

Suggested Readings

Aguilar, Jade. "Food choices and voluntary simplicity in intentional communities: What's race and class got to do with it?" *Utopian Studies* 26, no. 1 (2015) :79–100 DOI: 10.5325/utopianstudies.26.1.0079.

Bourne, Lesley T., Estelle V. Lambert, and Krisela Steyn. "Where does the black population of South Africa stand on the nutrition transition?" *Public Health Nutrition* 5, no. 1 (February 2002): 157–62, https://doi.org/10.1079/PHN2001288.

Fischler, Claude. "Food, self and identity." *Information (International Social Science Council)* 27, no. 2 (June 1988): 275–92 https//DOI:10.1177/053901888027002005.

Gossard, Marcia Hill and Richard York. "Social structural influences on meat consumption." *Human Ecology Review* 10, no.1 (Summer 2003): 1–9, https://www.jstor.org/stable/i24707080.

Jabs, Jennifer, Carol M. Devine, and Jeffrey Sobal. "Maintaining vegetarian diets: Personal factors, social networks and environmental resourses." *Canadian Journal of Dietetic Practice and Research* 59, no. 4 (Winter 1998) 183–89.

May, Julian and Juby Govender. "Poverty and inequality in South Africa." *Indicator South Africa* 15: 53–58, http://www.academia.edu/download/31219257/presentation.pdf (accessed April 15, 2018).

Newman, Latoya. "Vegan lifestyle gains favour." *IOL,* https://www.iol.co.za/lifestyle/food-drink/vegan-lifestyle-gains-favour-7575332 (Accessed April 2017).

Ross, Eleanor. "The intersection of cultural practices and ethics in a rights-based society: Implications for South African social workers." *International Social Work* 51, no. 3 (1998), 384–95, https:DOI:10.1177/0020872807088804.

Willett, Walter. "Lessons from dietary studies in Adventists and questions for the future." *The American Journal of Clinical Nutrition* 78, no. 3 (September 2003), 539S–43S, https://doi.org/10.1093/ajcn/78.3.539S.

Worsley, Anthony and Grace Skrzypiec. "Teenage vegetarianism: Prevalence, social and cognitive contexts." *Appetite* 30, no. 2 (April 1998) DOI:151–70 10.1006/appe.1997.011.

Notes

1. Bourne, Lesley T., Estelle V. Lambert, and Krisela Steyn. "Where does the black population of South Africa stand on the nutrition transition?" *Public Health Nutrition* 5, no. 1 (February, 2002): 157–62 https://doi.org/10.1079/PHN2001288.

2. Bourne, et al., "Black population on nutrition transition," 157–62.

3. Newman, Latoya. 2017. "Vegan lifestyle gains favour." *IOL,* https://www.iol.co.za/lifestyle/food-drink/vegan-lifestyle-gains-favour-7575332 (accessed April 2017).

4. Ross, Eleanor. "The intersection of cultural practices and ethics in a rights-based society: Implications for South African social workers." *International Social Work* 51, no. 3 (2008) 384–95, https://DOI.org:10.1177/0020872807088804.

5. May, Julian and Juby Govender. "Poverty and inequality in South Africa." *Indicator South Africa*, 15:53–58, http://www.academia.edu/download/31219257/presentation.pdf. (accessed April 15, 2018).

6. Gossard, Marcia Hill and Richard York. "Social structural influences on meat consumption." *Human Ecology Review 10*, no. 1 (Summer 2003), 1–9, https://www.jstor.org/stable/i24707080.

7. Aguilar, Jade. "Food choices and voluntary simplicity in intentional communities: What's race and class got to do with it?" *Utopian Studies* 26, no. 1: 79–100 (2015), https://DOI.org: 10.5325/utopianstudies.26.1.0079.

8. Willett, Walter. "Lessons from dietary studies in Adventists and questions for the future. *The American Journal of Clinical Nutrition* 78, no. 3 (September 2003) 539S–43S, https://doi.org/10.1093/ajcn/78.3.539S.

9. Worsley, Anthony and Grace Skrzypiec. "Teenage vegetarianism: Prevalence, social and cognitive contexts." *Appetite* 30, no. 2 (April 1998), https://DOI.org:151-70 10.1006/appe.1997.0118.

10. Jabs, Jennifer, Carol M. Devine, and Jeffrey Sobal. "Maintaining vegetarian diets: Personal factors, social networks and environmental resources. *Canadian Journal of Dietetic Practice and Research* 59, no 4 (Winter 1998) 183–89.

11. Fischler, Claude. "Food, self and identity." *Information (International Social Science Council)* 27, no. 2 (June 1988): 275–92, https//DOI/10.1177/053901888027002005.

CHAPTER 14

TURKEY

DO WORLDVIEWS CHANGE THROUGH EATING HABITS? INCARNATION OF A TURKISH VEGAN

ILKAY KANIK

Many people in Turkey consume dairy and meat daily, and red meat consumption is part of the Turkish dominant high culture. Despite this, veganism and vegetarianism have become more popular, and vegans and vegetarians in Turkey are constructing their own hybrid-identities. This study tells the story of a young Turkish woman who has constructed her own dietary culture, identity, social relationship via the means of veganism. With a descriptive approach of my study, I also analyzed secondary survey data related to the topic; a survey conducted by Yasemin Tuncay Son in her PhD dissertation "Veganism and Vegetarianism within the Framework of Bioethics." This study has revealed that vegans' and vegetarians' choices are individually formed.[1] In the last fifteen years the number of Turkish people that prefer to avoid animal products in their diet is increasing. Despite this growth, few academic studies have investigated Turkish culinary choices, consumption habits, lifestyles, and the difficulties faced by vegans and vegetarians.[2] There are no national-level statistical data about the numbers of vegans and vegetarians in Turkey, but there are some academic studies that focus on particular cities. One such study focuses on vegans and vegetarians living in Ankara, and revealed that they have an urban, well-educated and professional backgrounds, are most often women, between the ages of eighteen and thirty-four, single, and with no children.[3] When asked why they became vegan and vegetarian, participants from this study said that they were against "animal exploitation" and had ethical concerns such as: respect for sentient beings' life, conscientiousness, ecology, feminism, and living a healthy life among other reasons for their dietary choice.[4]

Overall, in Turkey vegans and vegetarians are marginalized as individuals for their dietary choice, and they have to defend their identity against such marginalization.[5] This chapter provides an example of this by exploring the experiences of a Turkish woman, Sedef T., who lives in Istanbul and works in the tourism industry. She became a vegan fifteen months prior to the interview, is happy about her dietary choice and is determined to continue as such. Sedef's life changed after reading a book on veganism: Yuval Noah Harari's book *Hayvanlardan Tanrılara: Sapiens.*[6] After reading Hariri's book, Sedef searched the Internet about veganism and learned how to become a vegan. Having read her first book on veganism, Sedef began to question her dietary choices, to reflect more systematically on them and to construct her new vegan identity by means of other media.[7] She began to think more about the exploitation and commercialization of animals, and the unacceptability of animals being kept forcefully in animal farms. "All milk bottles have smiling and happy animals on them and we are made to believe that milk products are just a normal and healthy part of our lives" says Sedef. After reading about the actual milk production she became determined to become a vegan. She explains this by saying that "just as humans do, animals give birth after nine months and their milk is just for their offspring. However, calves are separated from their mother just after the birth for the sake of profit maximization. Thus, calves and their mothers are not allowed to form sentimental ties. You can find moving passages in Harari's book and watch documentaries regarding animal welfare. How sad!" Her reflections are in line with other studies that have shown how veganism has more to do with animal rights than with health.[8] Sedef does not believe that becoming a vegan for health reasons gives us sufficient grounds to change our dietary choice. For Sedef, becoming a vegan for health reasons is an instance of selfishness and is an unattractive choice. By contrast, she thinks that a vegan should become so because of a conscious change in diet. For her being vegan is an ethical choice, thus she can be classified as an ethical vegan,[9] and he also describes her in that way: "I cannot eat a sentient being which can hear, see, understand, play games, interact and love just like as I do. This is like betraying my closest friend. Just for the sake of looking more beautiful or neat, I do not use cosmetic products that use animals in experiments. I am much more than this." In her opinion, health is merely a byproduct of a vegan lifestyle.

SOCIAL CONTEXT OF BEING VEGETARIAN IN TURKEY

When Sedef became vegan, it was not easy for her to defend her dietary choice as she did not know or interact with any other vegans or vegetarians in her neighborhood. Her family and boyfriend are carnivores and she found herself quarrelling with family members because they were worried that veganism is not a healthy dietary choice. Sedef's parents were concerned about her health. Especially Sedef's mother was trying to convince her that she could postpone her veganism and have eggs, cheese, and meat in her diet today. Sedef's friends were also, and perhaps even more critical of her: "My friends were making fun of me. They thought that I was trying to attract attention and look marginal. They challenged me by saying that veganism wouldn't be acceptable in Turkey, that I would starve and that I would change my dietary choice again in a short while." Placing vegan lifestyle at the center of her life, Sedef has tried to make people around her more aware of veganism. She explained to people around her why she made a particular choice and thus formed stronger ties with them. However, not all vegans and vegetarians in Turkey may have such positive experiences. Other vegans and vegetarians that I interviewed in the past had mentioned negative experiences regarding their dietary choice. Then again, as mentioned before, vegetarian dietary choices are becoming increasingly popular in Turkey, which can explain why today Sedef finds her way to explain and defend het dietary choice to others. Sedef mentions that the more people learn about veganism and vegetarianism the more positive attitudes people develop towards them: "Even if people around me are not vegans they learned how to respect my choice." Furthermore, they also got informed about veganism and started saying that "you are right."

What also supported Sedef was the increased media attention for veganism; especially the popular views on the inverse relation between health and eating meat have made it easier for Sedef to express herself and be understood.[10] Specialized social organizations also play an important role in getting a variety of identities accepted. Especially when they get a chance to showcase their activities through the means of media.[11] Several vegan and vegetarian NGOs in Turkey have made vegans and vegetarians more visible and acceptable. The first civil society movement that defended the rights of vegans and vegetarians—the Vegan and Vegetarian Association of Turkey—was established in March 2012. This association was initially a vegetarian one, but later also emphasized the vegans as a separate group under its organizational structure. The Vegan and Vegetarian Association of Turkey is a member of the Union of Vegetarians and the Union of European Vegetarians. Together they aim to inform people about the meaning of vegetarianism by telling people about the ethical, ecological, health, and social utility of vegetarianism. Lastly, also special events offer further support to vegetarianism. November 1 is being celebrated as vegan and vegetarian day both in the world and in Turkey. The county of Didim, in the province of Aydın, declared itself as a vegan county and organizes a vegan and vegetarian festival that welcomes local and international vegans and vegetarians. Following these trends, big cities like İstanbul and Ankara nowadays host lots of vegan and vegetarian restaurants.[12] Yet other parts of Turkey are still very much meat-centered; some regions have a strong tradition of meat-centered meals, and this geographical variation also influences any culinary identities. Sedef agrees that people's identities are determined by geography and adds that "when people ask me 'how you can go vegan while you come from Trace (Trakya in Turkish) a meat lover geography?' I say I can manage it."

Not just geography, but also religion plays a crucial role for vegetarianism in Turkey. Islam is the dominant religion in Turkey, and whether you are a Muslim or not determines what you eat and according to which ritual. Muslims who have sufficient wealth are religiously obliged to sacrifice an animal every year, while people that cannot afford to do this are given a share of the cooked animal. The annual sacrifice of a healthy animal, and sharing it with others is an important Muslim ceremony. It is a ritual and a means to socialize in Muslim families, and is crucial in the support of the family institution. Male children participate directly in the animal sacrifice ceremony by being present within it, whereas female children help their mothers to cook the meat. The male and female identities of children are formed within this religious context. The larger family also comes together to celebrate the animal sacrifice festival in the house of the eldest person in the family. It is also believed that the animal that is being sacrificed will spiritually protect the family both in this world and in the world to come. For this reason, choosing veganism and vegetarianism is a matter of revolt for those who grew up in

Muslim families. Sedef as a non-believer does not see any tension between her veganism and not consuming meat. She adds: "There are groups which are called Muslim Vegans. I presume, these vegans choose veganism not to protect the rights of animals *per se* but for environmental reasons. People coming from a Muslim background frequently ask me the following question: 'If you do not consume meat, what kind of a Muslim are you?' Such people assume that I am a Muslim without even recognizing my right to choose freely.' Sedef greatly informed herself about religion to accurately answer religiously-motivated questions. According to Sedef, sacrificing an animal is a remnant of shaman beliefs. According to shaman beliefs you have to sacrifice an animal to absolve yourself of your sins. Sedef explains: "It hurts me a lot to accept the anthropocentric belief that everything in the universe was created by God to serve human use. It is a great mistake for humans to assume that the World revolves around them. Furthermore, humans falsely assume that all food, animals and nature are presented to human use as a gift. Humans assume themselves as special in a diversified universe. Humans destruct and kill. I assume that is not what God means by anthropocentricism. Attributing such a negative meaning is a mockery of this concept."

Lastly, also gender influences the transition to vegetarian diets in Turkey. Socialization and hosting guests is very much separated between men and women in Turkey. Building social relationships with same-sex others revolves around food sharing. As guests, men are generally served meat or food that is mostly prepared from animal products. Women, by contrast, are served food that does not contain meat. For example, "kısır" a vegetarian food made up of pounded wheat and vegetables, is one such food. It is healthy and affordable. For this reason, it can be assumed that a vegetarian diet is more sustainable for women in Turkey. Sedef questions the socially accepted and valued relationship between male identity and being a carnivore. She criticizes this relationship and the unhealthy aspects of meat consumption. According to Sedef, it is absurd to think that meat consumption positively contributes to male identity formation, since consuming meat, in her knowledge, causes cardiovascular problems and has negative effects on testosterone levels in males.

IS IT POSSIBLE TO SHARE THE SAME MEAL?

After becoming a vegan or vegetarian the ritual of sharing a meal with others becomes different. "I presume, it was difficult for my lover, family and friends to prepare a rich breakfast for me. You know that a rich breakfast is a very important aspect of Turkish culinary culture. A rich Turkish breakfast includes a variety of cheese, eggs, honey etc. But they forget a variety of vegetables, marmalades and potatoes that enrich a vegan breakfast. They always ask me what I would like to have in the breakfast. I tell them my choice. I even bring my own food with me." Food sharing emphasizes the difference between those who do and do not eat meat, especially in a country like Turkey where meat takes a central place on the table, even at breakfast. Becoming vegetarian is for that reason never an individual choice; automatically family and friends get involved. For Sedef this was a positive experience: "My boyfriend is from Hatay and a carnivore. He tells me that his taste has been enriched since he met me." Sedef talks about a family ritual and how it changed after she became a vegan. Vegan dishes are also prepared for Sedef in large family gatherings. Large family gatherings have more meaning than just getting together for the sake of eating meat. Such meetings should serve the purpose of making family members happy and have chats over a meal. Sedef adds that "when eating a dish I do not want to make an animal suffer," and Sedef's family share her sensitivity and respect her concerns.

Going out for meals is also an important socialization event for Sedef and her urban-dwelling fellow vegans. The more they appear in public to eat vegan and vegetarian food and share their food with non-vegans and non-vegetarians the more they feel as part of the larger society. Nevertheless the number of vegan vegetarians' restaurants, cafés, and markets remains limited in big cities and is even non-existent in small cities. For this reason, it is pretty difficult to form a vegetarian lifestyle. Despite this difficulty, vegetarians persist in living the life they prefer. Having a meal with others plays a big role in the formation, strengthening, and persistence of social relationships. For it is a need that gives us joy. When Sedef and her vegetarian and non-vegetarian friends come together for a meal they often discuss the various reasons to eat or not eat meat. She notices that carnivores are often defensive and want to rationalize their choice for eating meat. Sedef is surprised by the way her friends react to her dietary choice. They question vegetarian dietary choices and wonder how a vegan diet tastes. Sedef got used to these reactions and learned how to tackle them. Sedef formed a strong vegan identity rather than isolating herself from her social environment. Sedef's positive attitude managed to transform people around her by rendering them as more understanding and empathetic to her dietary choices.

She further adds that socializing and sharing meals can be made easier with the type of food that is served. If the host or chef is liberal enough to include vegan and vegetarian food alongside meat it would be much easier to enjoy a meal together. In the Turkish cuisine, vegetarian dishes are not the main course but most often they are served as a side dish. For this reason, the culinary culture in Turkey is diverse enough so that people with different dietary choices can liberally choose the food they want to eat. As Sedef says: "Turkish cuisine is rich not only in red meat and poultry but also in vegetarian food. Turkish cuisine is a mixture of dishes rich in meat and vegetables. One can prepare only vegan or vegetarian dishes as well. My favorite dishes are green beans made of olive oil, eggplant, humus, falafel, rice and all salads. A diet that caters to the taste of both carnivores and vegetarians would be ideal, and the Turkish cuisine with its great variety of choices can offer this."

CONCLUSION

In conclusion, vegans and vegetarians in Turkey reconstruct their regional, ethnic, religious, and socio-sexual identities through their dietary choices. We can say that a vegan and vegetarian lifestyle creates a different life story. As is the case in Sedef's story this fact reveals itself both in a sympathetic under-standing and harsher confrontations. Sedef says that she values the positive attitude of her boyfriend and family. She received support from her family and friends for changing her dietary choice: "It seems I am lucky a person for receiving support from my family and friends. They accepted me for whom I am." Sedef further emphasizes that veganism made her a different person, and her identity has diverged from those that are not vegan. Veganism has changed her self-perception by rendering her a more sensitive and respectful person. She explains her transformation by saying that "ever since I became a vegan I consider myself as a more sensitive individual in my social rela-tionships, and as more respectful to animals and to my environment. Rather than consuming as if the natural resources are unlimited, I take a stand in my consumption by thinking about the future generations." Becoming vegan, she felt she became a better person, a nice reflection to end this story.

Suggested Readings

Aysu Altaş, "Vegetarianism and veganism: Current situation in Turkey in the light of examples in the world," *Journal of Tourism and Gastronomy Studies* 5/4 (2017): 403–21.

Silvia Ilonka Wolf, "We Are All Animals: The Emergence of Grassroots Nonhuman Animal Rights Movement in İstanbul" (Master's thesis. Sabancı University, 2015), http://research.sabanciuniv.edu/34374/.

Silvia Ilonka Wolf, "We are all animals: The emergence of grosstoots nonhuman animal rights movement in İstanbul," *Interface: A Journal For and About Social Movements*, 7(1), (May 2015): 40–69.

Tunçay Son, G. Y. and Bulut, M. "Yaşam Tarzı Olarak Vegan ve Vejetaryenlik." *International Journal of Human Sciences*, 13(1), (2016), 830–43.

Yasemin Tuncay Son, "Biyoetik Çerçevesinde Vegan ve Vejetaryenlik" (PhD diss., Ankara University, 2016), http://acikarsiv.ankara.edu.tr/eng/browse/29850/.

Notes

1. Yasemin Tuncay Son, "Biyoetik Çerçevesinde Vegan ve Vejetaryenlik" (PhD diss., Ankara University, 2016): 16, http://acikarsiv.ankara.edu.tr/eng/browse/29850/.
2. Yasemin Tuncay Son, "Biyoetik Çerçevesinde Vegan ve Vejetaryenlik" (PhD diss., Ankara University, 2016); Silvia Ilonka Wolf, "We Are All Animals: The Emergence of Grassroots Nonhuman Animal Rights Movement in İstanbul" (Master's thesis. Sabancı University, 2015), http://research.sabanciuniv.edu/34374/; Yasemin Tunçay Son, G. Y. and Bulut, M., "Yaşam Tarzı Olarak Vegan ve Vejetaryenlik" *International Journal of Human Sciences*, 13(1), (2016): 830–43; Aysu Altaş, "Vegetarianism and veganism: Current situation in Turkey in the light of examples in the world," *Journal of Tourism and Gastronomy Studies,* 5/4 (2017): 403–21.
3. Son. Ibid.
4. Son. Ibid., 145–46.
5. Son. Ibid.., 80.
6. Yuval Noah Harari, *Hayvanlardan Tanrılara-Sapiens* (Istanbul: Kolektif Kitap, 2016, 2st edition).
7. Nathan Stephens Griffin, *Understanding Veganism* (New York: Palgrave Macmillan, 2017), 7.
8. Jessica Greenebaum, "Veganism, identity and the quest for authenticity." *Food Culture and Society*. Vol. 15, Issue 1 (2012): 130.
9. Greenebaum, Ibid., 129.
10. "Kırmızı etin faydaları ve zararları nelerdir?" August 31, 2018, *haber7com*, accessed September 10, 2018, http://www.haber7.com/saglik/haber/2693801-kirmizi-etin-faydalari-ve-zararlari-nelerdir; Didem Seymen, Her gün kırmızı et, erken ölüm riskini artırıyor, *Sabah*, March 14, 2012; accessed September 10, 2018; Neslihan Tunç, "Aşırı et tüketimi iklimi bozuyor." *Sabah,* April 10, 2010, accessed September 10, 2018, https://www.sabah.com.tr/cumartesi/guncel/2010/04/10/asiri_et_tuketimi_iklimi_bozuyor; https://hthayat.haberturk.com/saglik/beslenme/haber/1054779-fazla-et-tuketiminin-zararlari.
11. John Hailey, "Indicators of Identity: NGOs and the Strategic Imperative of Assessing Core Values," *Development in Practice*, Vol. 10, Nos. 3 and 4, (2000): 402–406.
12. Restaurants, cafés, and markets for vegans and vegetarians in Istanbul: Zencefil; Bir Nevi Deli; Mahatma café & Restoran; Vegan İstanbul; Galata Kitchen; İyi Lokanta; Cafe 11; Rulo Lezzetler; Bi'nevi Karaköy; Kikero Falafel; Govinda İstanbul; Komşu Kafe; Collective; Ecoisthan Vegan & Vegetarian Restaurant; Nature & Peace, Cafe Zabata; Bombalara Karşı Sofralar; Cook & Book; Mahatma; Rulo Ezber Bozan Lezzetler; Tight Aggressive; Muhtelif Mekan Kadıköy; Aşina Kafe Mutfak; Vegan Bakkal; Naan Bakeshop

CHAPTER 15

UNITED KINGDOM

I AM NOT AWKWARD, I AM JUST A VEGETARIAN. TRIALS AND TRIBULATIONS OF A VEGETARIAN IN THE UK

CHRYSOSTOMOS APOSTOLIDIS

INTRODUCTION—VEGETARIANISM IN THE UK

In the UK, vegetarians account for approximately 10 percent of the total adult population, as people are increasingly embracing alternative ways of living and eating. This becomes even more prevalent among the young female demographic, with one in four young women reportedly cutting meat out of their diet. On the other hand, veganism remains a niche lifestyle, with only 1 percent of the overall UK population following a vegan diet.[1]

Like in many other Western countries, most UK vegetarians were not raised as such, but decided to convert from a meat-eating diet for a range of different reasons, including concerns about animal welfare, environmental sustainability, personal health, and taste.[2,3] Lifestyle campaigns and social media have played a key role in the growing interest in vegetarianism in the UK, as many consumers (especially young adults) have been influenced by campaigns and social media "celebrities" encouraging less meat-based diets.[4,5]

Although the above suggests that vegetarianism is an increasingly accepted lifestyle, UK remains primarily a nation of meat eaters. Even for people that have removed animal products from their diets, vegetarianism is not always an easy task. Research reports several personal and social challenges, such as meat cravings, nutritional concerns, social awkwardness, stigma and inconvenience, which vegetarians face in different aspects of their lives.[6] In this chapter, I will try to answer some of the key questions relating to the experiences of vegetarians in the UK, through an in-depth interview with a long-term vegetarian.

Laura (not her real name) is a representative of the young female vegetarian demographic in the UK. She gave up eating meat and fish ten years ago, when she was eighteen years old, and her diet is predominantly based on vegetables and carbohydrates, like pasta and rice. She is not completely dairy- and egg-free though, as she would still occasionally eat food products containing eggs, milk, or cheese, which categorizes Laura as a "lacto-ovo vegetarian," according to the Vegetarian Society.[7] Pulses and beans are the main protein sources in her diet, while she is not too keen on meat substitutes, as: "If they are trying to make it look like meat, then I am not interested in it. I love vegetables, so I always stick to vegetables."

MOTIVES FOR ADOPTING A VEGETARIAN DIET

Laura always struggled with the idea of eating animals and she never liked the taste of meat. Then she started feeling unwell just by the look of meat: "It just got too much at some point, so I decided to stay clear." Therefore, in Laura's case, the decision to adopt a vegetarian diet had less to do with environmental and health concerns and was motivated mainly by a disgust of eating meat. Disgust at the thought of eating animals is rather common in Western societies, especially among female consumers.[8] Although not directly linked to animal welfare concerns, disgust is reportedly higher for animals commonly classified as pets or perceived as possessing similar mental and emotional capacities as humans, which is also confirmed by Laura: "It's the association sometimes; I would never eat a rabbit for example. Looks too much like a pet."

BARRIERS IN THE ADOPTION OF A VEGETARIAN DIET

Despite vegetarianism recently gaining traction in the UK, Laura indicates that following a vegetarian lifestyle is not always convenient. Eating out remains one of the main challenges for vegetarians, despite the UK foodservice sector taking steps to embrace vegetarianism:[9] "If we're going somewhere that I haven't been before, I need to check out the menu. If it is a place that would normally have only one [vegetarian] option, if you don't like that option you have to go 'can I change this with that?,' which is awkward."

Getting enough protein in their diets can be another major challenge for vegetarians, particularly in countries like the UK, where consumers rely heavily on animal proteins.[10] In the question as to where she gets her protein from, Laura replies, "I don't, if I'm being honest. I've been told that I need to eat more protein, so I try to eat more beans." Although several plant-based protein food products have entered the UK market, aiming to substitute meat in consumers' diets, their market share remains limited, mainly due to aesthetic and value-for-money reasons.[11]

YOU ARE WHAT YOU EAT? HOW DO PEOPLE PERCEIVE THOSE WHO EAT VEGETARIAN?

Laura describes how meat eaters do not consider vegetarians as "normal" people, using a particular incident as an example: "I've had occasions where I just kept finding bits of meat in my food. Once, I raised it with the chef and he came out and yelled at me, because they were saying there is no meat in it. I found out they were using the same pan to cook some sort of pasta sauce that had meat in it and used the same pan to cook mine. [...] They said they only cater for 'normal' diets, so obviously I am not normal."

According to Laura, this is because many people still have an old-fashioned view on vegetarianism or they do not take vegetarians seriously: "People believe you are a hippie. When you are not familiar with any vegetarians you get this stereotypical, tree-hugging hippie image in your mind. It's an old-fashioned view, sort of 70s. I think many people also think it's a trend. Or it's a phase I've been going through; something I did to wind my parents up."

Laura adds that people's lack of knowledge and understanding of vegetarianism is evident in the way they describe vegetarians: "Sometimes, I think it's the way some people phrase it—you're awkward, you're fussy, you're picky—it's a little bit annoying. I'm not fussy, I'm not awkward, I'm not picky; I'm just a vegetarian." Stereotyping and stigmatization of their dietary patterns may encourage some vegetarians to develop ways to appear more "normal" and avoid tensions in social situations. Nonetheless, Laura highlights that despite what people think, she generally will not try to explain to others her vegetarian lifestyle choice: "If I'm asked I will tell them, but I'm not trying to push my views on anyone. I just think, you know what? You can think what you like, I'm not going to eat this food."

Nevertheless, in line with research reporting the increasing interest in less meat-based diets,[12] Laura also argues there seems to be a positive trajectory in the way people see vegetarians in the UK. "I think over the past ten years, society has changed, became more aware." According to Laura, animal welfare and health are the primary reasons for the changing perceptions of vegetarian diets: "Vegetarianism becomes a bit more prevalent, not only for the animal aspect of it, but also because people are trying to be healthier. I think it is becoming more accepted. More people can understand it—especially my generation. I have friends that when they hear I am a vegetarian they are like 'Oh, I'd like to be a vegetarian,' because people are a lot more aware now than previous generations." This statement also indicates that younger consumers may hold more positive views on vegetarian diets. The impact of age (as well as other socio-demographic characteristics, such as gender and income) on perceptions of vegetarianism have been identified also in earlier studies relating to vegetarianism in the UK.[13] Interestingly, Laura adds another aspect to this discussion, linking positive perceptions of vegetarianism with moral awareness resulting from people's profession, as she argues there is a strong presence of vegetarians among lawyers: "I'm in law and there is a lot of lawyers who are vegetarians. I think they see a link between human rights and animal rights. So law functions are usually well-catered for vegetarians."

When asked if she thinks that today vegetarians are the people that others look up to, Laura replies that it is a generation thing: "Some do, but I think it's limited. I think people in my generation do, as it is such a big thing now. They need to be healthier, as they see obesity levels rise and these issues are promoted more and more now. I think that's a greater incentive for people my age to be keen to reducing meat, and I have many friends who are saying 'I wish I could do it, but I could never give up my bacon sandwich.' Older generation no, they just see the whole idea of being a vegetarian as a fad." Social media and influencers have played an important role in raising the profile of vegetarian diets, particularly in younger demographics.[14] According to Janda and Trocchia,[15] although this type of social influence can elevate vegetarians to an aspirational reference group and result in an increasing interest in vegetarianism, its effectiveness may be short-lived, as people will not continue following a vegetarian lifestyle once they stop considering it trendy and unique.

VEGETARIAN VERSUS MEAT CHOICES, SOCIAL, AND PRACTICAL ISSUES

Laura explains that her family has always been supportive of her decision to become a vegetarian, even though sometimes they do not know how to deal with her dietary requirements. She clearly remembers the first time when she "came out" as a vegetarian to her family: "They were obviously a bit shocked when I told them at that time. I was still living at home and I knew the impact that it would have on my mom, as she would be the one that had to deal with this, because she was the one who had to cook two separate meals every night, so I was nervous to tell her."

Generally, Laura does not seek the support of other vegetarians, as people close to her are supportive of her dietary choices and the impact these choices have on cooking at home or eating out: "On the whole, my family are all very good about cooking for me. My husband is not a vegetarian, so he has to suffer sometimes, as he cannot go to the places he would like to go because they are not so good for me. He is very supportive however."

Although convenience has been reported as one practical issue related to vegetarian diets, Laura explains how food- and cooking-related activities take place in her (not completely meat-free) household: "At home I make the same dishes, but one just has veggies in it [. . .] I always use one side of the cooker for one utensil and the other side for another. I just have to remember always which is which." Of course, Laura's husband also had to learn how to deal with everyday things: "He's good now, as we are together for so long, so he is careful what he is using. So, if he wants to try my food he will always use my fork."

Although the discussion so far suggests that people are generally supportive to vegetarians, the uncertainty of how to cater for people avoiding meat can cause stress to vegetarians and their close ones, indicating that people may still lack the knowledge and mindfulness required in food-related interactions with people with different dietary requirements: "I'm always nervous about what's in things, even if it is my family cooking. Because everyone remembers about not giving me any actual meat, but I always have to think, what's in this, what does the gravy have in it?"

This can also make social occasions, like family and friend gatherings, quite stressful for vegetarians, indicating that vegetarianism is still considered a niche lifestyle: "Barbeques are always 'fun.' If you go to someone else's barbeque, you always wonder: have they actually kept my bit just vegetarian? Have they used the tongs for the burgers and then used them for my burger? [. . .] Another time I get really nervous is when I go to some-body's wedding and I'm like: Right, so I'll have to tell you that there is no vegetarian choice on the menu."

Therefore, in many cases, vegetarians have to accept that they will need to make sacrifices when attending such social occasions: "I'm quite good at recognizing that what I can eat will be quite limited, so when I go to something like a family do, and it's some sort of buffet, I recognise that what I'll be eating is some cherry tomatoes and probably not much else and I just get on with it."

VEGETARIAN VERSUS MEAT CHOICES, ETHICAL ISSUES

Following the subject of "awkward" social situations, the discussion contin-ues on what happens in cases where people with different dietary choices meet. Laura states emphatically "I will adjust as the vegetarian. Even if I am the host, I'll try to cook what other people enjoy eating. To be a good host you have to cook something that they [guests] enjoy." My next question to Laura is obvious; don't you think that this contradicts your values as a vegetarian? "Not really," she replies, "I do care about animals of course and I do wish animals were treated better, but in reality, I know that forcing vegetarian food on people will not fix it." There are however certain rules to what Laura considers acceptable: "I won't allow a few things and I apply this with my husband and guests as well; there's no veal, no foie gras, so anything that adds a level of cruelty to the animal. And of course, that goes with eating out as well. When it comes to more regular types of meat however, like pork, beef or chicken, I'm quite realistic and as long as I am not aware of any malpractice and they come from a reputable source then I am ok cooking it for others."

The above discussion relates to a long-standing debate regarding the stance vegetarians adopt toward the food choices of others. Although some vegetarians tend to object to others eating meat, as they consider ethical and/or health considerations should influence everyone's food choices, oth-ers see this as a personal lifestyle choice and thus other people should be allowed their own views.[16] In the question of whether she thinks that a vegetarian diet would be better for everyone, as they need to consider the ethical, environmental, and health impact of what they are eating, Laura replies that for her, everyone should be free to make their own choices: "To me, it's your health, it's your own decision, you can eat whatever you want. I guess I have a very realist's point of view on that. To me, if someone else wants to eat meat, I don't have a problem."

Interestingly, Laura indicates that ethical controversies do not only occur between meat eaters and vegetarians, but can also happen between different vegetarian groups, due to the loosely defined term of a "vegetarian diet": "I struggle with people that claim to be vegetarians and still eat fish. I'd rather if they called themselves just pescatarians, because they are not vegetarians, they still eat something with a face. [...] Another thing I always question, is when someone has turned to veganism or vegetarianism because of animal rights or animal welfare, but they wear leather [...] I have to look away and try to hold in a bit of a chuckle. I always think 'a bit of a hypocrite in your leather boots.'"

Rothgerber[17] argues that this "horizontal hostility" among non-meat eaters, is not only related to differences in their consumption patterns, but it is mainly influenced by the underlying motives for abstaining from meat. For example, ethically-motivated vegetarians may consider themselves as more dedicated than health-motivated vegetarians, as they may consider that the latter are less determined and morally-driven, which may influence their perceptions and interactions with different vegetarian groups.[18]

CONCLUSION

As vegetarianism and veganism are becoming increasingly popular in the UK, people seem to assimilate with once-niche food cultures. This is evident in our discussion with Laura, as she explains how perceptions of vegetarianism within the society and the food industry, are increasingly becoming more positive, creating better conditions for vegetarians. There is however no doubt, that the UK is a long way from being a predominantly vegetarian country, which creates several stressful situations for people avoiding meat. The interview highlights though, that vegetarians learn to deal with the challenges of a largely meat-eating society with the support of their families and friends.

The discussion also confirms that ethical and health concerns are not the only reasons for vegetarianism. In Laura's case, disgust to the look and taste of meat is the primary reason behind her meat avoidance, acknowledging though that vegetarian diets can convey several benefits for consumers' health, animal welfare, and the environment. That raises the question: Is vegetarianism a food ideology or a dietary trend? After my discussion with Laura, I realize that, in a heavily meat-eating country like the UK, it is the people who can actually endure against the personal and social adversities, that will be able to change the status quo and support a healthier, more ethical and more sustainable food system. Even if that comes with the risk of being called awkward.

Suggested Readings

Apostolidis, Chrysostomos, and Fraser McLeay. "Should we stop meating like this? Reducing meat consumption through substitution." *Food Policy* 65 (2016): 74–89.

Department for Environment, Food and Rural Affairs. 2018. "Family Food 2016/17: Summary." Accessed April 15, 2018, https://www.gov.uk/government/publications/family-food-201617/summary.

Fox, Nick and Katie Ward. "Health, ethics and environment: A qualitative study of vegetarian motivations." *Appetite* 50, no. 2–3 (2008): 422–29.

Hodson, Gordon and Megan Earle. "Conservatism predicts lapses from vegetarian/vegan diets to meat consumption (through lower social justice concerns and social support)." *Appetite* 120 (2018): 75–81.

Janda, Swinder and Philip J. Trocchia. "Vegetarianism: Toward a greater understanding." *Psychology & Marketing* 18, no. 12 (2001): 1205–40.

Mintel. 2017. "Meat-free Foods - UK - May 2017." Accessed April 17, 2018, http://academic.mintel.com/display/836747/.

Rothgerber, Hank. "Horizontal hostility among non-meat eaters." *PloS one* 9, no. 5 (2014): e96457.

Ruby, Matthew B. "Vegetarianism. A blossoming field of study." *Appetite* 58, no. 1 (2012): 141–50.

Ruby, Matthew B. and Steven J. Heine. "Too close to home: Factors predicting meat avoidance." *Appetite* 59, no. 1 (2012): 47–52.

Smart, Andrew. "Adrift in the mainstream: Challenges facing the UK vegetarian movement." *British Food Journal* 106, no. 2 (2004): 79–92.

Vegetarian Society. n.d. "What is a vegetarian?" Accessed April 21, 2018 https://www.vegsoc.org/page.aspx?pid=508.

Notes

1. "Meat-free Foods—UK—May 2017," Mintel, accessed April 17, 2018, http://academic.mintel.com/display/836747/.
2. Matthew B. Ruby, "Vegetarianism. A blossoming field of study," *Appetite* 58, no. 1 (2012): 142.
3. Andrew Smart, "Adrift in the mainstream: Challenges facing the UK vegetarian movement," *British Food Journal* 106, no. 2 (20–04): 8182.
4. Ibid, 88.
5. Mintel, "Meat-free Foods—UK—May 2017."
6. Gordon Hodson and Megan Earle, "Conservatism predicts lapses from vegetarian/vegan diets to meat consumption (through lower social justice concerns and social support)," *Appetite* 120 (2018): 78–79.
7. "What is a vegetarian?" Vegetarian Society, accessed April 21, 2018, https://www.vegsoc.org/page.aspx?pid=508.
8. Matthew B. Ruby and Steven J. Heine, "Too close to home: Factors predicting meat avoidance," *Appetite* 59, no. 1 (2012): 50.
9. Mintel, "Meat-free Foods—UK—May 2017."

10. "Family Food 2016/17: Summary," Department for Environment, Food and Rural Affairs, accessed April 15, 2018, https://www.gov.uk/government/publications/family-food-201617/summary.
11. Mintel, "Meat-free Foods—UK—May 2017."
12. Mintel, "Meat-free Foods—UK—May 2017."
13. Chrysostomos Apostolidis and Fraser McLeay, "Should we stop meating like this? Reducing meat consumption through substitution," *Food Policy* 65 (2016): 82–83.
14. Mintel, "Meat-free Foods—UK—May 2017."
15. Swinder Janda and Philip J. Trocchia, "Vegetarianism: Toward a greater understanding," *Psychology & Marketing* 18, no. 12 (2001): 1214.
16. Hank Rothgerber, "Horizontal hostility among non-meat eaters," *PloS one* 9, no. 5 (2014): e96457.
17. Hank Rothgerber, "Horizontal hostility among non-meat eaters," *PloS one* 9, no. 5 (2014): e96457.
18. Nick Fox and Katie Ward. "Health, ethics and environment: A qualitative study of vegetarian motivations," *Appetite* 50, no. 2–3 (2008): 426–27.

CHAPTER 16

UNITED STATES

EXPERIENCES AS A VEGAN IN THE UNITED STATES: THE EFFECTS OF DIET, IDENTITY, AND MORALITY ON SOCIAL RELATIONS

DANIEL L. ROSENFELD

A ccording to recent surveys, an estimated 3 to 5 percent of adults in the United States are vegetarian, with approximately half of that demographic being vegan.[1,2] The prevalence of vegetarianism, moreover, varies by region in the United States, tallying over 5 percent in the Northeast and as low as 2 percent in the South and the Midwest.[3] Vegetarianism also appears to be more common among women than men, unmarried adults than married adults, and liberals than conservatives.[4,5,6] These figures suggest that vegetarianism is a rather norm-defying practice in the United States, making it unsurprising that following a vegetarian diet can shape an individual's social experiences.[7,8] In this chapter, I share the experiences of Jonathan, a 23-year-old vegan from California, United

States, to whom the decision not to eat animal products embodies much more than what appears on his plate.

JONATHAN'S DIETARY PATTERN

While Jonathan reported having been vegan for one year, his initial considerations of vegan dieting began around two years ago. A few months after his sister went vegan, Jonathan found himself re-evaluating his own food choices. Cutting back on his meat intake progressively led toward following a fully vegetarian diet, which soon led toward a fully vegan diet. Jonathan had never planned on eschewing meat or animal products entirely; rather, veganism followed naturally. In retrospect, however, Jonathan described vegetarianism as a "stopping point along the way to veganism." As he learned more about the ethical and health implications of his food choices, forgoing meat while continuing to eat egg or dairy seemed contradictory to him. Essentially, Jonathan adopted a new dietary schema, categorizing foods no longer as vegetarian versus non-vegetarian but as plant-based versus animal-based.

JONATHAN'S DIETARY MOTIVATIONS

Jonathan's main two reasons for following a vegan diet are ethics and health—that is, moral objections to using animals for food and desires to optimize his physical health. These two motivations, he reported, are equally important to him. Secondary to these two motivations is concern about the environment. Yet Jonathan's motivations have evolved over time. Initially, Jonathan began shifting toward veganism for health reasons. It was not until a year later that he adopted a strictly vegan diet, after re-examining his moral stance on using animals for food. Jonathan reported that his newfound ethical motivation changed the way he thought about eating animal products to any extent: "By ethics, the biggest part is not doing harm to other sentient beings. If I were only doing this for health, then maybe I would treat myself to ice cream every now and then. But I've lost my taste for those types of things and even feel disgusted by them now."

JONATHAN'S BARRIERS IN ADOPTING A VEGAN DIET

Jonathan felt that adopting a vegan diet was fairly easy. He posed the following analogy to explain why he believes this was the case: Just as you will miss salt for the first few weeks of following a low-salt diet, and then get used to different flavors over time, so too will you naturally adjust to a diet without animal products. A vegan diet, he reported, became his "new normal," as he discovered an unexplored world of plant-based recipes and restaurants.

Still, Jonathan sees systemic barriers that make veganism challenging when eating at restaurants, both practically and socially: "Most restaurants put meat on a pedestal, filling all of their entrées with meat, making it implicitly glorified. And when every entrée has meat, my diet appears to be inherently abnormal. So there's a functional difficulty in that there's nothing I can eat here if I want to stay true to my diet and my beliefs. Then, of course, there's a social element on top, where I feel as if I'm viewed as deviant for behaving differently from this established norm of eating animal products."

VEGANISM AND IDENTITY: YOU ARE WHAT YOU (DON'T) EAT

Jonathan asserted that people view him differently for following a vegan diet, particularly when he is in situations that revolve around food. On a positive end, some people have told him they admire that he sticks to what he believes in. He reported that more commonly, however, people say things to him that they don't realize are offensive. "People make passive-aggressive comments about veganism, saying seemingly innocuous things that are actually quiet hurtful. The biggest thing is that being vegan just makes me abnormal. I'm now in this new category of people, while before I was just another person going to a restaurant or at a dinner table. Sometimes I just want to enjoy my meal and not necessarily have to bring up this aspect of my life."

Realizing that uncomfortable situations would often emerge when veganism entered the topic of conversation, Jonathan at one point decided to start saying he is vegetarian instead of vegan. He noticed that he faced significantly less backlash from labeling himself as vegetarian, as he believes people view veganism as more stigmatized, extreme, and rigid than they view vegetarianism. However, Jonathan soon returned to labeling himself as vegan, feeling that in calling himself vegetarian, he was misrepresenting his true self and what he believes in. "Just the phrase, 'I am a vegan,' describes what I am and what I do, so that makes it become a part of my identity. Eating is something you do every day and something important. I think that's why we give different diets certain labels. . . . Now I say I'm vegan because I believe more strongly that it's the right thing to do, the healthiest thing to do, and the best thing for the environment."

VEGANISM AND SOCIAL RELATIONS

While his family and friends have generally been supportive of his veganism, Jonathan reported that people make passive-aggressive remarks to him quite often across a variety of contexts. Some of these remarks are directed at vegan dieting itself. An avid cook, Jonathan enjoys devising creative ways to make plant-based versions of foods that are conventionally animal based. He feels that many people unjustifiably believe that eating animal products is normal and necessary—both for their health and for their food to taste good—and aims to cook plant-based foods that taste better than their animal-based counterparts to teach people differently. Yet before some people even taste what he has prepared, they dismiss it as weird and disgusting, exhibiting what Jonathan called a "knee-jerk reaction" to anything that goes against their expectations about food. Jonathan reported that while such comments may seem innocuous and understandable, he perceives them as having an underlying "aggressive undertone" that denigrates his lifestyle.

Jonathan's decision to be vegan also shapes how he navigates social gatherings that center on food. For one, he avoids attending barbecues and other events in which people glorify meat. He reported that such events make him feel not only left out but also uncomfortable. He admitted that he cannot help but judge people for eating animal products, which makes him feel guilty. Moreover, when at social gatherings, Jonathan always tries to sneak away if people start discussing veganism, or even food in general, anticipating that he will be dragged into the conversation and put on the defense. When this avoidance strategy is not an option, however, Jonathan draws upon humor in order to make situations less uncomfortable.

Jonathan regularly seeks out social support from his vegan sister, finding it helpful to hear her opinion on recent experiences he has had related to veganism. Typically, their conversations center on co-ruminating about microaggressive remarks they have received as well as affirming one another's moral and health beliefs. "It's often things like, 'Can you believe this person said this thing?' or 'Can you believe this restaurant served this thing?' And when I speak to her about this, I can feel like I'm not some crazy person in the world, or the only one who thinks this way."

VEGANISM AND MORALITY

Jonathan believes that criticality of veganism manifests itself most commonly in the desire for vegans to be flexible, as he reported having received numerous comments such as "Can't you just be flexible this one time?" from non-vegans. His commitment to following his diet strictly has created several uncomfortable and distressing social situations that could have been easily avoided by eating a small amount of egg or dairy. To Jonathan, however, being flexible would teach people that his moral beliefs are not all that important. "I think what makes veganism different [from other morally motivated behaviors] is that, in most cases, if someone has a strongly held belief or they're doing something because they think it's right, other people admire that person for sticking to their beliefs and ideals. Yet veganism seems to be a case where you're often doing something that's ethically motivated, and the more you go in that direction, the more other people feel uncomfortable and push back against it. . . . People might view someone else's being vegan as an attack on what they're doing themselves."

Proclaiming his moral motivation for eschewing animal products has led Jonathan to withstand many distressing interactions. Seeking to avoid such backlash, he tends to frame his diet in terms of its health aspects, rather than ethics, seeing health motivation as an "easier pill to swallow." Morality, he feels, is a more sensitive topic than health, which can make it quite uncomfortable to discuss at times. Jonathan also believes people are more critical of moral veganism than of moral vegetarianism. He reasons that most people do not see the same moral dilemma with eating eggs and dairy as they see with meat. Without acknowledging this dilemma, non-vegans may perceive vegans as irrationally extreme and outright weird.

Jonathan is recurrently disappointed by non-vegans' failures to recognize the moral rationale behind his food choices. He believes fervently that the ethical and environmental detriments of eating animal products make veganism different from other voluntary forms of restrictive dieting. He understands that chefs and hosts may face inconveniences in catering toward various dietary demands. To him, however, the question is not so much whether people should make an effort to accommodate vegans, but whether people should be eating or serving animal products at all. Jonathan believes that if people were to step back and think critically, nearly everyone would want to be vegan—they just haven't faced that reality yet.

CONCLUSION

Being vegan is central to Jonathan's identity. It shapes how he construes his relationships with his health, animals, and the environment; reflects on his moral principles; presents his self to other people; and views other people as either in-group or out-group. Jonathan's experiences also highlight that having a vegan identity reciprocally influences how other people view him, which he believes is typically through a more negative lens. Yet Jonathan reported that negative attitudes toward veganism manifest themselves through subtle jabs more often than through overt insults. These micro-aggressive comments, while perhaps intended innocuously, can feel as if they are direct attacks on Jonathan's core values and lifestyle. Consequently, Jonathan exhibited a low vegan identity in public regard, feeling that other people tend to view his veganism as an unfavorable part of his overall identity.[9] In many contexts, revealing his vegan identity to others would make him feel stigmatized.

Jonathan's experiences suggest that adverse social implications resulting from following a vegan diet may relate more strongly to moral, rather than health, aspects of food choice. He reported that people tend to have more negative perceptions not only of veganism than vegetarianism but also of morally motivated than health-motivated dieting. For this reason, he tends to emphasize his veganism as a health-motivated—rather than a morally motivated—choice, an impression management strategy that previous investigations into vegetarianism have likewise documented.[10,11]

Morality also played a role in how Jonathan's levels of vegan identity strictness and omnivorous regard shaped his social experiences.[12] In considering whether or not he should ever violate his diet, it was his moral stance against using animals for food that propelled him to adhere to his diet stringently. Moreover, feelings of disgust toward animal products followed his newfound moral beliefs and made him even more adverse to even small dietary violations. Maintaining this level of high dietary strictness, Jonathan feels, has made socializing as a vegan particularly stressful at times. Jonathan's strong moral motivation also led him to feel a low omnivorous regard, instinctively judging non-vegans for their food choices. He disliked the fact that he felt this way, as it became a negative aspect of his own self-perception.

Ultimately, the decision to follow a vegan diet in the United States is one of deviance. Practicing a lifestyle that becomes readily intertwined with matters of identity and morality, vegans may have adverse social experiences due to their food choices. Reflecting on these experiences may inform how vegans establish social support networks, plan their social activities, and reflect on who they truly are.

Suggested Readings

Adams, Carol J. *Living Among Meat Eaters: The Vegetarian's Survival Handbook* (New York: Lantern Books, 2009).

Colb, Sherry F. *Mind If I Order the Cheeseburger? And Other Questions People Ask Vegans* (New York: Lantern Books, 2013).

Iacobbo, Karen and Michael Iacobbo. *Vegetarian America: A History* (Westport, CT: Praeger Publishers, 2004).

Notes

1. Newport, Frank. "In U.S., 5% consider themselves vegetarians." Gallup, July 26, 2012, http://www.gallup.com/poll/156215/consider-themselves-vegetarians.aspx.

2. The Vegetarian Resource Group. "How many adults in the U.S. are vegetarian and vegan?" The Vegetarian Resource Group, 2012, http://www.vrg.org/nutshell/Polls/2016_adults_veg.htm.

3. Ibid.

4. Newport, Frank. "In U.S., 5% consider themselves vegetarians." *Gallup*, July 26, 2012, http://www.gallup.com/poll/156215/consider-themselves-vegetarians.aspx.

5. The Vegetarian Resource Group. "How many adults in the U.S. are vegetarian and vegan?" The Vegetarian Resource Group, 2012, http://www.vrg.org/nutshell/Polls/2016_adults_veg.htm.

6. Wrenn, Corey Lee. "Trump veganism: A political survey of American vegans in the era of identity politics." *Societies* 7 (2017): 32.

7. LeRette, Denise Elaine. "Stories of microaggressions directed toward vegans and vegetarians in social settings," PhD diss., Fielding Graduate University, 2014.

8. MacInnis, Cara C. and Gordon Hodson. "It ain't easy eating greens: Evidence of bias toward vegetarians and vegans from both source and target." Group Processes & Intergroup Relations 20 (2017): 721–44.

9. Rosenfeld, Daniel L., and Anthony L. Burrow. "The unified model of vegetarian identity: A conceptual framework for understanding plant-based food choices." *Appetite* 112 (2017): 78–95.

10. Greenebaum, Jessica B. "Managing impressions: 'Face-saving' strategies of vegetarians and vegans." *Humanity & Society* 36 (2012): 309–25.

11. Wilson, Marc Stewart, Ann Weatherall, and Carly Butler. "A rhetorical approach to discussions about health and vegetarianism." *Journal of Health Psychology* 9 (2004): 567–81.

12. Rosenfeld, Daniel L. and Anthony L. Burrow. "The unified model of vegetarian identity: A conceptual framework for understanding plant-based food choices." *Appetite* 112 (2017): 78–95.

CONCLUSION

CHARLOTTE J. S. DE BACKER
AND MARYANNE L. FISHER

This is a book that has important consequences for everyone. The narratives clearly show that how we view each other, based on dietary choice, divides us from one another and has deep, meaningful implications for our social lives. This book is not "about vegetarians"; this book is instead about us, how we perceive ourselves and those around us, and the various ways we create groups, form friendships, and tolerate or exclude each other.

We discussed in the Introduction how vegetarians are often viewed with suspicion and seen as a group of choosy, doctrine-driven people (usually women) who want everyone to stop eating meat.[1] Our collection of stories contained in the chapters of this book are from vegetarians around the globe, and after reading them, we have to conclude that this perception of vegetarians is simply inaccurate. Vegetarians are a diverse group of people, who are driven by often very different motives to not eat meat and with many of them living very distinct lifestyles from one another.

Several people interviewed in the stories of this book did not want to be identified by a specific label. Some explained that they did not self-identify as vegetarian or vegan because they occasionally consumed animal (derived) products. Others mentioned that the concepts of being "vegetarian" or "vegan" are so fuzzy that it is hard to use them for self-identification

185

purposes, and instead suggest that the phrase "I'm following a 'plant-based' diet" as a far clearer, cleaner distinction.

The link between labels and identity is at best a tenuous one and certainly quite contentious. Some individuals expressed clear dislike about being "put in a box" of any kind. We agree that it, after reading the narratives, it is problematic to create a contrast between vegetarian, vegan, or plant-based diet followers versus omnivores. Most omnivores will not eat all that is edible for human beings, and consequently have no more right to claim this term than those who skip meat, animal products, or any other foods. The negative perceptions we described at the start may be the consequence of putting people into boxes based on what they eat. A member of a social media group for plant-based diet followers[2] recently wrote that when she prepares plant-based meals for family, friends, and even strangers without the specific notion that these dishes are plant-based/vegan, people seem to show greater appreciation for the food. Putting a label on something or someone creates the opportunity for people to use a stereotype,[3] which has obvious negative connotations and can be unnecessarily limiting. At the same time, using labels and categories serve a very important role in helping us to understand the complexity of something, such as dietary choices.

Dietary choices are convoluted and multi-faceted, and to comprehend the social consequences of not eating meat, we drew a line between diets that included meat and those without. We called those in the latter group "vegetarian," which we felt accommodated all the different subtypes of non-meat diets. Here, though, we feel the need to emphasize the diversity of this group, the one we labeled "vegetarian," must be acknowledged at all times. The stories we collected reveal that at the very least, there is a clear distinction between vegetarians and vegans to the extent they should be treated as separate groups. Several chapters highlighted that being vegan is frequently more challenging than being vegetarian on many levels, ranging from health and knowledge issues to social consequences.

For both vegans and vegetarians, however, a seemingly simple decision to no longer eat meat (and other animal products) appears to be much harder than many anticipate. While one might have the very noble motive to not harm any animal, other humans can be harsh and difficult, which leads to challenging practical consequences and less than pleasant reactions to one's dietary choice. All stories had a few experiences in common, including the fact that many individuals who follow a vegetarian (or vegan, etc.) diet feel isolated at times. Their testimonies showcase how dietary choices influence our social interactions in ways we have not fully captured or explored prior to this book.

We are inspired by the stories collected in this book, and we have a few final concluding remarks to share based on our observations. We first summarize some general thoughts, highlighting parallels and differences in the narratives. From these stories, we derive both suggestions for future scientific research and suggestions for practical arrangements that can help to ease the social consequences of becoming or being vegetarian. Our goal is to ultimately help reduce the divide between vegetarians and omnivores and be a catalyst for deeper, positive, social connections.

THIS BOOK IS ABOUT YOU, ME, AND EVERYONE ELSE

As we stated at the start of this chapter, this book is not about vegetarians. This book is about you, and me, and everyone else. Whether you do or do not eat meat, you are directly involved in what this book is about: you are part of the broader social context in which we can study vegetarian diet choices. Moreover, while this book is about meat and meatless diets, it could easily have been about other exclusion-based diets. There are many parallels to be drawn between the topic of this book and the social consequences of people with food allergies and intolerances, or people who choose to avoid any food like dairy, nuts, gluten, fats, sugar, or anything else. Any exclusion diet can lead to the social consequences highlighted in this book.

There is one important difference, though, as people with allergies and intolerances may experience less negative comments than vegetarians. One of our interviewees explained: "food-related allergies are taken into account when preparing meals to others, and the needs of vegans could be taken into account the same way."[4] If one cannot eat certain foods because of health issues, people may be more tolerant to their choice and lenient toward the consequences because they did not *choose* this restriction. If people make a personal choice, for whatever reason, to not eat certain foods, however, they are met with criticism, a lack of understanding, and behavior that may be seen as bullying.

Exclusion diets are trending, and the number of vegetarians and vegans is growing worldwide. All of the countries in the chapters show an increase in vegetarian and vegan diets, or at least they have become more prevalent in the past few years. This pattern leads us to wonder if we are at a turning point where vegetarianism is on its way out of a minority position in the future, although vegetarians remain a minority group at the moment.[5] Whether you are part of this minority group or not, this book applies to you, because everyone will benefit by being more mindful of the simple question: do you eat meat?

TO EAT OR NOT EAT MEAT

Whether to eat or not eat meat is the question all people interviewed for this book have asked themselves. None of the vegetarians interviewed for this book were born and raised a vegetarian, and all have made a conscious decision to adopt the diet later in life. Or should we say conscious decisions, adding the plural, because several people interviewed for this book switched back and forth between being vegetarian, vegan, flexitarian, and omnivore. The stories reveal that for many, the decision to eat or not eat meat is not a clear dichotomy, nor is it something fixed. People play around with their dietary choices and identities, and both internal and external factors influence these switches in diet. Many vegetarians start to alter their diet away from meat in their teen years, yet some were as young as nine[6] years old. Little is known about the age at which turning to vegetarianism is most common, or perhaps possible as a conscious individual decision. It is known that children develop a memory for food around the age of eight to nine,[7] which coincides with the youngest ages reported in this book. This link may be a coincidence, but it would be worthwhile to further investigate at what age children can and do start to make conscious decisions to not eat meat. It is known that certain childhood factors, like having a pet, influence these conscious vegetarian choices.[8] A vegetarian woman from the Netherlands quit eating meat when she was given some chickens as pets during her childhood. Watching a pig being roasted triggered the Israeli woman interviewed in this book, leading to her decision to no longer eat meat when she was only nine years old. We know that animal concerns are crucial in explaining vegetarianism; they set vegetarians apart from all those who do eat meat, even compared those who consciously reduce their meat intake.[9] Next to animal concerns, health motives and environment concerns have been identified as major drivers of vegetarianism.[10] Motivations for vegetarianism and sex differences in vegetarian diets and attitudes have been well studied.[11] In this book, we contend many aspects of the social consequences of vegetarian diet choices can only be fully understood if we take one's motives into mind. Motives for vegetarianism may, however, not always be highly personal, but influenced by several cultural aspects that also need to be considered.

Food is culture, and behaviors involving food can only be fully understood when studied in a broader cultural context. The stories collected from different parts of the world emphasize this relationship between food and culture very clearly. Here we highlight a few factors that need to be considered in order to understand vegetarian dietary choices. To start, religious aspects must be taken into account if one wants to understand vegetarianism. Whether someone is an atheist, a Christian, Muslim, Jew, or follower of any other religion may matter, and often plays a highly significant role in dietary decisions. The Jewish Kosher rules, for example, can make animal consumption quite complex because of the strict divide between meat and dairy. The stories from Israel clearly illustrate that vegetarianism may make life easier for Kosher-keeping Jews. Kosher rules to strictly separate dishes and even sinks for meat and dairy are much easier to follow for vegans especially, as such steps are no longer required. Some individuals may thus turn to vegetarianism for practical reasons, which is not always captured by researchers who have tended to focus on the classical motives related to personal health and moral concerns. Moreover, in line with the Kosher rules, foods in Israel—or other Jewish diaspora communities—are clearly labeled as "containing meat" or "containing dairy," which makes it also easier for vegetarians and vegans to select their food. Furthermore, some Jewish biblical accounts lead a vegetarian diet to be seen as an ideal, and as a result, some Jews aspire to evolve toward meatless communities again. For these individuals, being vegetarian is not so much about not eating any animals, but rather it is about their religious identity.[12] In the South African chapter, the Hindu woman and Adventist man both explained how their religion made their vegetarian diet choice easier, because their religion supports their behavior. Yet other religious traditions can create barriers rather than support. Among Muslims, for example, turning to vegetarianism is sometimes perceived as an insult toward the family. For Muslims, sacrificing an animal and sharing it with family and friends is a crucial religious moment, and a family member who becomes a vegetarian threatens the core of these beliefs.[13] Muslims worldwide do become vegetarian and vegan and unite in groups like the Muslim Vegans (see https://veganmuslims.com).

Not just religion, but also other cultural backgrounds and heritage can majorly impact on one's decision to eat or not eat meat. Jews sometimes compare the killing of animals to what happened during the Holocaust, and this comparison motivates many Jewish people to stop eating meat.[14] Culinary traditions must also be considered. Several chapters[15] highlighted how regional food traditions influence the barriers towards meatless diets. In some regions, meat dishes are so central to the local cultural heritage that not eating meat almost serves as an act of rebellion. In Turkey, for example, some regions thrive on meat-centered dishes, whereas other regions care less about these meat-based cuisines. Some regions even declare themselves as being "vegetarian" and host vegetarian festivals.[16]

Living in a big city versus a small town in the countryside can have a significant influence, both in terms of access to vegetarian food choices as well as the attitudes of other inhabitants. In general, large cities are more accommodating to vegetarians.[17] Similarly, geography can matter in terms of crossing regional borders, and perhaps even language borders, as they may impose challenges to people who restrict their diet. Some mentioned that their travels caused them some stress, because of their vegetarian diet: not knowing what foods to expect, not knowing the names of meat in other languages, or not being able to communicate the required details about ingredients with the person preparing food can create tension.[18]

Lastly, not everyone can financially afford to be vegetarian, which is a critical factor to consider when discussing dietary choice. It is important to remember that for many lower income families, fruits and vegetables are simply too expensive[19] which means they may be prohibited from selecting a non-meat-based diet. The South African chapter was one of the few that emphasized this often silenced, yet important issue. Whereas higher income groups can afford to become vegetarian because of animal concerns, or other moral and environmental motivations, lower income groups may not have this luxury. Alternatively, lower income individuals may be more preoccupied with health issues, and subsequently use health as the main driver for turning to a vegetarian diet. These possibilities highlight how motives are not always equal to personal choices or attitudes, but subject to contextual constraints as well.

Furthermore, socioeconomic status may not only influence dietary choices because of practical or financial reasons, but also the attitudes toward other vegetarians may differ according to socioeconomic status. Again, in the South African chapter, those interviewed said that higher income groups are more supportive toward vegetarians, whereas the lower income groups are less considerate and more critical. This class-related bias raises another obstacle for lower-income families, as they also potentially face more in-group criticism. In the South African context specifically, the divide between higher- and lower-income groups is still strong, and interrelated to ethnicity. Vegetarian communities in South Africa can be very elite and dominated by white, Western people. The vegetarian Hindu woman from South Africa felt some disdain toward her, as she did not meet these elite or white criteria. Interestingly, as she added, this feeling was akin to "lip service"; it is in marked contrast to (some) vegetarians' moral attitudes to treat all living beings alike and equal.

This relationship between diet and socioeconomic class is undoubtedly a topic that requires further attention. Historically, meat has been considered a luxury food and a status symbol. For example, in the South African case, older generations are generally resistant toward vegetarian diets because they have experienced times where eating meat was a luxurious privilege. For these individuals, vegetarian diets may be unappealing because they remind them of when they were less affluent. Indeed, in several cultures until the end of the twentieth century, meat eaters as well as vegetarians associated meat with luxury, or at least special occasions.[20] Popular Western culture readily displays the image of large geese or turkeys being consumed for Christmas or other holidays, with the message that it is not truly a holiday feast unless these foods are available. Thus, the resistance of older generations toward the diets of younger generations who increasingly favor vegetarian foods is understandable. For these younger generations the act of not eating meat may actually be the new status symbol, as it delivers the message, "Look, I can afford to be vegetarian."

The fact that food is used as a status symbol is not new; after all, taste is an expression of Bourdieu's cultural capital.[21] By which we mean that food is used as an expression of social class; people eat fancy food or exclusive food to demonstrate that they are well off or unique. That is what is scarce becomes the luxury good; when meat was scarce it signaled luxury, while now that meat consumption is the norm, meatless diets have become a status symbol. We can wonder how this may evolve in the future; if the majority of people become vegetarian, will those who express their wealth via food consumption switch to eating meat? In-vitro meat offers a special situation to pay particular attention toward, as it will be very costly when it is introduced on the market. It could be predicted that those who turned vegetarian to express their prestige may be among the first to start consuming this new, expensive type of meat.

KNOWING WHAT TO EAT AND HOW TO MAKE IT

Food signals status and, hence, it also represents power. Power comes in many forms, including knowledge, as those with more knowledge may be more powerful. A strong example of this relationship between power and knowledge is the Italian chapter. The divide between "senior" and "junior" vegetarians was discussed; switching to a vegetarian diet requires new skills and knowledge to be acquired. Strict vegetarian and vegan diets, especially, require high levels of food literacy[22] and control: people need to plan, select, prepare, and eat only the desired foods.

For vegetarians, the main question is simply whether foods or meals contain meat or not. For vegans, the question may at face value seem more difficult, as this diet demands additional restrictions of dairy and eggs. However, as Jonathan[23] pointed out, the difficulty may be a misperception, as vegans also only need to make the simple distinction between "animal-based" and "plant-based" foods. More and more people are opting to say that they eat a partial or exclusive "plant-based" diet, rather than labeling themselves as vegetarian or vegan. This term ("plant-based") may in time ease the tensions around foods that are and are not part of one's diet. For vegetarians (and vegans), knowing what to eat, how to prepare it, and then how to consume it within social settings represents the accumulation of important knowledge and skills.

The Italian vegetarians and vegans interviewed for this book mentioned how, in their opinion, only vegetarians with years of experience know how to cook tasty meals and have acquired a clear taste preference for vegetarian foods. Vegetarians with a lack of knowledge and experience, in contrast, may feel less confident to make their own meals, and may turn to ready-made meals, despite the fact that there might be limited options available. Shop-bought foods and meals increasingly have simplified their food labels to include words such as "vegetarian" or "vegan" that ease the process of selecting the right foods. Moreover, it is not only junior or inexperienced vegetarians who may benefit from ready-made foods labeled in this way; those who are attempting to share meals with vegetarians may select these items in order to be more inclusive. Thus, interestingly, these ready-made meals not only save junior vegetarians time and frustrations, but they are also used to overcome social barriers. In addition, vegetarian ready-made meals often look highly similar to meat-based ready-made meals, and by consuming these items when eating in the company of meat-eaters, vegetarians may avoid "standing out" or receiving judgment and potential criticism.

People have generally become estranged from what they eat due to the rise of industrial (highly) pre-processed foods. A surprising amount of processed foods contain traces of animal products, and we are not always aware of these ingredients. Many processed soups, candies, snacks, and even bread or wine are often treated with, or include, animal or milk proteins. A popular processed soup company in Canada and the United States, Campbells, has "vegetable soup" with the primary ingredient of beef broth, and hence, consumers have to search for "vegetarian vegetable" soup. Likewise, marshmallows, gummy candies, jelly beans, among other treats, rely on gelatin derived from horses, while isinglass, derived from fish swim bladders, is used for clarification of wine and beer. Vegetarians and vegans often feel pressure to carefully read lists of ingredients and closely monitor what they purchase and eat, and the people around them may also feel this same pressure. Eating at friends' or family members' houses can be daunting and create tensions, if one has to ask, for example, the ingredients of a sauce.[24] In the chapter about Israel, Hadar referred to an omnivore colleague who could not date a vegan, because that would be "too complex." In many of the chapters, the lack of knowledge around food literacy was mentioned as a barrier preventing one from adopting a vegetarian diet, and a source of potential conflict with others. It is difficult for inhabitants of meat-centered countries like Brazil to eat less meat and more plant-based meals when there is a dearth of information available on vegetarian or vegan diets, which foods can be included or not, and an overall lack of knowledge about plant-based foods.[25] The lack of others' food knowledge while serving food was mentioned several times as a potential obstacle to vegetarians, particularly while dining out. Some people still think that vegetarians eat chicken or fish, at least on some occasions, and many have little knowledge about vegan diets. Even chefs may barely know what vegetarians and vegans do or do not eat, as was illustrated by the Irish chef who was unaware of the fact that vegans do not eat cheese.[26] Several chapters mentioned that people are typically unaware that vegans will not eat honey, despite the fact that it is clearly an animal-based product. Friends, family, and even romantic partners of those interviewed in this book have reported frustration when they do not know what foods vegetarians may eat. Yet, what would happen if we re-educate ourselves about food? In the Turkish chapter, Sedef experienced less resistance to her vegan dietary choice once she started to explain her diet to those who initially criticized her.[27] Improving our food knowledge, where foods come from, and our food literacy more generally, could thus be a simple though crucial step to overcoming some of the barriers to being vegetarians, or being inclusive of vegetarians.

To the best of our knowledge, no one has investigated whether improving food literacy could ease some of the misconceptions and stereotypes surrounding vegetarians and their dietary decisions. Researchers should empirically test if a lack of knowledge about vegetarian food, and levels of food literacy, moderate or mediate the known moral disengagement[28] and divide between meat eaters and vegetarians. (Food literacy here is conceptualized as the skills and knowledge about how to plan meals, selecting the right foods, cooking the foods into meals, and enjoying food consumption.)

If so, then an option to reduce existing frictions and stereotypes between omnivores and vegetarians would be to increase people's food literacy. Overall, levels of food knowledge and skills related to food production and meal preparation are poor in many parts of the world,[29] which has important implications for decreased personal health.[30]

There is one further suggestion about the need for food literacy, which we make with great care: we posit that it may also support social relations and ease conflicts over food choices. Research is required, but if this prediction is accurate, then individuals could have more successful and harmonious relations with others when they improve their knowledge about food. If so, then this emphasis on social relations could be used as a strategy to educate people about food. Few people like to be told what to eat in order to improve their personal health, but people are willing to change their food literacy when they are told to focus on the social aspects of food and eating[31] and their lifestyle. People want to enjoy food; consuming food in the presence of others may be even more pleasant if we know, with confidence, what others are able to enjoy eating.

CONFLICT AND COPING

While a lack of knowledge can be an obstacle for vegetarians to feel included and accepted, it is not the only factor. Apostolidis writes in the chapter about the United Kingdom that it is not just about knowing what vegetarians do and do not eat, but also, and perhaps even more so, about being mindful about their decisions to restrict their diet. While most vegetarians struggle with these negative reactions primarily at the start of their transition to a vegetarian diet,[32] others experience these comments for long periods of time. The lack of empathy of omnivores toward vegetarians surfaced in the majority of the stories in this book; there were reports of negative reactions and rude insults,[33] with people asking them if they have "become crazy,"[34] calling vegetarians marginal and attention-seekers.[35] Even family members and close friends often have an "aggressive undertone" that denigrates the lifestyle of vegetarians.[36] Vegetarians are considered "not normal"; some were even yelled at in a restaurant that only served meals for "normal people."[37] Some vegetarians felt they had become "a problem" rather than just a human being with different personal choices.[38] It also occasionally felt as though friends and family members were waiting for their vegetarian friend or child to switch back to "normal," as if following a vegetarian diet is a phase, much like puberty.[39] Interviewees used terms such as "coping" with reactions and comments, and defending themselves by "attacking" those who criticize them.[40] All of those interviewed did not want to get involved in discussions and quarrels about their dietary decisions but were often left with no other choice than defending themselves, as they were confronted with similar comments and remarks over and over again.

Some of the vegetarians and vegans interviewed for this book felt isolated at times. One of the Fisher sisters wrote: "I found these moments unpleasant, as I felt that I am attending social gatherings for a sense of community, not to feel isolated or individuated."[41] Others were even deliberately excluded from social gatherings, like barbecues (BBQ), because "what would a vegetarian do at a BBQ?"[42] Repeated negative comments, and either intentional or unintentional social isolation toward vegetarians by the meat eaters, who are still dominant by way of majority, echoes of bullying. If bullying is defined as "repetitive aggressive behaviour with an imbalance of power,"[43] then being confronted over and over again with negative remarks and being individuated, particularly as initiated by those who are in the majority, meets this criteria.

The stories in this book reveal that vegetarians develop several coping strategies to deal with these potentially aggressive situations. A first and simple coping strategy we observed is that vegetarians relax their dietary rules to avoid social conflict. They cook and serve meat when their omnivore friends come for dinner, with the hopes of pleasing them: "I will adjust as the vegetarian. Even if I am the host, I'll try to cook what other people enjoy eating. To be a good host you have to cook something that they [guests] enjoy."[44] Some not only relax their dietary rules when cooking for others, but also for themselves. Vegetarians allow themselves to "sin" and consume animal products, especially the ones that cannot be observed directly on their plate, such as in a soup or sauce. This may contradict their core values of "not killing an animal for meat," but they put this aside, knowing that "forcing vegetarian food on people will not fix it."[45]

Not being too strict and following a more open, relaxed animal-free diet makes one's social life much easier. Campbell and Campbell have been telling us this message for decades in their popular China Study books[46] on the health benefits of animal-free diets. Vegetarians driven by health or ecological concerns may have an easier time relaxing their dietary rules, as compared to those driven by animal concerns, however. There is evidence that sustainable diets, that are nutritionally adequate and that have a low environmental impact are not necessarily meatless diets.[47] These findings can therefore be used to provide justification for health- or environmentally-driven vegetarians to consume animal products in very small amounts on rare occasions, as this does not drastically erode their decision to follow a healthy or environmentally-friendly diet. For vegetarians driven by animal concerns, however, this option to "sin" and eat animal products on occasion is less feasible. Any consumption of animal products, no matter how small or rare, goes against their basic principle to not kill or harm an animal for food. For them, this first coping strategy of catering to an omnivore's dietary preference and include meat is thus not an option. Apart from motives, this coping strategy may also be influenced by personality traits, such as a need for approval, which is a possibility that deserves further attention. We posit that those vegetarians who feel a strong need for another's approval will most likely be flexible in their dietary decisions and in accommodating others. We further predict that the more someone wants to be socially approved (need for approval), the less likely they will want to switch to a vegetarian diet in the first place, unless others approve of this decision.

A second coping strategy observed among the vegetarians interviewed for this book is purposeful seeking approval, or at least social support, by others making the same decisions. In several chapters, interviewees mentioned they sought contact with fellow vegetarians, especially in online environments. Online support groups are considered important in that they offer both emotional support and practical tips, like where to find vegetarian restaurants. The social support seems crucial to build confidence, which in turn can lead to coping strategies where vegetarians manage to stay in control of what they eat. This exertion of control is key, as not all vegetarians interviewed were willing to "give in" and be flexible.[48] In the domain of health sciences, it is known that online support groups can empower people,[49] and it may be worthwhile to further investigate if this pattern applies to vegetarian or other dietary choices as well.

Those who feel empowered are the ones who will bring their own foods to social gatherings,[50] or call family, friends, and even restaurants in advance to make sure they will cater vegetarian or vegan food.[51] In doing these activities, some used another coping strategy: they consciously lied about their reasons to be vegetarian, or at least omit their moral motives. In most cases, they instead reported they are vegetarian because of health reasons: "people seem to be more likely to accept that it is not completely [a vegan's] 'fault' that she is being 'difficult,' as it is a health issue, rather than a conviction."[52] Similar reports were made in the interviews in Finland, Ireland, and the United States. One person even went one step further and told those around her that she was meat intolerant; she experienced increased social acceptance when she gave this reason for following a vegetarian diet.[53] Meat allergies do exist, and although they are extremely rare they are increasing,[54] and hence, must be taken into account. The difference in reactions to various motives to defend one's vegetarian choices also opens up new opportunities for research. Are meat eaters more or less tolerant toward vegetarians who are intolerant to meat, driven by health motives, motivated by environmental issues, or taking into account animal concerns? This question is particularly interesting given that meat eaters often feel cognitive dissonance when confronted with vegetarians.[55] Researchers could test whether meat eaters' dissonance is greater when confronted with vegetarians who are driven by animal concerns, as compared to vegetarians driven by ecological concerns or health; meat intolerances in particular should result in the least dissonance.

Lastly, vegetarians in the narratives reported a more extreme use of a coping strategy, which not only lead to avoiding conflict, but social gatherings in general. Some just avoid the eating part of an event by eating food at home before going to any social gathering.[56] Others avoid any restaurant outings with people.[57] Barbecues in particular were mentioned several times as events that vegetarians try to avoid.

In the most extreme cases, vegetarians distance themselves completely from critical omnivores, even if these are family members.[58] That is to say, people will avoid any social contact with others, simply because they differ in what they eat. This highlights the fact that what we eat matters much more than we often think. Food not only fuels our bodies, it fuels our lives, and our social interactions in particular.

BUFFET TIME: LET'S CATER FOR EVERYONE'S TASTE

Dietary choices do not have to lead to bullying behavior and coping strategies. In the Austrian chapter, Ulrike refers to barbecues as the perfect occasions for meat lovers and vegetarians to mingle, at least when everyone respects one another's choices. A barbecue is like a buffet: It is about the preparation of a variety of dishes that can cater to everyone's demands. The Finnish chapter also mentioned that buffet-style dinners work best, because everyone is then given a chance to eat what they want and avoid dishes that do not meet one's dietary needs.

Ulrike from the Austrian story is vegan and married a meat lover. At their wedding, they created a buffet that could cater to everyone's dietary demands. Their wedding is an excellent example of striking a balance, as they offered a variety of dishes people could choose from. The buffet allowed for commensality and food sharing to occur. Although vegetarians may skip some of the dishes due to their dietary restrictions, and omnivores may skip dishes for other reasons (taste related, neophobia, and so on), some of the dishes may appeal to everyone and allow for some genuine food sharing. The importance of food sharing for social interaction cannot be over-emphasized: sharing a dish provides an occasion where we are reminded to not be greedy and take all of the food, and where we are reminded to treat others fairly, regardless of who they are and what they do or do not eat.

Like Laura, a vegetarian in the UK, said: "it's your own decision, you can eat whatever you want. I guess I have a very realist's point of view on that. To me, if someone else wants to eat meat, I don't have a problem." If everyone had an attitude like Laura, this book would not exist: there would be no stories of people who at times feel isolated simply due to their diet. Many stories we collected illustrate that vegetarians and vegans do not fit the stereotype of being a uniform dogmatic, stubborn group of people who want to force everyone to stop eating meat. Almost all of the vegetarians interviewed for this book reported that they made a conscious and ethical decision to not harm anyone, no human beings, and no other animals. Some even said they felt that they had become a better, more empathic person since becoming vegetarian.[59] As the interviewees from the Netherlands said: vegetarians do not need overt social support from (significant) others; simply taking a plant-based diet for granted and quietly respecting vegetarians for who they are is sufficient. Respecting dietary choices and not allowing them to become grounds for social rejection is all that is needed to avoid feelings of isolation.

Our goal was not to endorse one particular dietary decision over any other, but instead to focus on how a restricted diet infringes on one's social interactions and relationships. We could easily have explored many foods that people routinely avoid or exclude, such as gluten, sugar, alcohol, and so on. We decided to investigate vegetarianism due to its long history and its prevalence cross-culturally. Food is intimately linked to identity and culture, but despite individual differences and socio-cultural influences, we uncovered several universal experiences. The most worrisome one, from the standpoint of psychological and physical well-being, is that vegetarians often feel isolated within their social and familial network. Therefore, we want to conclude this book with three simple take-away messages to stop the growing divide between those who do and those who do not eat meat:

1. **Empathize. Stop judging based on dietary choices**. You are what you eat, and others are what they eat, but we do not need to judge each other based on dietary choices. People vary in their decisions to follow a particular diet, and those decisions are inherently related

to who they are as individuals. There are other characteristics and aspects that reveal our identity: our clothes, hairdos, house interiors, and music preferences. We do not criticize others because we dislike their green sofa, or at least not in the same degree to which we criticize others based on what they eat. If instead of criticizing other's dietary choices we became more tolerant and inclusionary, we could reduce feelings of isolation or the one's need to use coping strategies.

2. **Increase your food literacy**. Across the globe people struggle more and more to plan meals, select the right foods, to know where foods are sourced from, and to turn foods into delicious meals that are eaten in the company of others. Food fuels our bodies, our minds, our lives, and must be taken seriously. Knowing how to make meals, understanding what you eat, as well as knowing what others eat, will improve our social life in meaningful ways.

3. **Share food**. Eating alone is not nearly as enjoyable as eating with others. Sharing food has many known benefits, including the building and maintaining of skills related to sociality. If we share our food with others, and let them share food with us, we will discover new flavors and our relationships will be nourished, too.

Humans are a species marked by individual differences and preferences. Ultimately, we are united by the fact that we have a variety of foods available to us, and the cognitive capacities to decide which of these foods to consume and avoid. Our social relationships are part of the very foundation of our experience as humans, and the stories from around the globe collected in this book clearly show how diet significantly impacts on our social lives.

Suggested Readings

Bosmans Jade and Ilja Van Damme. "'Naar buiten, stedeling! Zie wat groeit in het laboratorium van Onze-Lieve-Heer': Het vegetarisme van het natuurgeneeskundig Hygiënisch Gesticht Van den Broeck en het denken over het geïndustrialiseerde voedselsysteem in het Antwerpse interbellum." *Stadsgeschiedenis* 11, no. 1 (2016).

Campbell, Thomas Colin and Thomas M. Campbell. "*The China Study: Startling implications for diet, weight loss and long-term health*" (2004). Dallas, TX: Benbella Books.

Cassady, Diana, Karen M. Jetter, and Jennifer Culp. "Is price a barrier to eating more fruits and vegetables for low-income families?" *Journal of the American Dietetic Association* 107, no. 11 (2007): 1909–15.

De Backer, Charlotte J. S., and Liselot Hudders. "From meatless Mondays to meatless Sundays: Motivations for meat reduction among vegetarians and semi-vegetarians who mildly or significantly reduce their meat intake." *Ecology of food and nutrition* 53, no. 6 (2014): 639–57.

Devine, Patricia G. "Stereotypes and prejudice: Their automatic and controlled components." *Journal of personality and social psychology* 56, no. 1 (1989): 5.

Fox, Nick and Katie Ward. "Health, ethics and environment: A qualitative study of vegetarian motivations." *Appetite* 50, no. 2–3 (2008): 422–29.

Graça, João, Maria Manuela Calheiros, and Abílio Oliveira. "Attached to meat? (Un) Willingness and intentions to adopt a more plant-based diet." *Appetite* 95 (2015): 113–25.

Hamilton, Malcolm. "Disgust reactions to meat among ethically and health motivated vegetarians." *Ecology of Food and Nutrition* 45, no. 2 (2006): 125–58.

Kenyon, Paul and Margo Barker. "Attitudes towards meat-eating in vegetarian and non-vegetarian teenage girls in England—An ethnographic approach." *Appetite* 30, no. 2 (1998): 185–98.

Livingstone, Barbara, James Robson, and Gavin Wallace. "Issues in dietary intake assessment of children and adolescents." *British Journal of Nutrition* 92, no. S2 (2004): S213–S222.

McGowan, Laura, Martin Caraher, Monique Raats, Fiona Lavelle, Lynsey Hollywood, Dawn McDowell, Michelle Spence, Amanda McCloat, Elaine Mooney, and Moira Dean. "Domestic cooking and food skills: A review." *Critical Reviews in Food Science and Nutrition* 57, no. 11 (2017): 2412–31.

Perignon, Marlene, Florent Vieux, Louis-Georges Soler, Gabriel Masset, and Nicole Darmon. "Improving diet sustainability through evolution of food choices: Review of epidemiological studies on the environmental impact of diets." *Nutrition Reviews* 75, no. 1 (2017): 2–17.

Phull, Surinder, Wendy Wills, and Angela Dickinson. "The Mediterranean diet: Socio-cultural relevance for contemporary health promotion." *The Open Public Health Journal* 8 (2015b): 35–40.

Rosenfeld, Daniel. "The psychology of vegetarianism: Recent advances and future directions." *Appetite* (2018): 125–38.

Rothgerber, Hank. "Efforts to overcome vegetarian-induced dissonance among meat eaters." *Appetite* 79 (2014): 32–41.

Rothgerber, Hank and Frances Mican. "Childhood pet ownership, attachment to pets, and subsequent meat avoidance. The mediating role of empathy toward animals." *Appetite* 79 (2014): 11–17.

Smith, Peter K. "Bullying: Definition, types, causes, consequences and intervention." *Social and Personality Psychology Compass* 10, no. 9 (2016): 519–32.

Tiu Wright, Len, Clive Nancarrow, and Pamela M. H. Kwok. "Food taste preferences and cultural influences on consumption." *British Food Journal* 103, no. 5 (2001): 348–57.

Vidgen, Helen Anna and Danielle Gallegos. "Defining food literacy and its components." *Appetite* 76 (2014): 50–59.

van Uden-Kraan, Cornelia F., Constance H. C. Drossaert, Erik Taal, Erwin R. Seydel, and Mart A. F. J. van de Laar. "Participation in online patient support groups endorses patients' empowerment." *Patient Education and Counseling* 74, no. 1 (2009): 61–69.

Wilson, Jeffrey M. and Thomas A. E. Platts-Mills. "Meat allergy and allergens." *Molecular Immunology* 100 (2018): 107–12.

Notes

1. See the preface of this book and the chapter about Italy.
2. Kept anonymous for privacy reasons.
3. See Patricia G. Devine, "Stereotypes and prejudice: Their automatic and controlled components." *Journal of Personality and Social Psychology* 56, no. 1 (1989): 5.
4. Taken from the Finish chapter.
5. See, e.g., the chapter from The Netherlands where Hans Dagevos carefully explains that vegetarianism has been on the rise in the past too.
6. See chapters on Israel and The Netherlands.
7. Barbara Livingstone, James Robson, and Gavin Wallace, "Issues in dietary intake assessment of children and adolescents." *British Journal of Nutrition* 92, no. S2 (2004): S213.
8. Hank Rothgerber and Frances Mican, "Childhood pet ownership, attachment to pets, and subsequent meat avoidance. The mediating role of empathy toward animals." *Appetite* 79 (2014): 11.
9. Charlotte De Backer and Liselot Hudders. "From meatless Mondays to meatless Sundays: Motivations for meat reduction among vegetarians and semi-vegetarians who mildly or significantly reduce their meat intake." *Ecology of Food and Nutrition* 53, no. 6 (2014): 639.
10. See, e.g., Nick Fox and Katie Ward, "Health, ethics and environment: A qualitative study of vegetarian motivations." *Appetite* 50, no. 2–3 (2008): 422.
11. For a good recent overview see Daniel Rosenfeld, "The psychology of vegetarianism: Recent advances and future directions." *Appetite* (2018): 125.
12. See the Australian chapter about a Jewish community in Perth.
13. See Turkish chapter.
14. See chapters about Israel and the Jewish community in Australia.
15. See, e.g., chapters from Brazil, Canada, South Africa, and Turkey.
16. See Turkish chapter.
17. See, e.g., chapters from Canada, Finland, and Turkey.
18. See chapters from Canada and Finland.
19. Diana Cassady, Karen M. Jetter, and Jennifer Culp, "Is price a barrier to eating more fruits and vegetables for low-income families?" *Journal of the American Dietetic Association* 107, no. 11 (2007): 1909–15.
20. Pail Kenyon and Margo Barker, "Attitudes towards meat-eating in vegetarian and non-vegetarian teenage girls in England—an ethnographic approach." *Appetite* 30, no. 2 (1998): 185.
21. Len Tiu Wright, Clive Nancarrow, and Pamela M. H. Kwok, "Food taste preferences and cultural influences on consumption." *British Food Journal* 103, no. 5 (2001): 348.
22. Helen Anna Vidgen and Danielle Gallegos, "Defining food literacy and its components." *Appetite* 76 (2014): 50.
23. See U.S. chapter.
24. See British chapter.
25. See Brazilian chapter.
26. See the story in the Irish chapter.

27. See Turkish chapter.

28. Rothgerber, "Efforts to overcome vegetarian-induced dissonance among meat eaters."

29. See an overview paper by Laura McGowan, et al., "Domestic cooking and food skills: A review." *Critical reviews in food science and nutrition* 57, no. 11 (2017): 2412.

30. Vidgen Gallegos, "Defining food literacy and its components."

31. Surinder Phull, Wendy Wills, and Angela Dickinson, "The Mediterranean diet: Socio-cultural relevance for contemporary health promotion." *The Open Public Health Journal* 8 (2015b): 35.

32. See Italian chapter about the difference between junior and senior vegetarians.

33. See South African chapter.

34. See Brazilian chapter.

35. See Turkish chapter.

36. See U.S. chapter.

37. See British chapter.

38. See Italian chapter.

39. See U.S. chapter.

40. See Belgian chapter.

41. See Canadian chapter.

42. See South African chapter.

43. E.g., Peter Smith, "Bullying: Definition, types, causes, consequences and intervention." *Social and Personality Psychology Compass* 10, no. 9 (2016): 519.

44. Taken from Laura's interview in the UK chapter.

45. See especially the stories from the Australian, Canadian, and UK chapters.

46. Campbell and Campbell, "*The China Study: Startling Implications for Diet, Weight Loss and Long-Term Health,*" 242–44.

47. Marlene Perignon, et al., "Improving diet sustainability through evolution of food choices: Review of epidemiological studies on the environmental impact of diets." *Nutrition Reviews* 75, no. 1 (2017): 2.

48. See Italian and U.S. chapters especially.

49. E.g., Cornelia van Uden-Kraan et al., "Participation in online patient support groups endorses patients' empowerment." *Patient Education and Counseling* 74, no. 1 (2009): 61.

50. See, e.g., the Canadian stories.

51. See Irish and UK chapters especially.

52. Taken from the Belgian chapter.

53. See chapter about Ireland.

54. Jeffrey M. Wilson, and Thomas A. E. Platts-Mills. "Meat allergy and allergens." *Molecular Immunology* 100 (2018): 107.

55. Hank Rothgerber, "Efforts to overcome vegetarian-induced dissonance among meat eaters." *Appetite* 79 (2014): 32.

56. See Brazilian chapter.

57. See chapters from Ireland, the Netherlands, and the U.S.

58. See South African chapter.

59. See Sedef's account in the Turkish chapter.

INDEX

ABOUT THE AUTHORS

Chrysostomos Apostolidis is a Senior Lecturer of Marketing in Newcastle Business School, Newcastle upon Tyne, which he joined in 2012. He specializes in social marketing, ethical marketing, and sustainable consumer behavior and has published several articles, book chapters, and conference papers in this area. His main research interest is in the impact of marketing and digital marketing on sustainable and ethical consumer behavior.

Ulrike Atzmüller-Zeilinger is a plant-based blogger based in Vienna. She writes about various vegan topics, her lifestyle, and whatever else comes to her mind on her blog, Cookies&Style, since 2013 and has worked as an editor for a vegan online magazine since 2019. She was nominated for the Austrian Food Blog Award in 2015 and published a vegan recipe e-book two years ago.

Leesa Costello is a Senior Lecturer and Researcher in the School of Medical and Health Sciences at Edith Cowan University in Western Australia, specializing in the field of Health Communication. While her track record has been around social networking, online community and social media strategies for health promotion, she developed an interest in plant-based nutrition during her PhD research which was designed to help heart patients adopt healthier lifestyles. She is recognized as a qualitative scholar with the International Institute for Qualitative Methodology and has lead research projects underpinned by netnographic, ethnographic, phenomenological, and narrative forms of inquiry. Her research portfolio is punctuated by diverse health topics including child health nutrition, blue space, body image, loneliness and isolation, domestic violence, homelessness, maternal health, blood donation, social marketing, environmental behavior, and plant-based nutrition. Leesa has produced numerous peer-reviewed articles, some of which are published in high-ranking journals such as *Children & Youth Services Review*, *Health Information & Libraries Journal* and *Nurse Education Today*.

Hans Dagevos (PhD) is senior scientist at Wageningen University & Research in the Netherlands. He approaches and analyzes the world of food from the perspective of the sociology of consumption. This has resulted in numerous publications ranging from scholarly papers and research reports, books and book chapters, to book reviews and weblogs that he (co)authored and (co)edited. His latest research interests are in the fields of food transition toward sustainable diets (particularly protein transition away from meat-rich diets), circular economy and consumption, social innovation, and sustainable food policy.

Julie Dare is a Senior Lecturer and Public Health researcher in the School of Medical and Health Sciences, Edith Cowan University, in Perth, Western Australia. She has demonstrated research expertise in ethnographic, phenomenological, case study and narrative methodologies across a range of qualitative and mixed methods of interdisciplinary projects. She has a particular interest in the social context underpinning health behaviors such as alcohol use among older people, and the adoption of whole food plant-based diets and has co-authored articles exploring issues associated with vegetarianism and veganism, and the role of social media in supporting the adoption and maintenance of a whole food plant-based diet. Julie has also led projects investigating social engagement and social isolation among older adults and is currently involved in research ranging from an exploration of social capital in a community center, to promoting social engagement and well-being among frail older adults through exercise programs in residential aged-care facilities. Julie has authored a book chapter exploring gender in mediated communication environments and had numerous peer-reviewed articles published in journals including *Health and Social Care in the Community, European Journal of Cultural Studies,* and *Health Care for Women International.*

Charlotte De Backer is Associate Professor at the University of Antwerp, Department of Communication Sciences. She leads a group of scholars that study the interactions between media and food consumption (FOOMS— Food, Media & Society, see https://www.uantwerpen.be/en/projects/

food-media-society/). In collaboration with her colleagues and PhD students she studies how media do and can influence our eating habits, with a strong focus on food media other than traditional advertisements. Think of TV cooking shows, social media, food influencers, and so on. Attention is also paid to what strategies work best to endorse healthy eating habits, focusing on storytelling and social context factors. And, she also studies how the foods we eat influence our identity and social behavior: what we eat, who we eat with, and whether we share foods may matter more than we think. See: https://www.uantwerpen.be/en/staff/charlotte-debacker/.

Sara Erreygers, PhD, works as a student counselor at the Study Advice and Student Counselling Service of the University of Antwerp.

Joanne Fisher is an Independent Scholar and self-proclaimed foodie living in Vancouver, Canada.

Maryanne L. Fisher, PhD, is a Full Professor in the Department of Psychology at Saint Mary's University in Halifax, Canada, and an Affiliate Faculty at Kinsey Institute in Indiana. She is an award-winning teacher and has published over 100 scientific articles, mostly pertaining to women's attractiveness and intrasexual mating competition. She authored *A Very Short Introduction to Evolutionary Psychology* (upcoming), edited the *Oxford Handbook of Women and Competition* (2017), and was the lead co-editor of *Evolution's Empress: Darwinian Perspectives on the Nature of Women* (2013).

Lelia Green is Professor of Communications in the School of Arts and Humanities, Edith Cowan University, Perth. She has conducted "vegangelical" research over a number of years, reflecting upon her own experience of becoming vegan in 2007. Her books include *The Internet: An Introduction to New Media* (2010); *Digitising Early Childhood* (co-editor, 2019); and *Narratives in Research and Interventions on Cyberbullying among Young People* (co-editor, 2019).

Maeve Henchion (MAgrSc, PhD) is a Principal Research Officer in Teagasc (the Irish agriculture and food development authority), Adjunct Professor in the School of Agriculture & Food Science, University College Dublin, and Head of the Department. of Agrifood Business and Spatial Analysis which includes budget responsibility of €1.5m/yr and a team of up to forty researchers, post-docs, and PhD students. Her research interests include innovation, farmer, industry, and consumer acceptance of technologies, and sustainable production and consumption. Orcid: http://orcid.org/0000-0001-7842-1516.

Piia Jallinoja is professor (medical sociology) at the Tampere University. She has studied various health, lifestyle, and food-related phenomena from a sociological perspective, such as discourses of healthy lifestyle and lifestyle change, low-carbohydrate dieters, debates over dietary fats in the media, and rise of veganism in the 2010s.

Helmut Jungwirth is Associate Professor at the Institute of Molecular Biosciences and business manager of the Center for Society, Knowledge and Communication. Since 2016 he has been professor of science communications and a member of the science comedy "Science Busters."

Ilkay Kanik is an Assistant Professor in the Gastronomy and Culinary Arts Department at Beykent University in Istanbul, Turkey. She has published several articles, chapters, and the following books on food culture in Turkey: *Gastro Gösteri* (in Turkish), *Gastro Endişe* (in Turkish), and *Gastro Sinema* (in Turkish). She visited the New School, New York, as a research scholar in 2013–2015.

Pamela Kerschke-Risch, PhD, is a sociologist and criminologist at the University of Hamburg where she teaches Sociology and Master of International Criminology. Her main research topics are food and nutrition as well as victimological questions concerning food-related offenses. She carried out the project "Gender-specific Aspects of Food Choices" using different quantitative online surveys and qualitative interviews. Moreover, she conducted the first sociological study with 850 vegans in Germany. Dr. Kerschke-Risch published papers on the subject of food crime from a consumer's perspective as well as vegan food choices.

Anthonieta Looman Mafra is Associate Professor at Universidade Potiguar, Brazil. She has been studying Evolutionary Psychology for the last nine years and published on this subject, including the paper "Investment in Beauty, Exercise, and Self-esteem: Are They Related to Self-perception as a Romantic Partner?" published in *Evolutionary Psychological Science*; the chapter "Limited Reproductive Potential" of the *Encyclopedia of Evolutionary Psychological Science*; and a review of the book *Evolutionary Perspectives on Human Sexual Psychology and Behavior* published in *Human Ethology Bulletin*.

Alessandra Micalizzi is lecturer at SAE Institute of Milan and Adjunct Professor at IUSTo of Turin. She teaches Marketing, Communication Information and Media Practices, Psychology of Communication. Her area of research deals with the use of digital contexts to share emotions. She took part in several projects such as "Trend Food 3SC 2016" and "consumers' perception of the use of palm oil in baby food industry." Among her most recent publications there is *Happy-Net: The Internet as Technology with High Potential of Happiness* (2018).

Asher Myerson was born in Melbourne but has lived in Perth since 2006. Asher went on a leadership gap year program in Israel with his youth movement, Habonim Dror. Living in Israel, his promised land for a year greatly affected and inspired him. Asher has been a passionate leader in Habonim Dror Perth since returning from Israel at the end of 2015 and is the current chairperson. He studies Physics and Philosophy at UWA and often works at Carmel School doing informal education, among other part-time work with Elevate Education.

Mari Niva is professor of food culture at the University of Helsinki (2018–2021). Her field of expertise is in the study of food culture, food choices, and the social and cultural aspects of eating. In international and national projects, she has studied eating patterns in the Nordic countries, the consumption and future prospects of meat and plant-based proteins, and weight management as a practice. Currently her research focuses on insect eating, veganism, and political food consumption.

Yandisa Ngqangashe is a PhD Candidate at the University of Antwerp, faculty of Social Science, Department of Communication Studies. Her research is on how food-related media can be used to promote positive eating behaviors in adolescents. She has published work on this subject focusing on the nutritional content of foods portrayed by TV cooking shows and the experimental effects of exposure to existing TV cooking shows that endorse fruits and vegetables.

Elisabeth Oberzaucher has served as scientific director of the research institute Urban Human since 2015. She is a tenured lecturer at the University of Vienna and has been teaching courses at various other institutions since 2001. In 2015, she was awarded the Ig Nobel Prize in Mathematics. See: www.oberzaucher.eu.

Talia Raphaely, originally from Cape Town, South Africa, now lives in Perth, Western Australia, and has over thirty years of international experience in increasing sustainable outcomes. She works closely with multicultural and heterogeneous groups in diverse settings, including academia, media, research-based organizations, government bodies and political organizations, community-based organizations and industry. She is recognized for her work on flexitarianism, collaboration, empowerment, and sustainability humanistic education. Her co-edited, Scopus indexed academic work, *The Impact of Meat Consumption on Health and Environmental Sustainability,* was the 2017 Winner of three Gourmand International Book Awards: 1) Best Sustainable Food Book in the World; 2) Best Australian Sustainable Food Book (2013); and Best Australian Vegetarian Food Book (2017).

Sigal Tifferet is a senior lecturer at the Ruppin Academic Center. Her main research interests are gender differences, evolutionary psychology, and social network sites.

Annukka Vainio is associate professor of Behavioral Change toward Sustainability at Helsinki Institute of Sustainability Science (HELSUS), University of Helsinki. Her academic background is in social psychology. The aim of her research is to understand the agency of consumers/citizens, as well as that of other actors in sustainability transformations. She seeks to understand how unsustainable practices are related to ethics, beliefs, and habits and to find effective ways to overcome these barriers.

Laurence Verheijen is an assistant data manager at the Flemish Audiovisual Fund. She is responsible for the optimization of the internal database and by extension, for analysis of the sector.

Daniel L. Rosenfeld is currently a Ph.D. student in Health Psychology at UCLA. Daniel's research centers on vegetarianism and meat consumption, particularly as they relate to identity, morality, and cognitive dissonance.